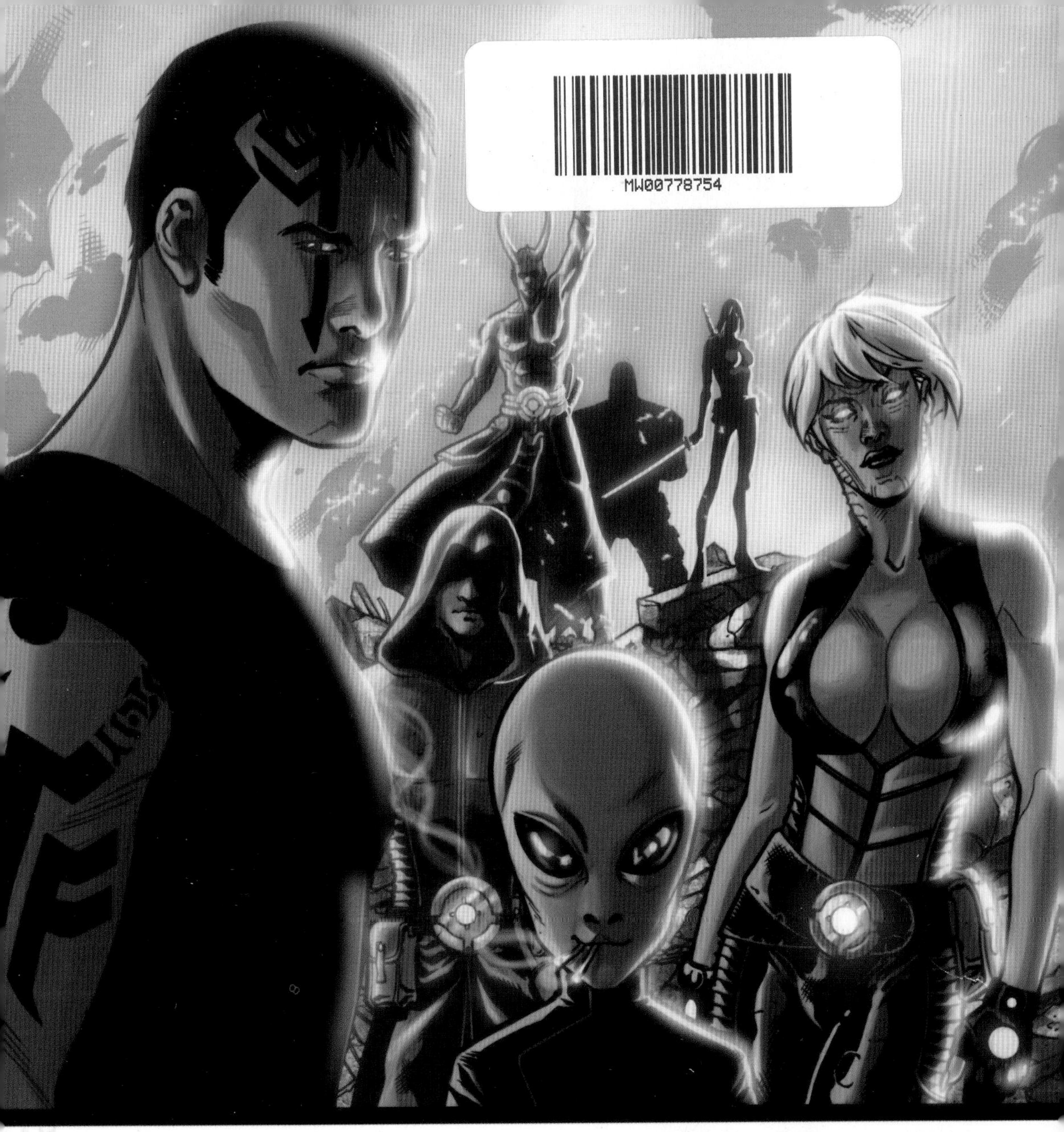

RYALL · WALTZ · MESSINA

INFESTATION OUTBREAK

WRITTEN BY
CHRIS RYALL
AND TOM WALTZ

ART BY
DAVID MESSINA

COLORS BY
SCARLETGOTHICA

INKS BY
GAETANO CARLUCCI

LETTERS BY
SHAWN LEE AND CHRIS MOWRY

SERIES EDITS BY
BOBBY CURNOW

COVER BY
DAVID MESSINA

COLLECTION EDITS BY
JUSTIN EISINGER AND ALONZO SIMON

COLLECTION DESIGN BY
CHRIS MOWRY

Groom Lake created by Chris Ryall and Ben Templesmith • CVO created by Alex Garner

ISBN: 978-1-61377-107-5

14 13 12 11   1 2 3 4

Ted Adams, CEO & Publisher
Greg Goldstein, Chief Operating Officer
Robbie Robbins, EVP/Sr. Graphic Artist
Chris Ryall, Chief Creative Officer/Editor-in-Chief
Matthew Ruzicka, CPA, Chief Financial Officer
Alan Payne, VP of Sales

Become our fan on Facebook facebook.com/idwpublishing
Follow us on Twitter @idwpublishing
Check us out on YouTube youtube.com/idwpublishing
www.IDWPUBLISHING.com

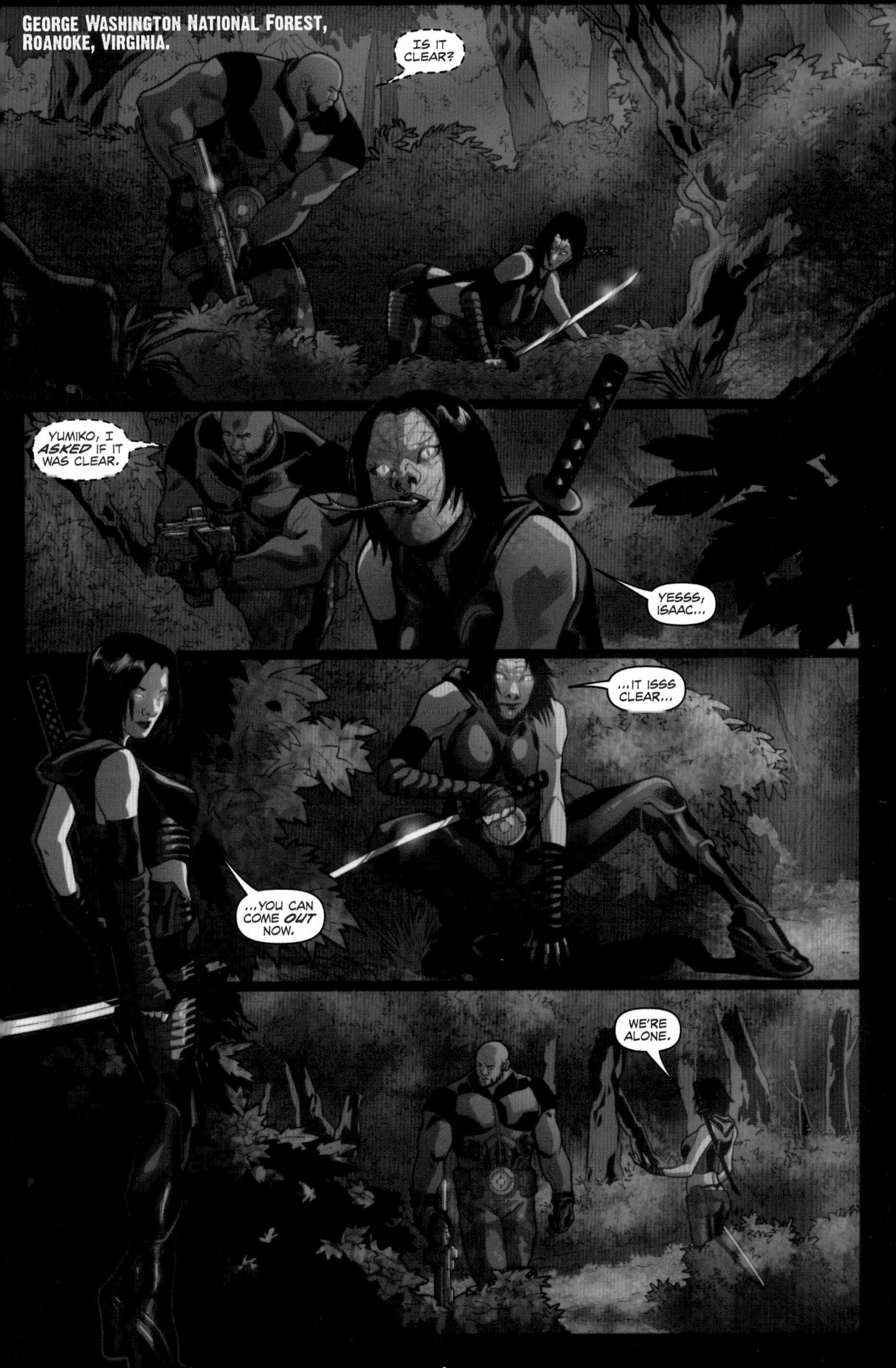
GEORGE WASHINGTON NATIONAL FOREST, ROANOKE, VIRGINIA.
IS IT CLEAR?
YUMIKO, I ASKED IF IT WAS CLEAR.
YESSS, ISAAC...
...IT ISSS CLEAR...
...YOU CAN COME OUT NOW.
WE'RE ALONE.

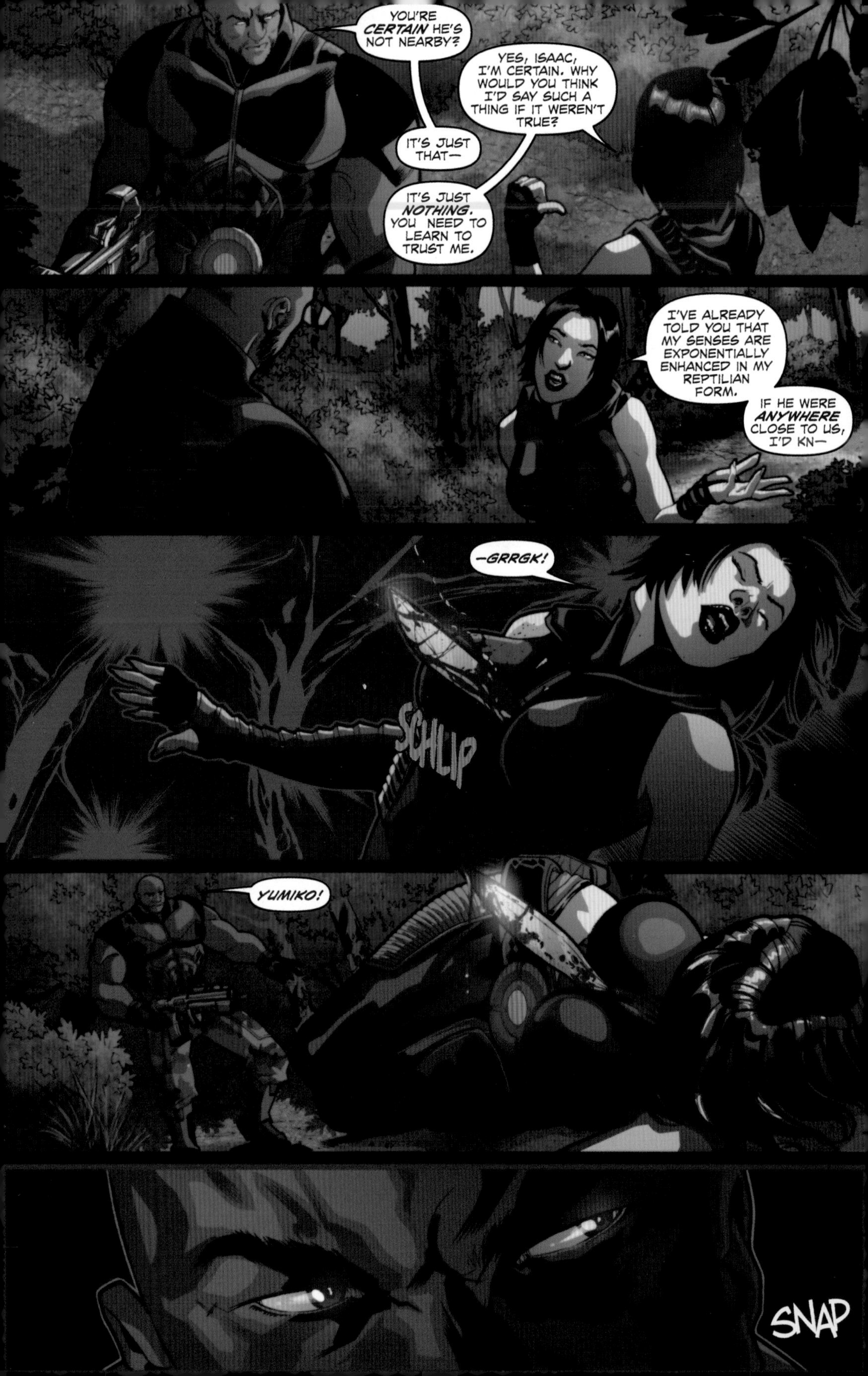
YOU'RE *CERTAIN* HE'S NOT NEARBY?
YES, ISAAC, I'M CERTAIN. WHY WOULD YOU THINK I'D SAY SUCH A THING IF IT WEREN'T TRUE?
IT'S JUST THAT—
IT'S JUST *NOTHING*. YOU NEED TO LEARN TO TRUST ME.
I'VE ALREADY TOLD YOU THAT MY SENSES ARE EXPONENTIALLY ENHANCED IN MY REPTILIAN FORM.
IF HE WERE *ANYWHERE* CLOSE TO US, I'D KN—
—GRRGK!
SCHLIP
YUMIKO!
SNAP

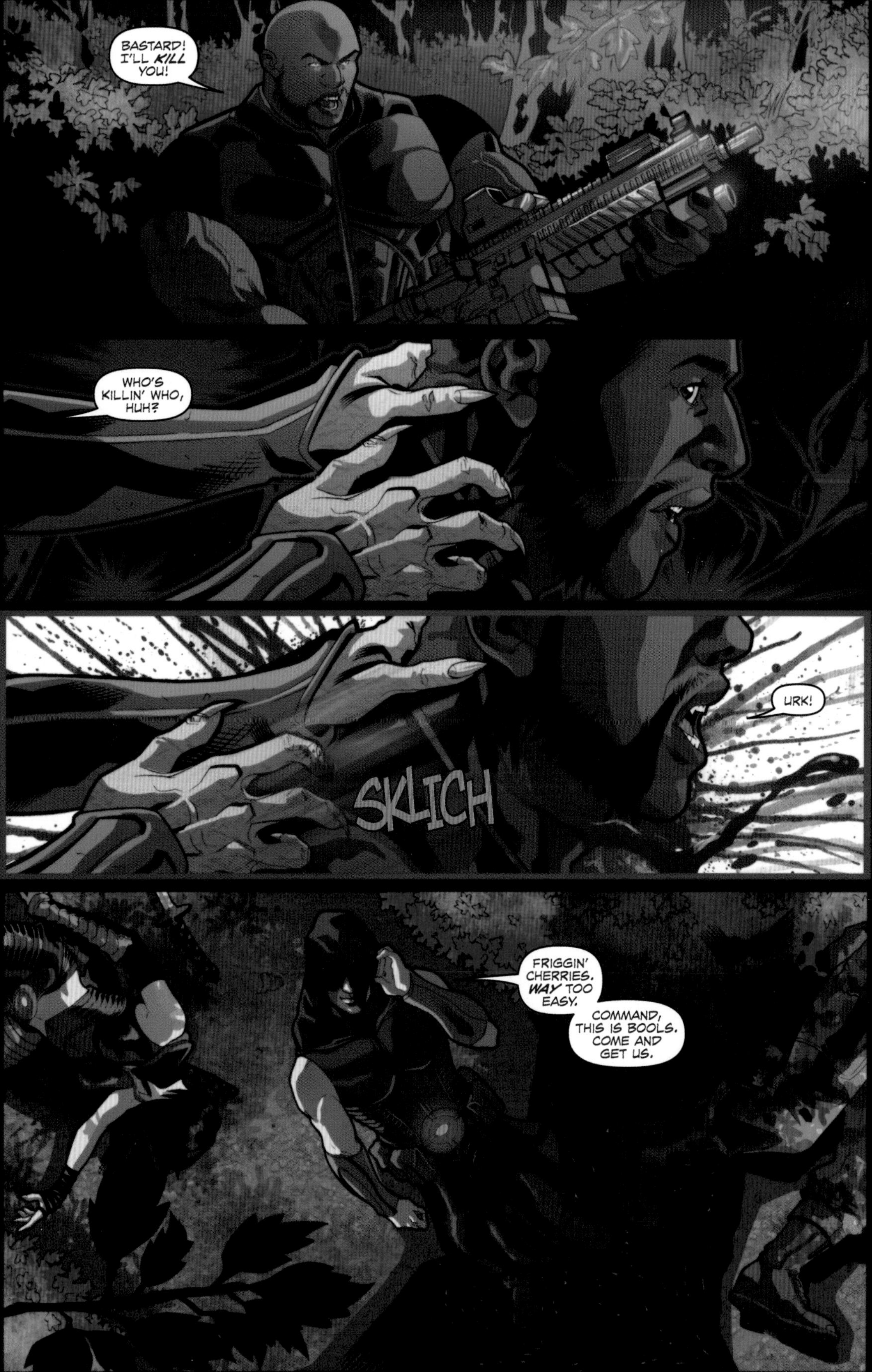
BASTARD! I'LL KILL YOU!
WHO'S KILLIN' WHO, HUH?
URK!
SKLICH
FRIGGIN' CHERRIES. WAY TOO EASY.
COMMAND, THIS IS BOOLS. COME AND GET US.

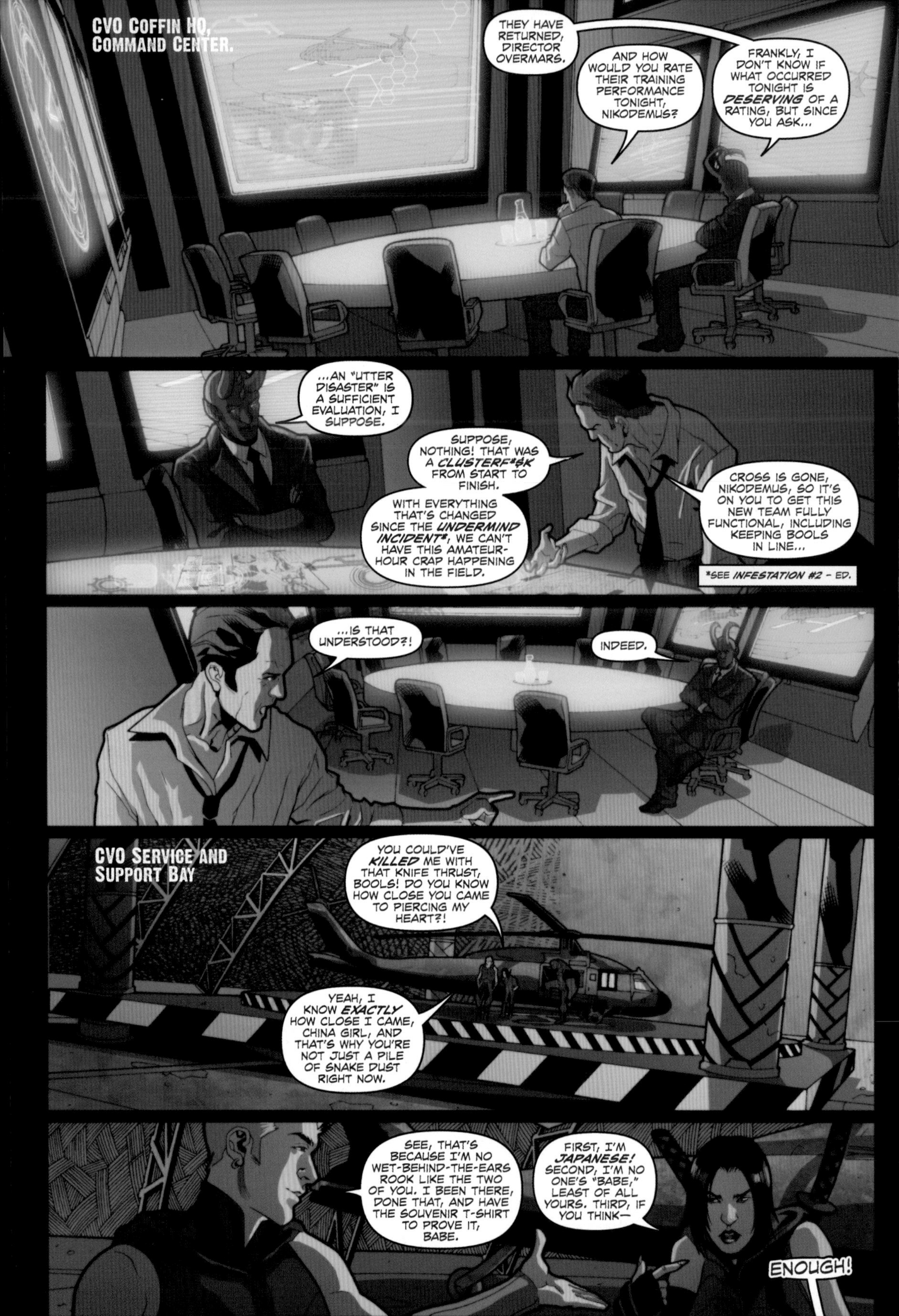
CVO Coffin HQ, Command Center.
THEY HAVE RETURNED, DIRECTOR OVERMARS.
AND HOW WOULD YOU RATE THEIR TRAINING PERFORMANCE TONIGHT, NIKODEMUS?
FRANKLY, I DON'T KNOW IF WHAT OCCURRED TONIGHT IS DESERVING OF A RATING, BUT SINCE YOU ASK...
...AN "UTTER DISASTER" IS A SUFFICIENT EVALUATION, I SUPPOSE.
SUPPOSE, NOTHING! THAT WAS A CLUSTERF*$K FROM START TO FINISH.
WITH EVERYTHING THAT'S CHANGED SINCE THE UNDERMIND INCIDENT*, WE CAN'T HAVE THIS AMATEUR-HOUR CRAP HAPPENING IN THE FIELD.
CROSS IS GONE, NIKODEMUS, SO IT'S ON YOU TO GET THIS NEW TEAM FULLY FUNCTIONAL, INCLUDING KEEPING BOOLS IN LINE...
*SEE INFESTATION #2 - ED.
...IS THAT UNDERSTOOD?!
INDEED.
CVO Service and Support Bay
YOU COULD'VE KILLED ME WITH THAT KNIFE THRUST, BOOLS! DO YOU KNOW HOW CLOSE YOU CAME TO PIERCING MY HEART?!
YEAH, I KNOW EXACTLY HOW CLOSE I CAME, CHINA GIRL, AND THAT'S WHY YOU'RE NOT JUST A PILE OF SNAKE DUST RIGHT NOW.
SEE, THAT'S BECAUSE I'M NO WET-BEHIND-THE-EARS ROOK LIKE THE TWO OF YOU. I BEEN THERE, DONE THAT, AND HAVE THE SOUVENIR T-SHIRT TO PROVE IT, BABE.
FIRST, I'M JAPANESE! SECOND, I'M NO ONE'S "BABE," LEAST OF ALL YOURS. THIRD, IF YOU THINK—
ENOUGH!

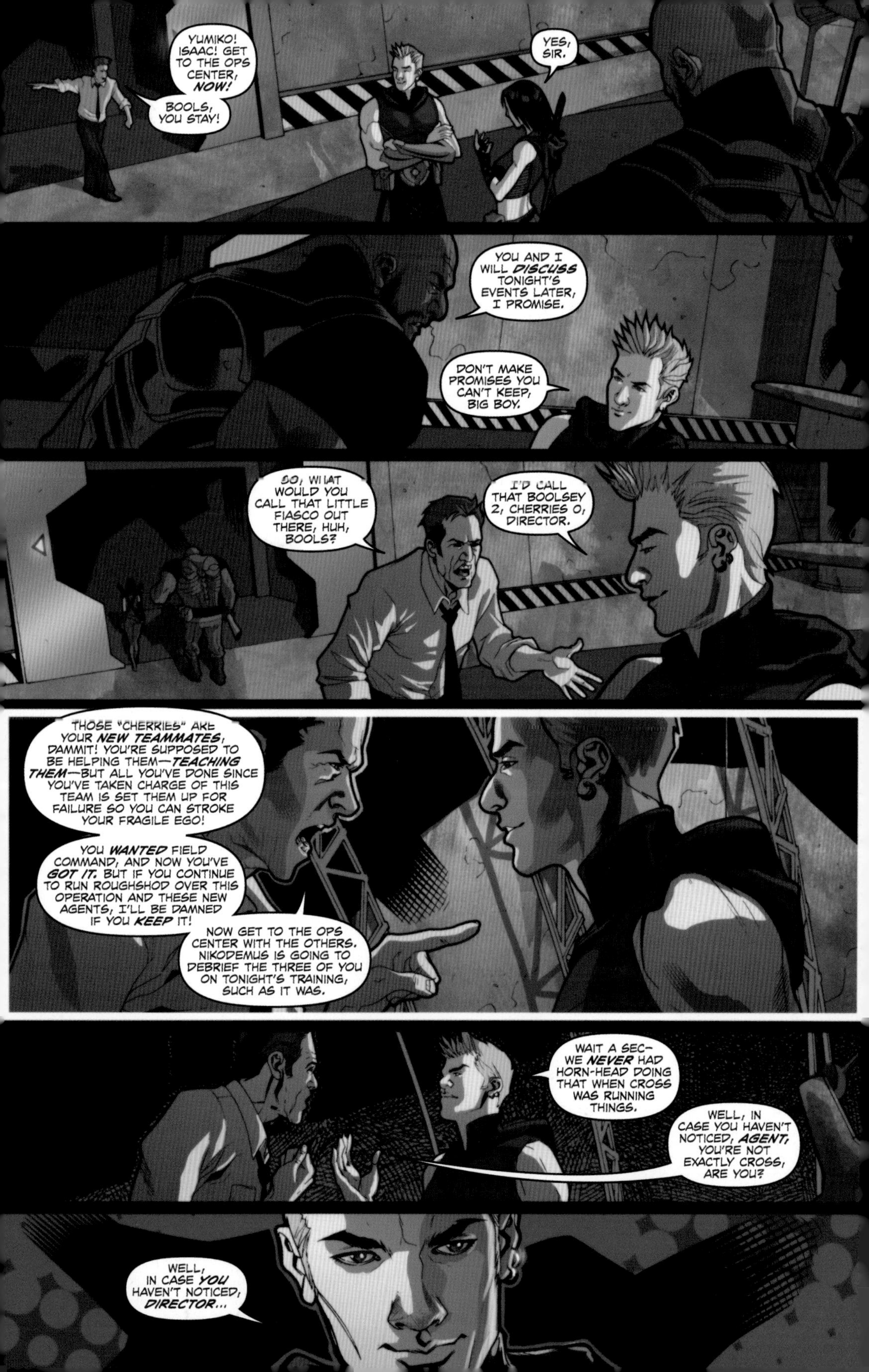
YUMIKO! ISAAC! GET TO THE OPS CENTER, NOW!
BOOLS, YOU STAY!
YES, SIR.
YOU AND I WILL DISCUSS TONIGHT'S EVENTS LATER, I PROMISE.
DON'T MAKE PROMISES YOU CAN'T KEEP, BIG BOY.
SO, WHAT WOULD YOU CALL THAT LITTLE FIASCO OUT THERE, HUH, BOOLS?
I'D CALL THAT BOOLSEY 2, CHERRIES 0, DIRECTOR.
THOSE "CHERRIES" ARE YOUR NEW TEAMMATES, DAMMIT! YOU'RE SUPPOSED TO BE HELPING THEM—TEACHING THEM—BUT ALL YOU'VE DONE SINCE YOU'VE TAKEN CHARGE OF THIS TEAM IS SET THEM UP FOR FAILURE SO YOU CAN STROKE YOUR FRAGILE EGO!
YOU WANTED FIELD COMMAND, AND NOW YOU'VE GOT IT. BUT IF YOU CONTINUE TO RUN ROUGHSHOD OVER THIS OPERATION AND THESE NEW AGENTS, I'LL BE DAMNED IF YOU KEEP IT!
NOW GET TO THE OPS CENTER WITH THE OTHERS. NIKODEMUS IS GOING TO DEBRIEF THE THREE OF YOU ON TONIGHT'S TRAINING, SUCH AS IT WAS.
WAIT A SEC—WE NEVER HAD HORN-HEAD DOING THAT WHEN CROSS WAS RUNNING THINGS.
WELL, IN CASE YOU HAVEN'T NOTICED, AGENT, YOU'RE NOT EXACTLY CROSS, ARE YOU?
WELL, IN CASE YOU HAVEN'T NOTICED, DIRECTOR...

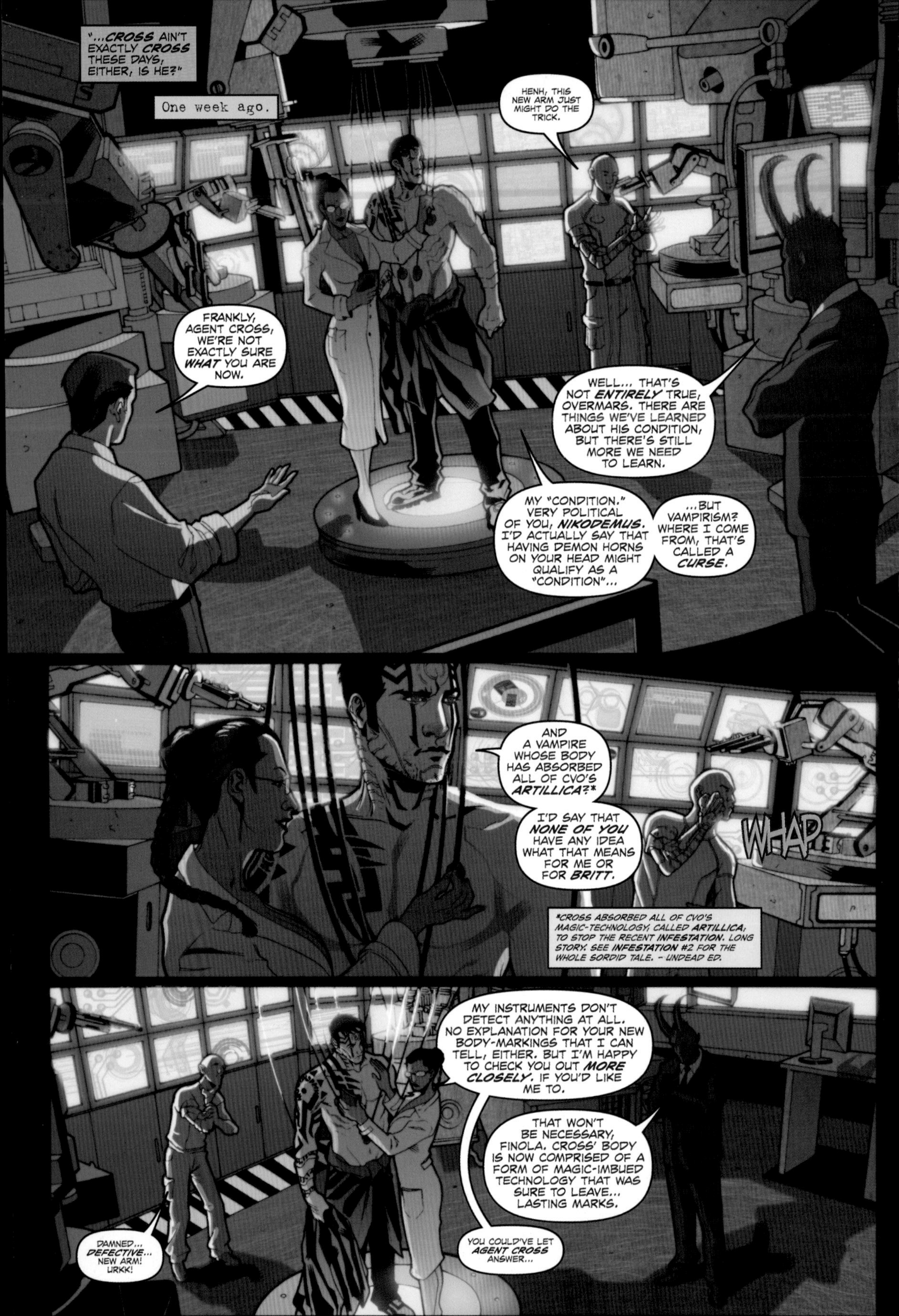

"...CROSS AIN'T EXACTLY CROSS THESE DAYS, EITHER, IS HE?"
One week ago.
HENH, THIS NEW ARM JUST MIGHT DO THE TRICK.
FRANKLY, AGENT CROSS, WE'RE NOT EXACTLY SURE WHAT YOU ARE NOW.
WELL... THAT'S NOT ENTIRELY TRUE, OVERMARS. THERE ARE THINGS WE'VE LEARNED ABOUT HIS CONDITION, BUT THERE'S STILL MORE WE NEED TO LEARN.
MY "CONDITION." VERY POLITICAL OF YOU, NIKODEMUS. I'D ACTUALLY SAY THAT HAVING DEMON HORNS ON YOUR HEAD MIGHT QUALIFY AS A "CONDITION"...
...BUT VAMPIRISM? WHERE I COME FROM, THAT'S CALLED A CURSE.
AND A VAMPIRE WHOSE BODY HAS ABSORBED ALL OF CVO'S ARTILLICA?*
I'D SAY THAT NONE OF YOU HAVE ANY IDEA WHAT THAT MEANS FOR ME OR FOR BRITT.
WHAP
*CROSS ABSORBED ALL OF CVO'S MAGIC-TECHNOLOGY, CALLED ARTILLICA, TO STOP THE RECENT INFESTATION. LONG STORY. SEE INFESTATION #2 FOR THE WHOLE SORDID TALE. - UNDEAD ED.
MY INSTRUMENTS DON'T DETECT ANYTHING AT ALL. NO EXPLANATION FOR YOUR NEW BODY-MARKINGS THAT I CAN TELL, EITHER. BUT I'M HAPPY TO CHECK YOU OUT MORE CLOSELY. IF YOU'D LIKE ME TO.
THAT WON'T BE NECESSARY, FINOLA. CROSS' BODY IS NOW COMPRISED OF A FORM OF MAGIC-IMBUED TECHNOLOGY THAT WAS SURE TO LEAVE... LASTING MARKS.
DAMNED... DEFECTIVE... NEW ARM! URKK!
YOU COULD'VE LET AGENT CROSS ANSWER...

SPEAKING OF BRITT, IF I'M BACK ON MY FEET, WHY ISN'T SHE? *WHERE* IS SHE?

BRITT IS STILL.... RECUPERATING.

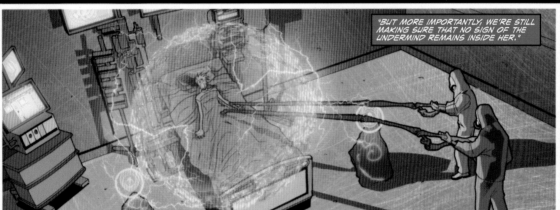

"BUT MORE IMPORTANTLY, WE'RE STILL MAKING SURE THAT NO SIGN OF THE UNDERMIND REMAINS INSIDE HER."

WE CAN'T CLEAR HER RETURN TO THE TEAM UNTIL WE KNOW FOR SURE. THERE ARE CONCERNED ENTITIES THAT PRECLUDE—

"CONCERNED ENTITIES," OVERMARS? *I'M* A CONCERNED ENTITY. AND I WOULD'VE HOPED YOU WOULD BE, TOO.

SOUNDS LIKE WE'VE TURNED A CORNER, OVERMARS. WITHOUT BRITT, YOU DON'T HAVE ME. AND WITHOUT ME, WHAT HAVE YOU GOT? *NOTHING.* THE UNDERMIND IS *GONE,* BUT IT TOOK CVO WITH IT.

I BEG TO DIFFER. CVO IS FAR FROM DONE—IN FACT, AS WE SPEAK, AGENT BOOLS IS, WELL, REBUILDING THE TEAM. HE IS DETERMINED TO PROVE HIMSELF A LEADER. HE'LL BE FIELD-TESTING NEW AGENTS VERY SOON—

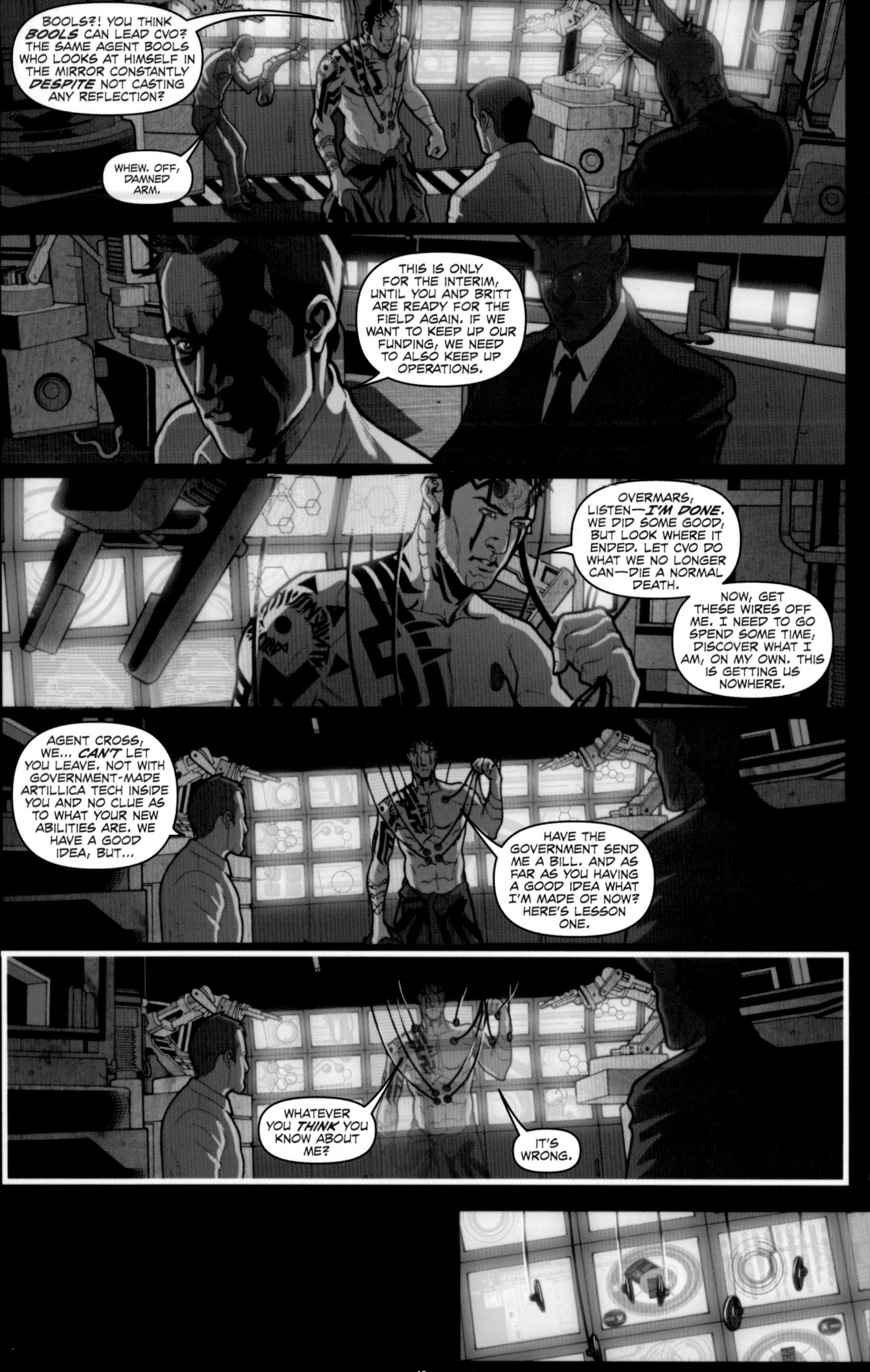
BOOLS?! YOU THINK BOOLS CAN LEAD CVO? THE SAME AGENT BOOLS WHO LOOKS AT HIMSELF IN THE MIRROR CONSTANTLY DESPITE NOT CASTING ANY REFLECTION?
WHEW. OFF, DAMNED ARM.
THIS IS ONLY FOR THE INTERIM, UNTIL YOU AND BRITT ARE READY FOR THE FIELD AGAIN. IF WE WANT TO KEEP UP OUR FUNDING, WE NEED TO ALSO KEEP UP OPERATIONS.
OVERMARS, LISTEN—I'M DONE. WE DID SOME GOOD, BUT LOOK WHERE IT ENDED. LET CVO DO WHAT WE NO LONGER CAN—DIE A NORMAL DEATH.
NOW, GET THESE WIRES OFF ME. I NEED TO GO SPEND SOME TIME, DISCOVER WHAT I AM, ON MY OWN. THIS IS GETTING US NOWHERE.
AGENT CROSS, WE... CAN'T LET YOU LEAVE. NOT WITH GOVERNMENT-MADE ARTILLICA TECH INSIDE YOU AND NO CLUE AS TO WHAT YOUR NEW ABILITIES ARE. WE HAVE A GOOD IDEA, BUT...
HAVE THE GOVERNMENT SEND ME A BILL. AND AS FAR AS YOU HAVING A GOOD IDEA WHAT I'M MADE OF NOW? HERE'S LESSON ONE.
WHATEVER YOU THINK YOU KNOW ABOUT ME?
IT'S WRONG.

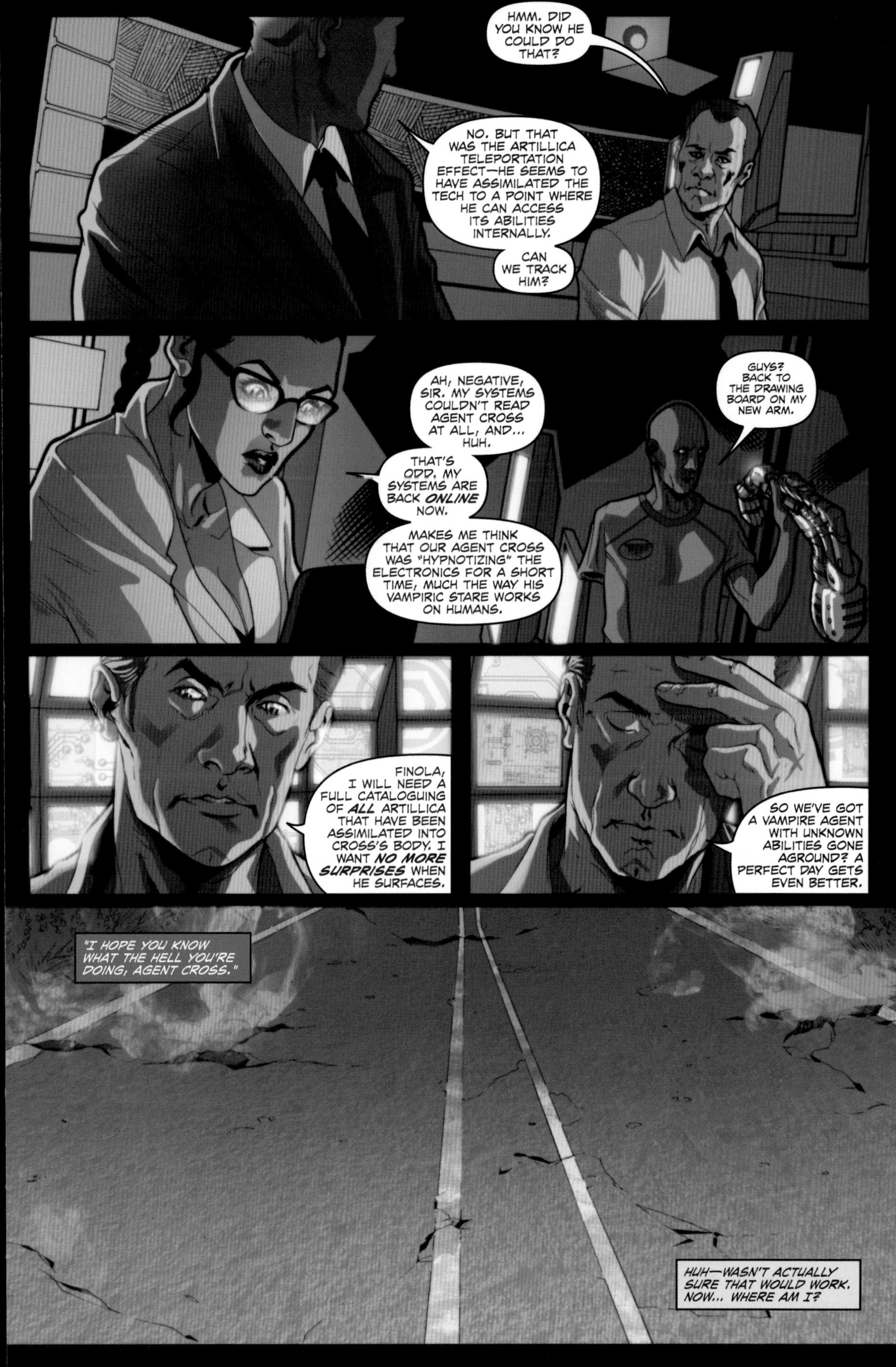

HMM. DID YOU KNOW HE COULD DO THAT?
NO. BUT THAT WAS THE ARTILLICA TELEPORTATION EFFECT—HE SEEMS TO HAVE ASSIMILATED THE TECH TO A POINT WHERE HE CAN ACCESS ITS ABILITIES INTERNALLY.
CAN WE TRACK HIM?
AH, NEGATIVE, SIR. MY SYSTEMS COULDN'T READ AGENT CROSS AT ALL, AND... HUH.
THAT'S ODD. MY SYSTEMS ARE BACK ONLINE NOW.
MAKES ME THINK THAT OUR AGENT CROSS WAS "HYPNOTIZING" THE ELECTRONICS FOR A SHORT TIME, MUCH THE WAY HIS VAMPIRIC STARE WORKS ON HUMANS.
GUYS? BACK TO THE DRAWING BOARD ON MY NEW ARM.
FINOLA, I WILL NEED A FULL CATALOGUING OF ALL ARTILLICA THAT HAVE BEEN ASSIMILATED INTO CROSS'S BODY. I WANT NO MORE SURPRISES WHEN HE SURFACES.
SO WE'VE GOT A VAMPIRE AGENT WITH UNKNOWN ABILITIES GONE AGROUND? A PERFECT DAY GETS EVEN BETTER.
"I HOPE YOU KNOW WHAT THE HELL YOU'RE DOING, AGENT CROSS."
HUH—WASN'T ACTUALLY SURE THAT WOULD WORK. NOW... WHERE AM I?

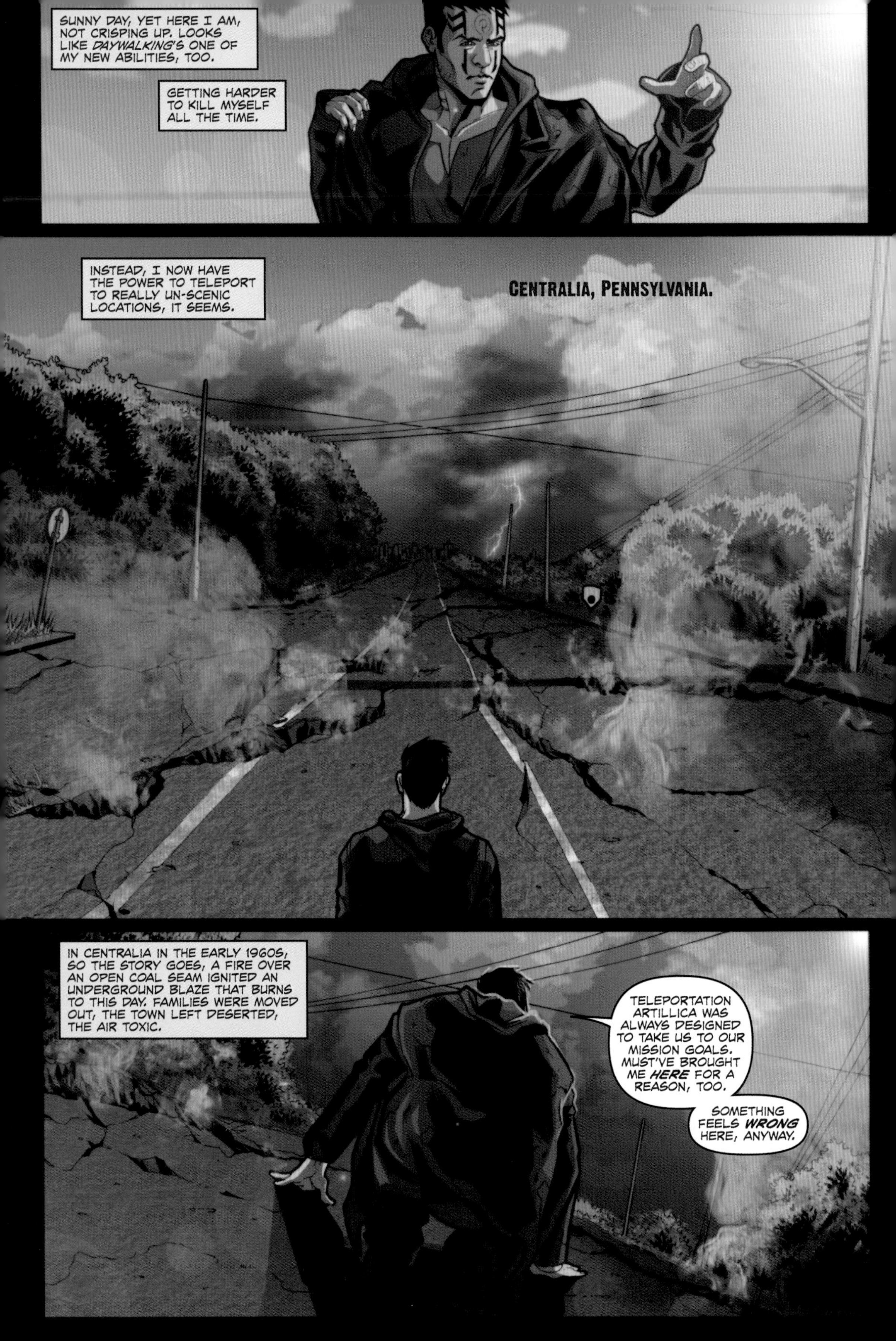
SUNNY DAY, YET HERE I AM, NOT CRISPING UP. LOOKS LIKE *DAYWALKING*'S ONE OF MY NEW ABILITIES, TOO.
GETTING HARDER TO KILL MYSELF ALL THE TIME.
INSTEAD, I NOW HAVE THE POWER TO TELEPORT TO REALLY UN-SCENIC LOCATIONS, IT SEEMS.
CENTRALIA, PENNSYLVANIA.
IN CENTRALIA IN THE EARLY 1960S, SO THE STORY GOES, A FIRE OVER AN OPEN COAL SEAM IGNITED AN UNDERGROUND BLAZE THAT BURNS TO THIS DAY. FAMILIES WERE MOVED OUT, THE TOWN LEFT DESERTED, THE AIR TOXIC.
TELEPORTATION ARTILLICA WAS ALWAYS DESIGNED TO TAKE US TO OUR MISSION GOALS. MUST'VE BROUGHT ME *HERE* FOR A REASON, TOO.
SOMETHING FEELS ***WRONG*** HERE, ANYWAY.

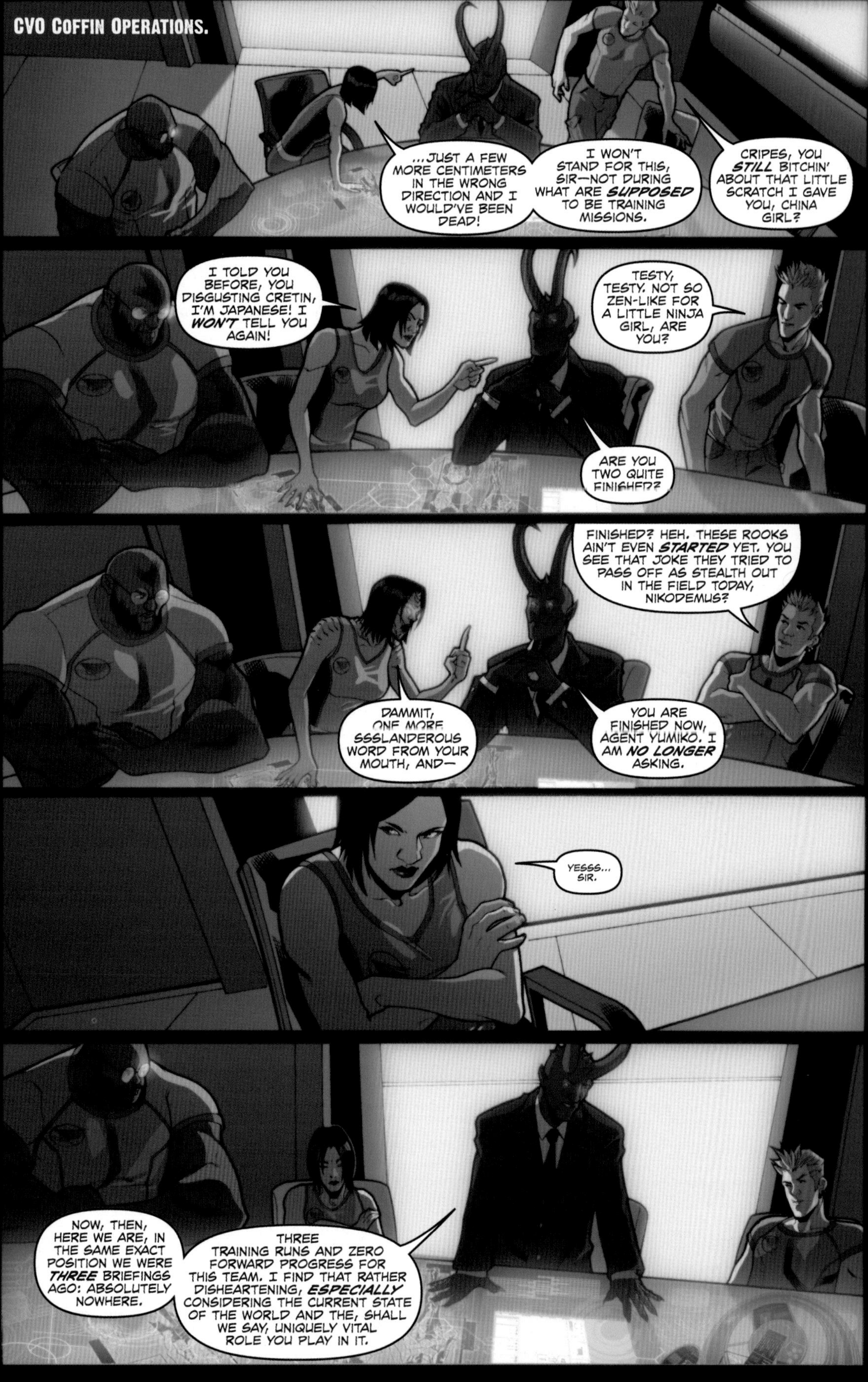
CVO Coffin Operations.
...JUST A FEW MORE CENTIMETERS IN THE WRONG DIRECTION AND I WOULD'VE BEEN DEAD!
I WON'T STAND FOR THIS, SIR—NOT DURING WHAT ARE SUPPOSED TO BE TRAINING MISSIONS.
CRIPES, YOU STILL BITCHIN' ABOUT THAT LITTLE SCRATCH I GAVE YOU, CHINA GIRL?
I TOLD YOU BEFORE, YOU DISGUSTING CRETIN, I'M JAPANESE! I WON'T TELL YOU AGAIN!
TESTY, TESTY. NOT SO ZEN-LIKE FOR A LITTLE NINJA GIRL, ARE YOU?
ARE YOU TWO QUITE FINISHED?
FINISHED? HEH. THESE ROOKS AIN'T EVEN STARTED YET. YOU SEE THAT JOKE THEY TRIED TO PASS OFF AS STEALTH OUT IN THE FIELD TODAY, NIKODEMUS?
DAMMIT, ONE MORE SSSLANDEROUS WORD FROM YOUR MOUTH, AND—
YOU ARE FINISHED NOW, AGENT YUMIKO. I AM NO LONGER ASKING.
YESSS... SIR.
NOW, THEN, HERE WE ARE, IN THE SAME EXACT POSITION WE WERE THREE BRIEFINGS AGO: ABSOLUTELY NOWHERE.
THREE TRAINING RUNS AND ZERO FORWARD PROGRESS FOR THIS TEAM. I FIND THAT RATHER DISHEARTENING, ESPECIALLY CONSIDERING THE CURRENT STATE OF THE WORLD AND THE, SHALL WE SAY, UNIQUELY VITAL ROLE YOU PLAY IN IT.

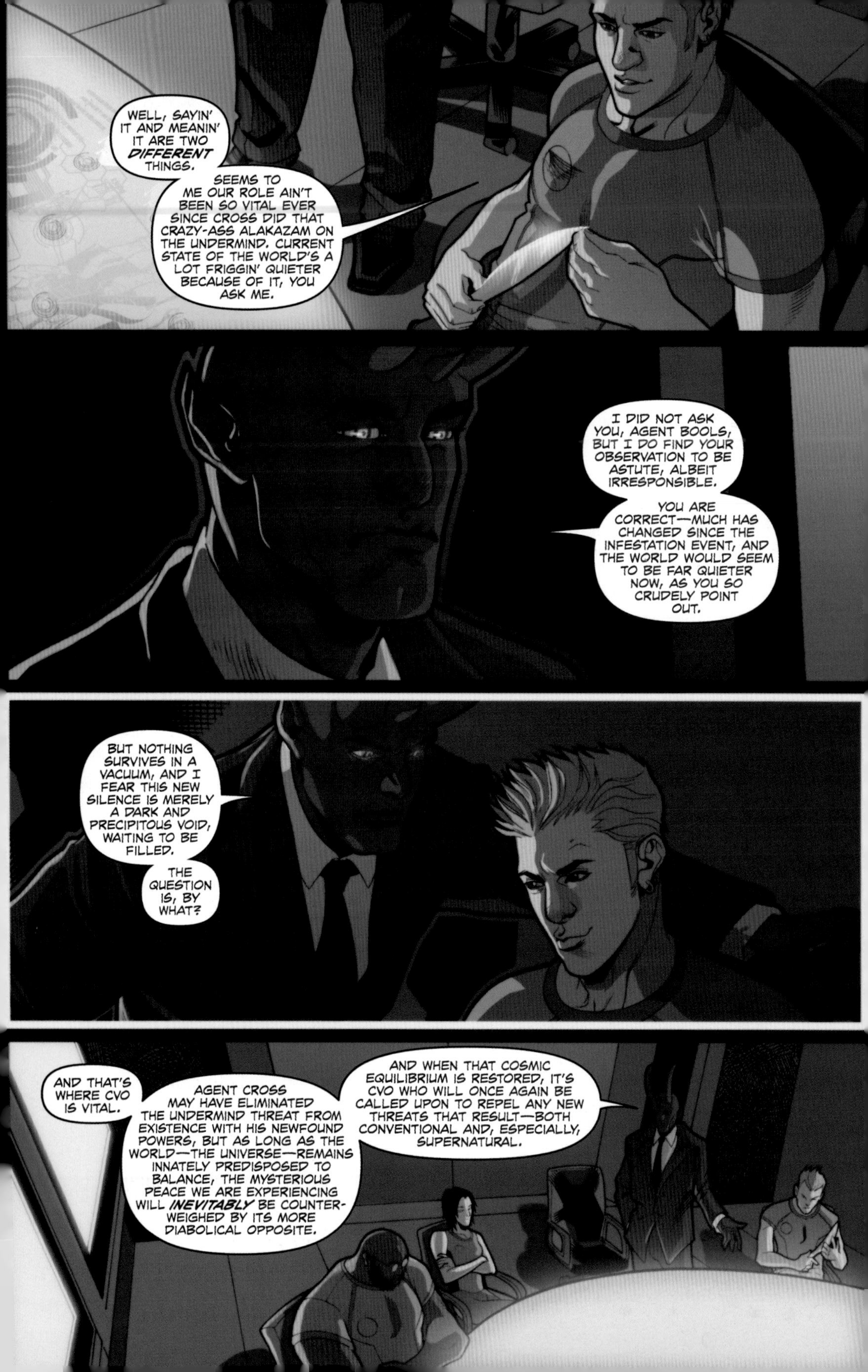
WELL, SAYIN' IT AND MEANIN' IT ARE TWO *DIFFERENT* THINGS.
SEEMS TO ME OUR ROLE AIN'T BEEN SO VITAL EVER SINCE CROSS DID THAT CRAZY-ASS ALAKAZAM ON THE UNDERMIND. CURRENT STATE OF THE WORLD'S A LOT FRIGGIN' QUIETER BECAUSE OF IT, YOU ASK ME.
I DID NOT ASK YOU, AGENT BOOLS, BUT I DO FIND YOUR OBSERVATION TO BE ASTUTE, ALBEIT IRRESPONSIBLE.
YOU ARE CORRECT—MUCH HAS CHANGED SINCE THE INFESTATION EVENT, AND THE WORLD WOULD SEEM TO BE FAR QUIETER NOW, AS YOU SO CRUDELY POINT OUT.
BUT NOTHING SURVIVES IN A VACUUM, AND I FEAR THIS NEW SILENCE IS MERELY A DARK AND PRECIPITOUS VOID, WAITING TO BE FILLED.
THE QUESTION IS, BY WHAT?
AND THAT'S WHERE CVO IS VITAL.
AGENT CROSS MAY HAVE ELIMINATED THE UNDERMIND THREAT FROM EXISTENCE WITH HIS NEWFOUND POWERS, BUT AS LONG AS THE WORLD—THE UNIVERSE—REMAINS INNATELY PREDISPOSED TO BALANCE, THE MYSTERIOUS PEACE WE ARE EXPERIENCING WILL *INEVITABLY* BE COUNTER-WEIGHED BY ITS MORE DIABOLICAL OPPOSITE.
AND WHEN THAT COSMIC EQUILIBRIUM IS RESTORED, IT'S CVO WHO WILL ONCE AGAIN BE CALLED UPON TO REPEL ANY NEW THREATS THAT RESULT—BOTH CONVENTIONAL AND, ESPECIALLY, SUPERNATURAL.

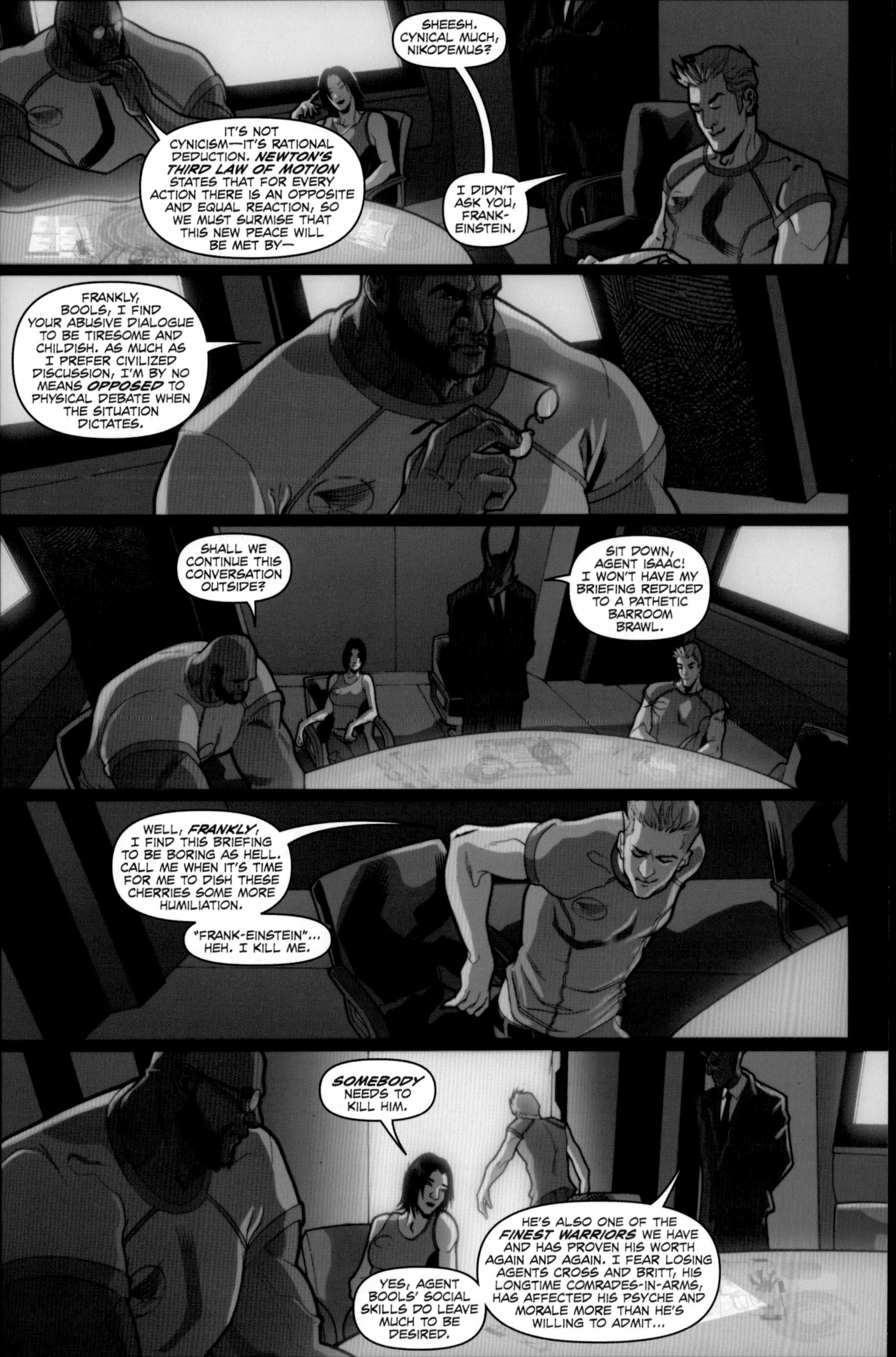
SHEESH. CYNICAL MUCH, NIKODEMUS?
IT'S NOT CYNICISM—IT'S RATIONAL DEDUCTION. NEWTON'S THIRD LAW OF MOTION STATES THAT FOR EVERY ACTION THERE IS AN OPPOSITE AND EQUAL REACTION, SO WE MUST SURMISE THAT THIS NEW PEACE WILL BE MET BY—
I DIDN'T ASK YOU, FRANK-EINSTEIN.
FRANKLY, BOOLS, I FIND YOUR ABUSIVE DIALOGUE TO BE TIRESOME AND CHILDISH. AS MUCH AS I PREFER CIVILIZED DISCUSSION, I'M BY NO MEANS OPPOSED TO PHYSICAL DEBATE WHEN THE SITUATION DICTATES.
SHALL WE CONTINUE THIS CONVERSATION OUTSIDE?
SIT DOWN, AGENT ISAAC! I WON'T HAVE MY BRIEFING REDUCED TO A PATHETIC BARROOM BRAWL.
WELL, FRANKLY, I FIND THIS BRIEFING TO BE BORING AS HELL. CALL ME WHEN IT'S TIME FOR ME TO DISH THESE CHERRIES SOME MORE HUMILIATION.
"FRANK-EINSTEIN"... HEH. I KILL ME.
SOMEBODY NEEDS TO KILL HIM.
YES, AGENT BOOLS' SOCIAL SKILLS DO LEAVE MUCH TO BE DESIRED.
HE'S ALSO ONE OF THE FINEST WARRIORS WE HAVE AND HAS PROVEN HIS WORTH AGAIN AND AGAIN. I FEAR LOSING AGENTS CROSS AND BRITT, HIS LONGTIME COMRADES-IN-ARMS, HAS AFFECTED HIS PSYCHE AND MORALE MORE THAN HE'S WILLING TO ADMIT...

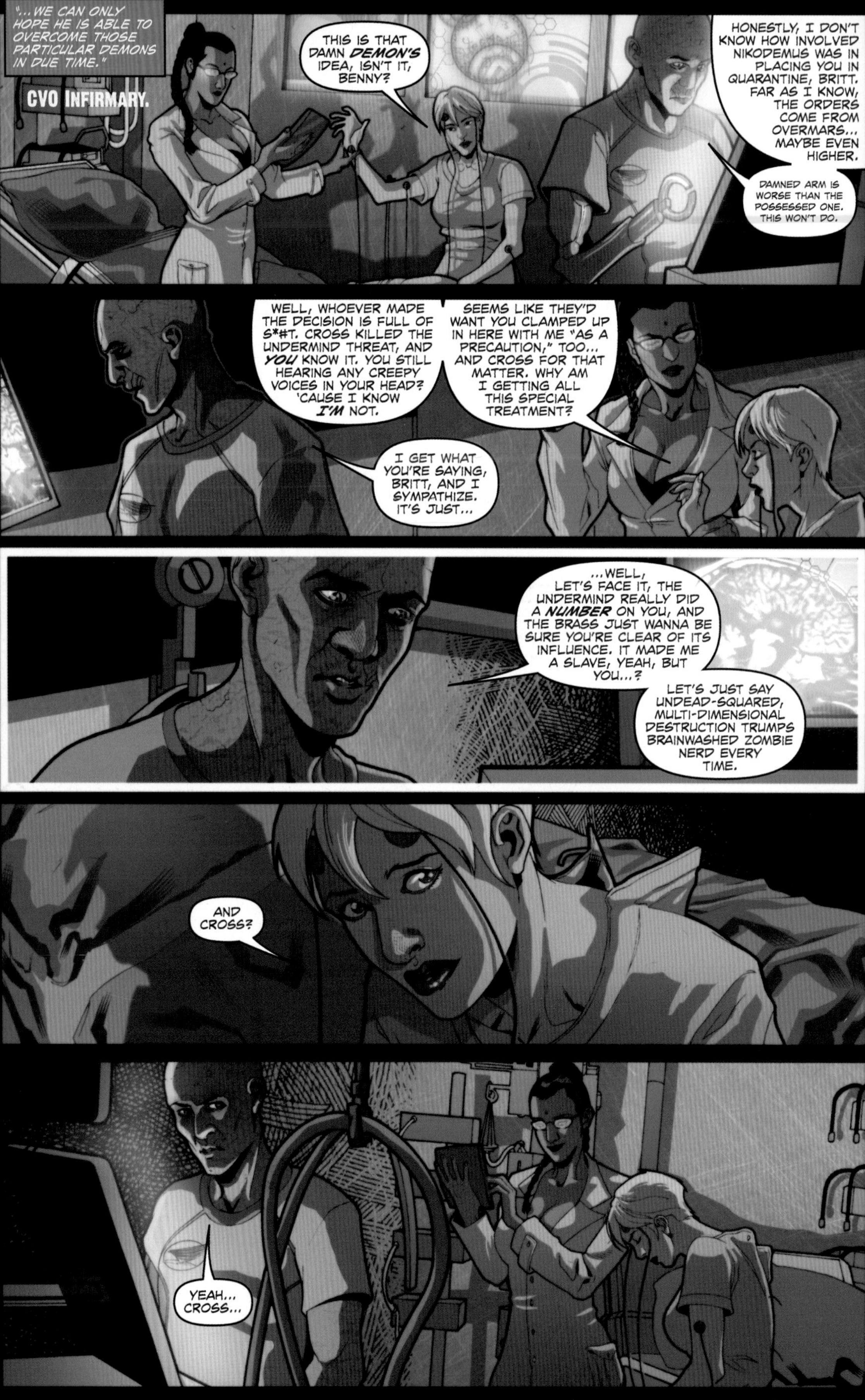
"...WE CAN ONLY HOPE HE IS ABLE TO OVERCOME THOSE PARTICULAR DEMONS IN DUE TIME."
CVO INFIRMARY.
THIS IS THAT DAMN DEMON'S IDEA, ISN'T IT, BENNY?
HONESTLY, I DON'T KNOW HOW INVOLVED NIKODEMUS WAS IN PLACING YOU IN QUARANTINE, BRITT. FAR AS I KNOW, THE ORDERS COME FROM OVERMARS... MAYBE EVEN HIGHER.
DAMNED ARM IS WORSE THAN THE POSSESSED ONE. THIS WON'T DO.
WELL, WHOEVER MADE THE DECISION IS FULL OF S*#T. CROSS KILLED THE UNDERMIND THREAT, AND YOU KNOW IT. YOU STILL HEARING ANY CREEPY VOICES IN YOUR HEAD? 'CAUSE I KNOW I'M NOT.
SEEMS LIKE THEY'D WANT YOU CLAMPED UP IN HERE WITH ME "AS A PRECAUTION," TOO... AND CROSS FOR THAT MATTER. WHY AM I GETTING ALL THIS SPECIAL TREATMENT?
I GET WHAT YOU'RE SAYING, BRITT, AND I SYMPATHIZE. IT'S JUST...
...WELL, LET'S FACE IT, THE UNDERMIND REALLY DID A NUMBER ON YOU, AND THE BRASS JUST WANNA BE SURE YOU'RE CLEAR OF ITS INFLUENCE. IT MADE ME A SLAVE, YEAH, BUT YOU...?
LET'S JUST SAY UNDEAD-SQUARED, MULTI-DIMENSIONAL DESTRUCTION TRUMPS BRAINWASHED ZOMBIE NERD EVERY TIME.
AND CROSS?
YEAH... CROSS...

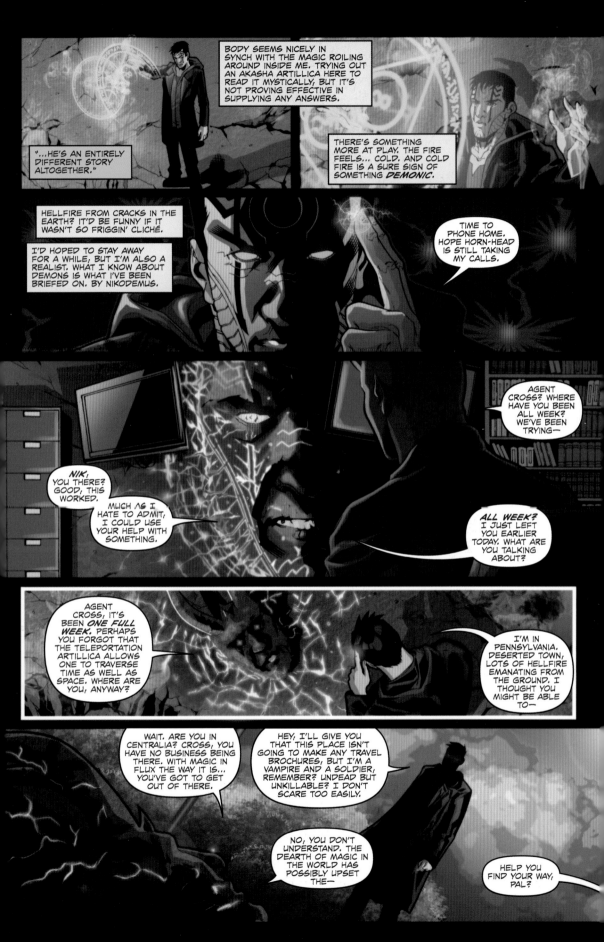

BODY SEEMS NICELY IN SYNCH WITH THE MAGIC ROILING AROUND INSIDE ME. TRYING OUT AN AKASHA ARTILLICA HERE TO READ IT MYSTICALLY; BUT IT'S NOT PROVING EFFECTIVE IN SUPPLYING ANY ANSWERS.

"...HE'S AN ENTIRELY DIFFERENT STORY ALTOGETHER."

THERE'S SOMETHING MORE AT PLAY. THE FIRE FEELS... COLD. AND COLD FIRE IS A SURE SIGN OF SOMETHING *DEMONIC.*

HELLFIRE FROM CRACKS IN THE EARTH? IT'D BE FUNNY IF IT WASN'T SO FRIGGIN' CLICHÉ.

I'D HOPED TO STAY AWAY FOR A WHILE, BUT I'M ALSO A REALIST. WHAT I KNOW ABOUT DEMONS IS WHAT I'VE BEEN BRIEFED ON. BY NIKODEMUS.

TIME TO PHONE HOME. HOPE HORN-HEAD IS STILL TAKING MY CALLS.

AGENT CROSS? WHERE HAVE YOU BEEN ALL WEEK? WE'VE BEEN TRYING—

NIK, YOU THERE? GOOD, THIS WORKED.

MUCH AS I HATE TO ADMIT, I COULD USE YOUR HELP WITH SOMETHING.

ALL WEEK? I JUST LEFT YOU EARLIER TODAY. WHAT ARE YOU TALKING ABOUT?

AGENT CROSS, IT'S BEEN *ONE FULL WEEK.* PERHAPS YOU FORGOT THAT THE TELEPORTATION ARTILLICA ALLOWS ONE TO TRAVERSE TIME AS WELL AS SPACE. WHERE ARE YOU, ANYWAY?

I'M IN PENNSYLVANIA. DESERTED TOWN, LOTS OF HELLFIRE EMANATING FROM THE GROUND. I THOUGHT YOU MIGHT BE ABLE TO—

WAIT. ARE YOU IN CENTRALIA? CROSS, YOU HAVE NO BUSINESS BEING THERE. WITH MAGIC IN FLUX THE WAY IT IS... YOU'VE GOT TO GET OUT OF THERE.

HEY, I'LL GIVE YOU THAT THIS PLACE ISN'T GOING TO MAKE ANY TRAVEL BROCHURES, BUT I'M A VAMPIRE AND A SOLDIER, REMEMBER? UNDEAD BUT UNKILLABLE? I DON'T SCARE TOO EASILY.

NO, YOU DON'T UNDERSTAND. THE DEARTH OF MAGIC IN THE WORLD HAS POSSIBLY UPSET THE—

HELP YOU FIND YOUR WAY, PAL?

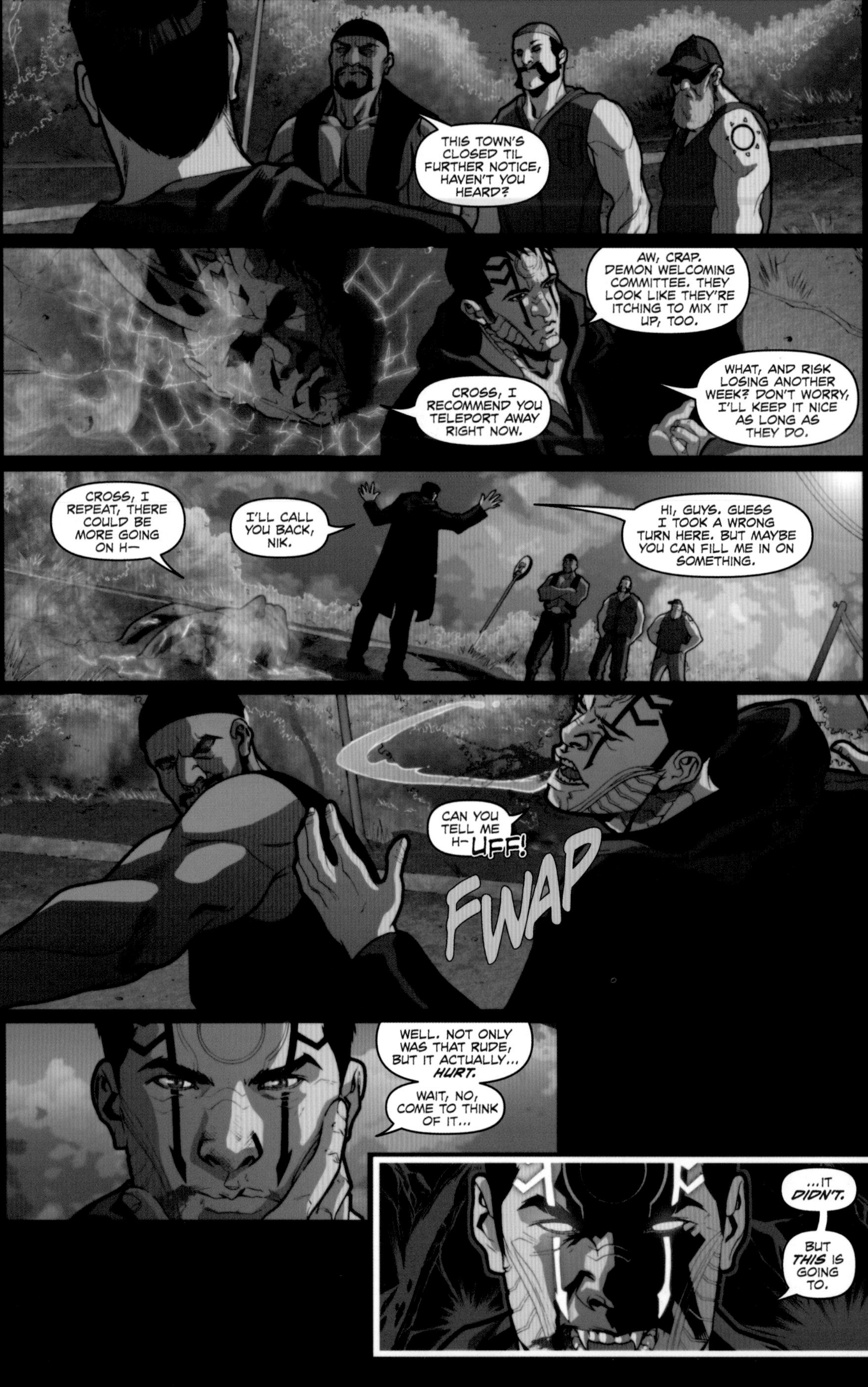
THIS TOWN'S CLOSED TIL FURTHER NOTICE, HAVEN'T YOU HEARD?
AW, CRAP. DEMON WELCOMING COMMITTEE. THEY LOOK LIKE THEY'RE ITCHING TO MIX IT UP, TOO.
CROSS, I RECOMMEND YOU TELEPORT AWAY RIGHT NOW.
WHAT, AND RISK LOSING ANOTHER WEEK? DON'T WORRY, I'LL KEEP IT NICE AS LONG AS THEY DO.
CROSS, I REPEAT, THERE COULD BE MORE GOING ON H—
I'LL CALL YOU BACK, NIK.
HI, GUYS. GUESS I TOOK A WRONG TURN HERE. BUT MAYBE YOU CAN FILL ME IN ON SOMETHING.
CAN YOU TELL ME H—UFF!
FWAP
WELL. NOT ONLY WAS THAT RUDE, BUT IT ACTUALLY... *HURT.*
WAIT, NO, COME TO THINK OF IT...
...IT *DIDN'T.*
BUT *THIS* IS GOING TO.

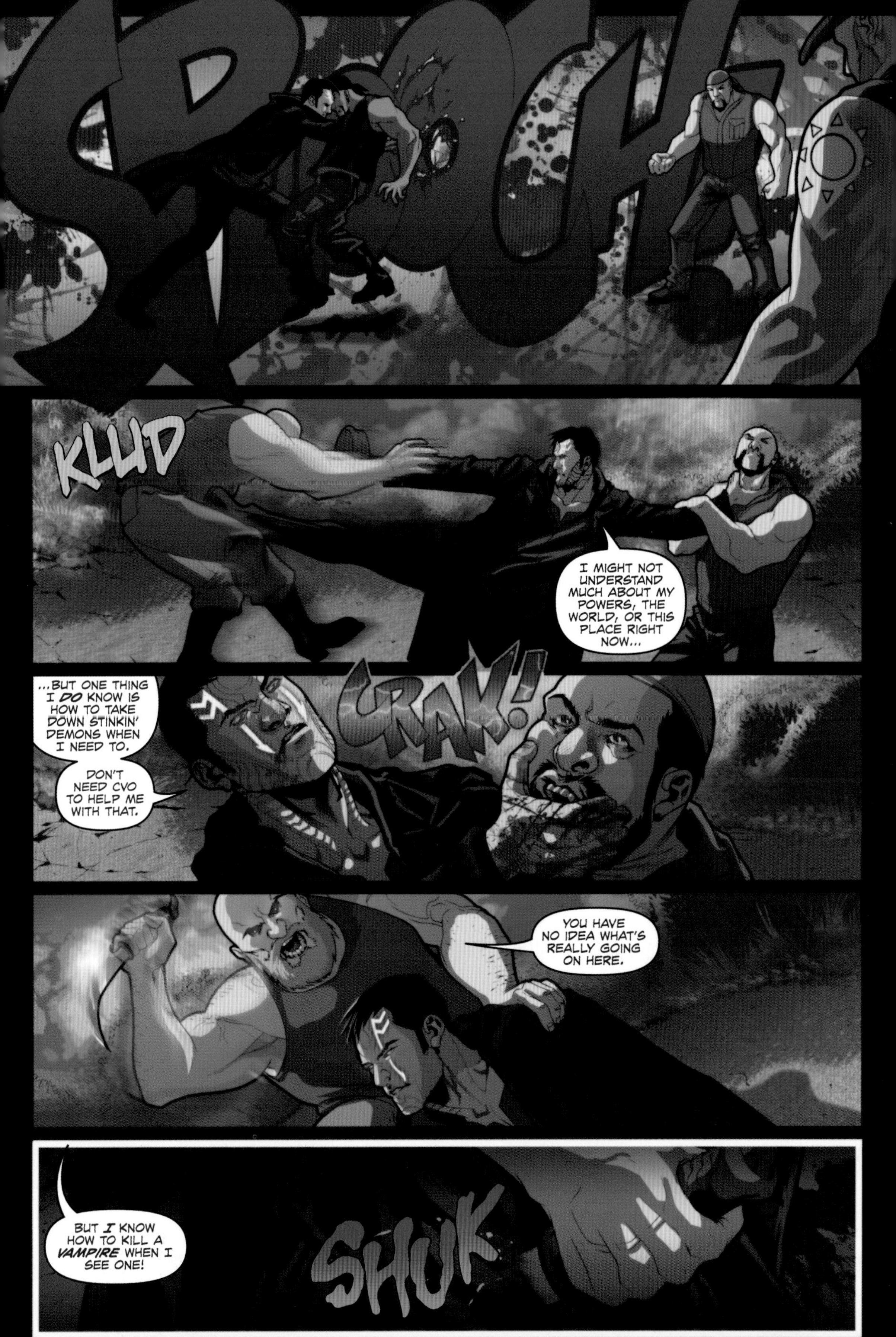
SPLOOCH!
KLUD
I MIGHT NOT UNDERSTAND MUCH ABOUT MY POWERS, THE WORLD, OR THIS PLACE RIGHT NOW...
...BUT ONE THING I DO KNOW IS HOW TO TAKE DOWN STINKIN' DEMONS WHEN I NEED TO.
CRAK!
DON'T NEED CVO TO HELP ME WITH THAT.
YOU HAVE NO IDEA WHAT'S REALLY GOING ON HERE.
BUT I KNOW HOW TO KILL A VAMPIRE WHEN I SEE ONE!
SHUK

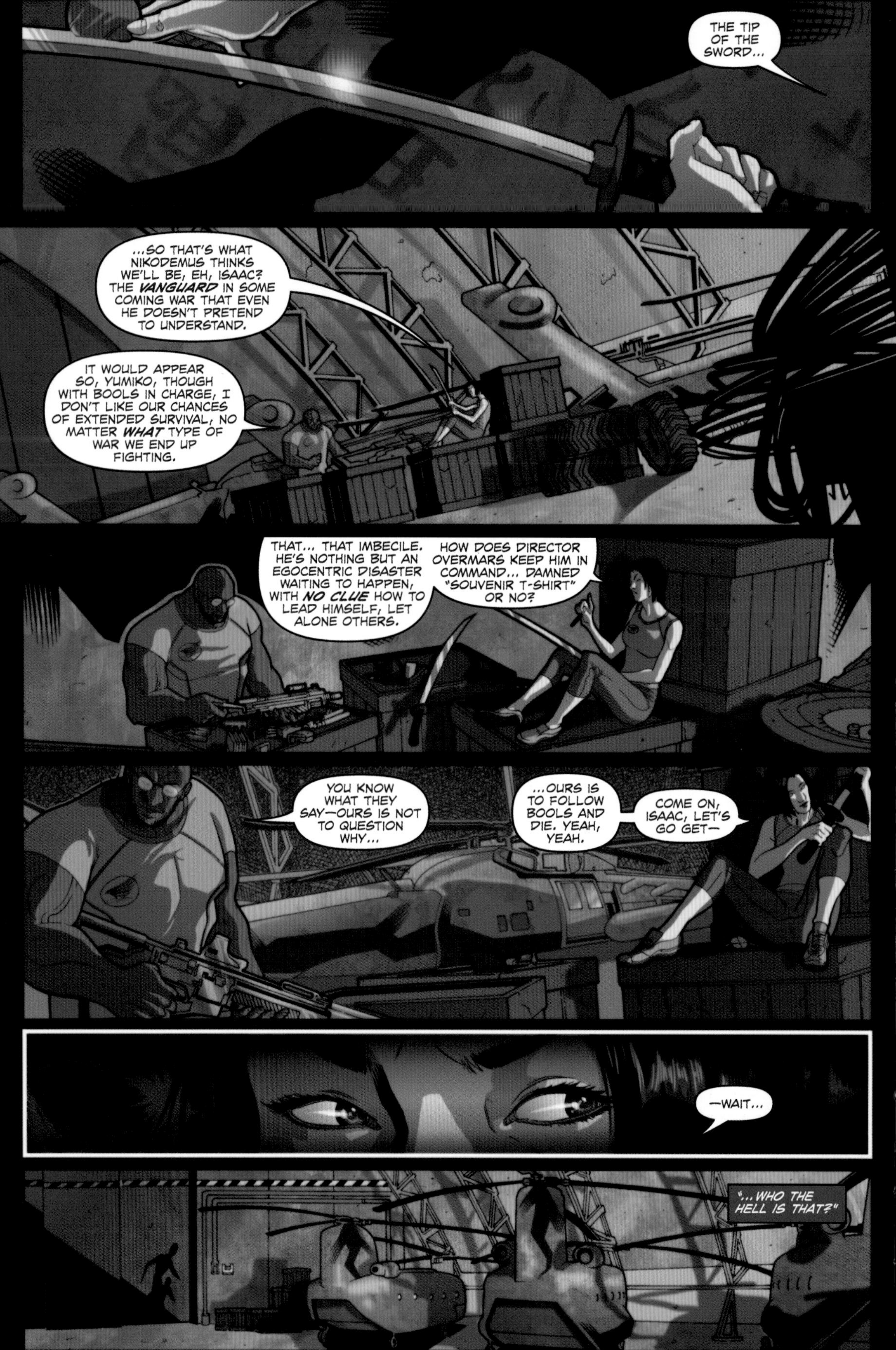
THE TIP OF THE SWORD...
...SO THAT'S WHAT NIKODEMUS THINKS WE'LL BE, EH, ISAAC? THE VANGUARD IN SOME COMING WAR THAT EVEN HE DOESN'T PRETEND TO UNDERSTAND.
IT WOULD APPEAR SO, YUMIKO, THOUGH WITH BOOLS IN CHARGE, I DON'T LIKE OUR CHANCES OF EXTENDED SURVIVAL, NO MATTER WHAT TYPE OF WAR WE END UP FIGHTING.
THAT... THAT IMBECILE. HE'S NOTHING BUT AN EGOCENTRIC DISASTER WAITING TO HAPPEN, WITH NO CLUE HOW TO LEAD HIMSELF, LET ALONE OTHERS.
HOW DOES DIRECTOR OVERMARS KEEP HIM IN COMMAND... DAMNED "SOUVENIR T-SHIRT" OR NO?
YOU KNOW WHAT THEY SAY—OURS IS NOT TO QUESTION WHY...
...OURS IS TO FOLLOW BOOLS AND DIE. YEAH, YEAH.
COME ON, ISAAC, LET'S GO GET—
—WAIT...
"...WHO THE HELL IS THAT?"

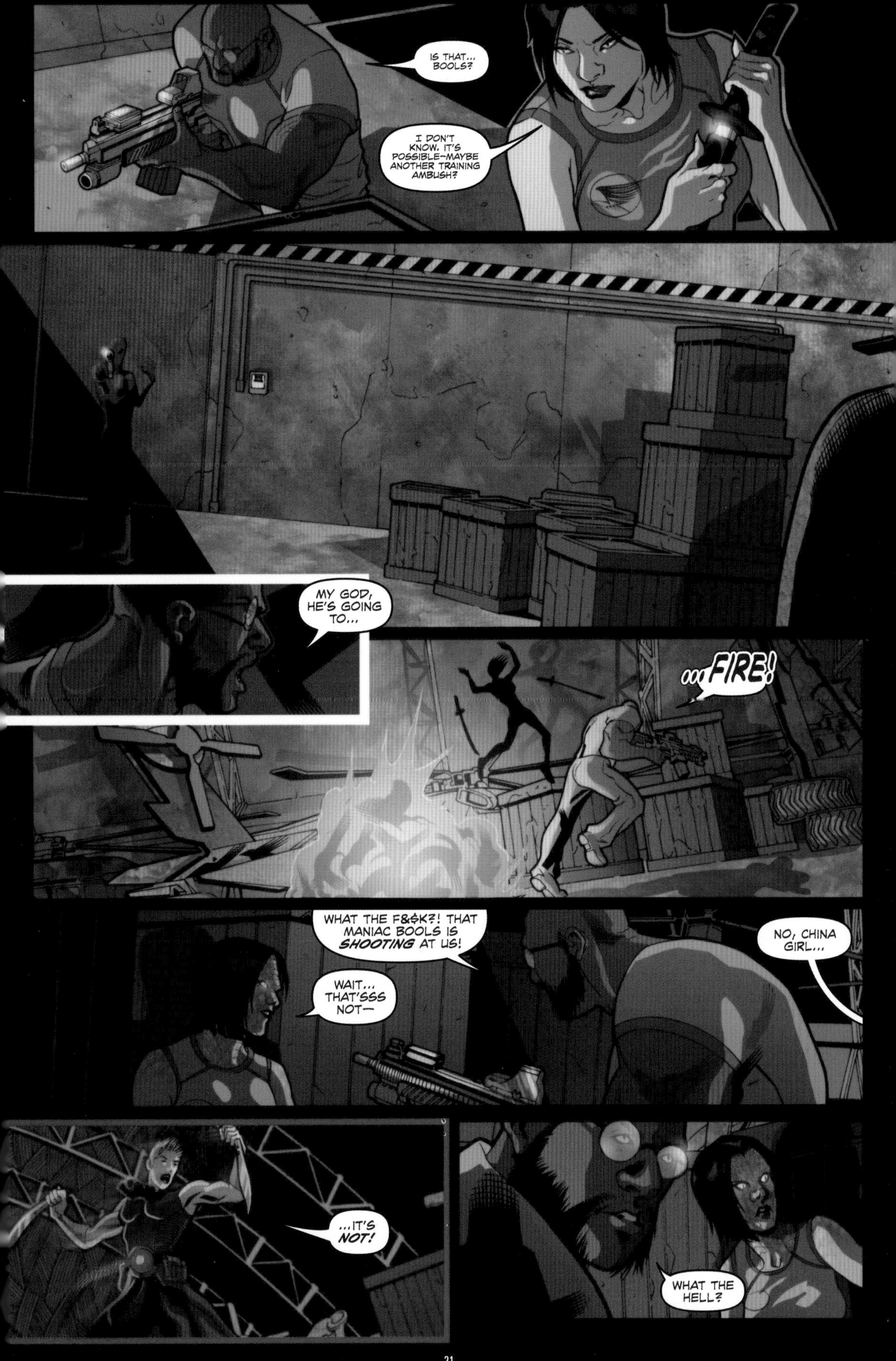
IS THAT... BOOLS?
I DON'T KNOW. IT'S POSSIBLE—MAYBE ANOTHER TRAINING AMBUSH?
MY GOD, HE'S GOING TO...
...FIRE!
WHAT THE F&$K?! THAT MANIAC BOOLS IS SHOOTING AT US!
WAIT... THAT'SSS NOT—
NO, CHINA GIRL...
...IT'S NOT!
WHAT THE HELL?

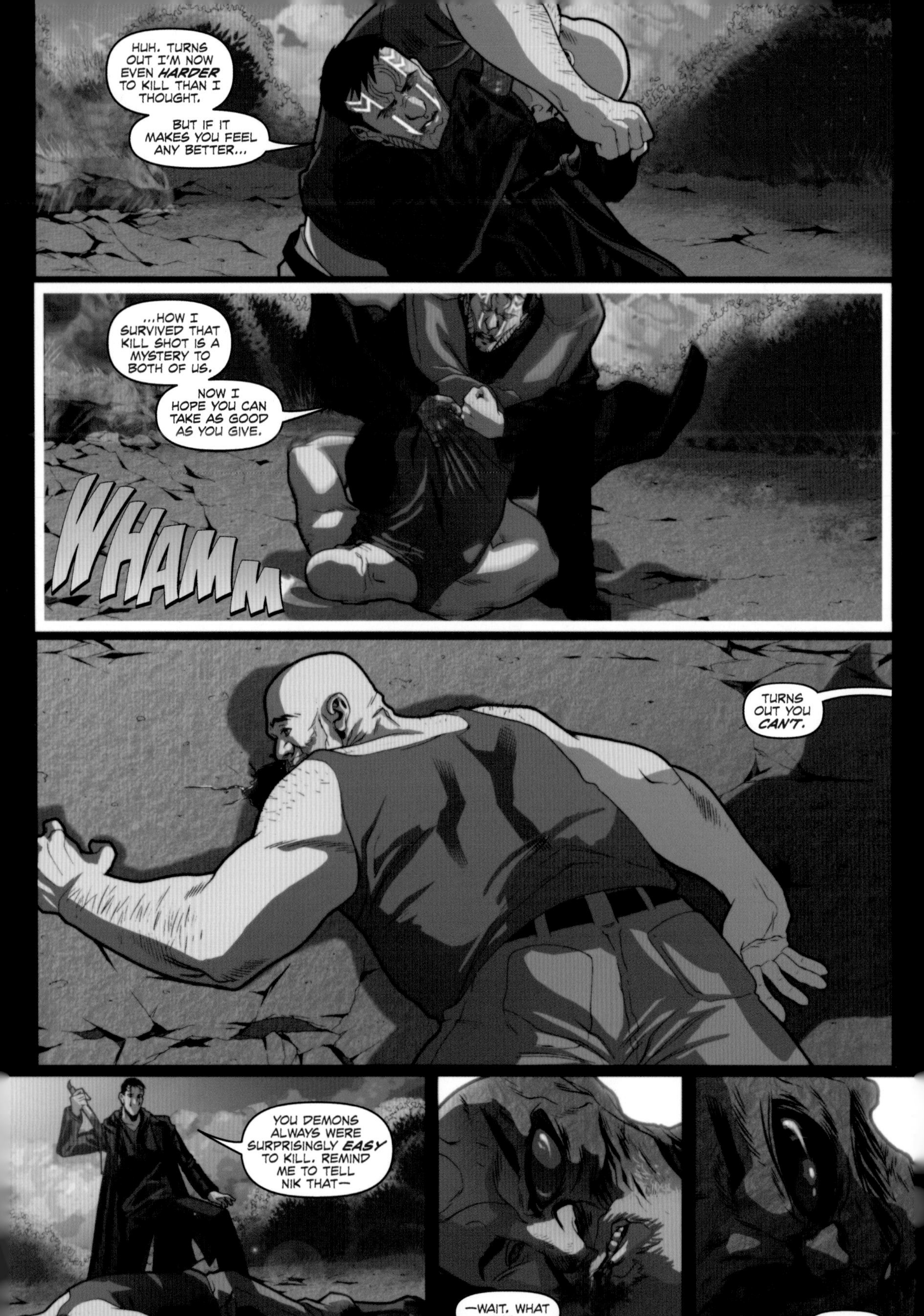
HUH. TURNS OUT I'M NOW EVEN **HARDER** TO KILL THAN I THOUGHT.
BUT IF IT MAKES YOU FEEL ANY BETTER...
...HOW I SURVIVED THAT KILL SHOT IS A MYSTERY TO BOTH OF US.
NOW I HOPE YOU CAN TAKE AS GOOD AS YOU GIVE.
WHAMM
TURNS OUT YOU **CAN'T**.
YOU DEMONS ALWAYS WERE SURPRISINGLY **EASY** TO KILL. REMIND ME TO TELL NIK THAT—
—WAIT. WHAT THE—
—**HELL?**

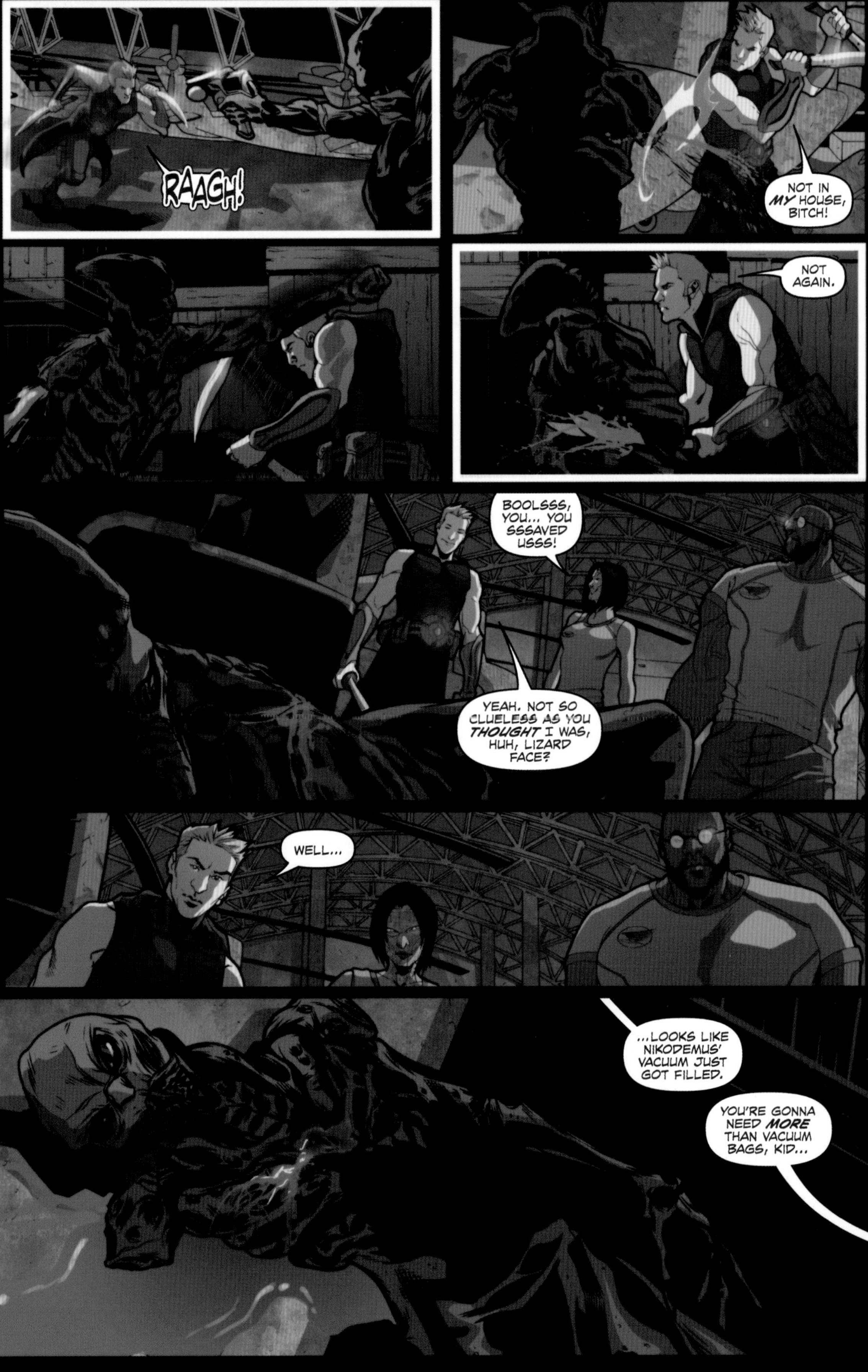
RAAGH!
NOT IN *MY* HOUSE, BITCH!
NOT AGAIN.
BOOLSSS, YOU... YOU SSSAVED USSS!
YEAH. NOT SO CLUELESS AS YOU *THOUGHT* I WAS, HUH, LIZARD FACE?
WELL...
...LOOKS LIKE NIKODEMUS' VACUUM JUST GOT FILLED.
YOU'RE GONNA NEED *MORE* THAN VACUUM BAGS, KID...

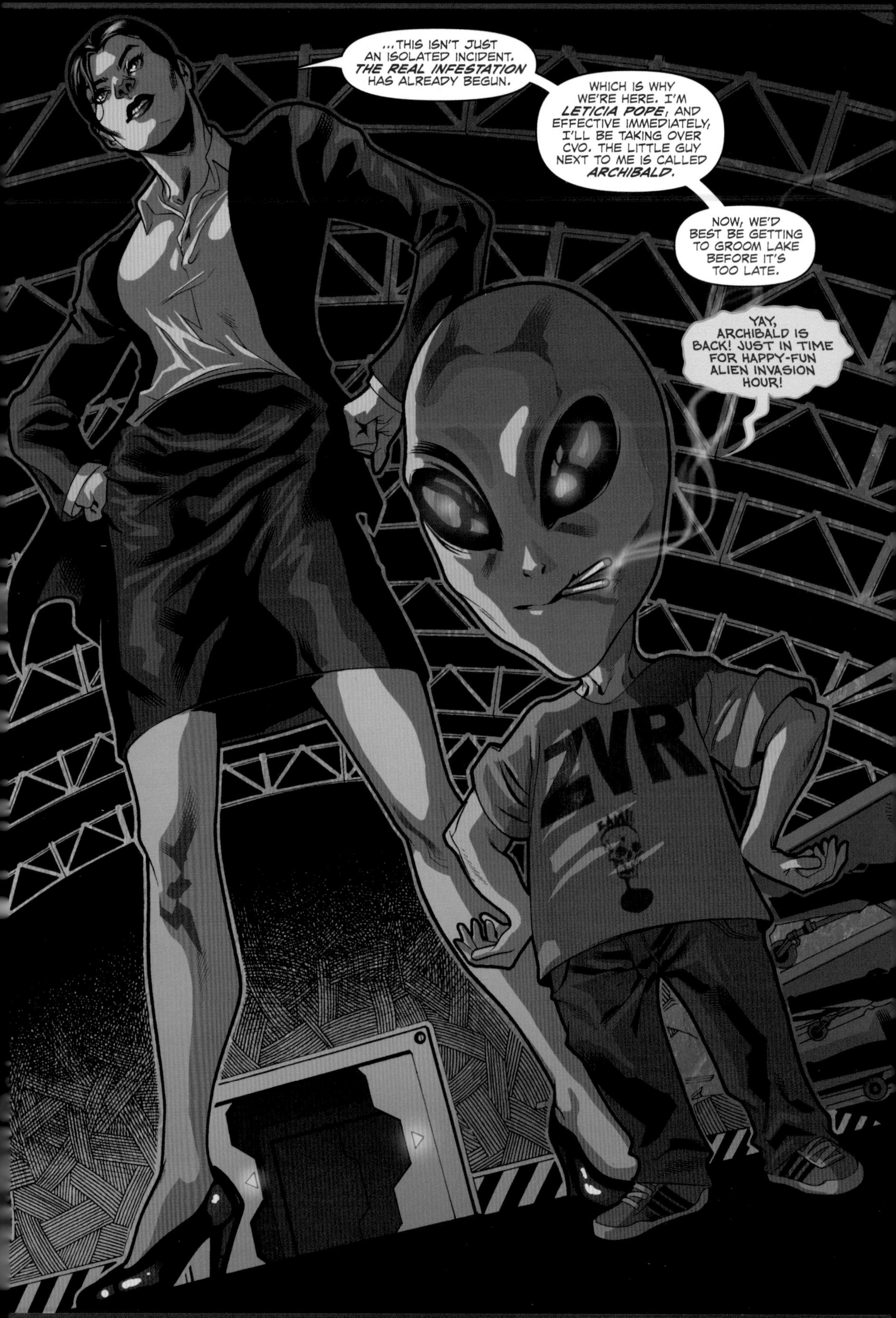
...THIS ISN'T JUST AN ISOLATED INCIDENT. THE REAL INFESTATION HAS ALREADY BEGUN.
WHICH IS WHY WE'RE HERE. I'M LETICIA POPE, AND EFFECTIVE IMMEDIATELY, I'LL BE TAKING OVER CVO. THE LITTLE GUY NEXT TO ME IS CALLED ARCHIBALD.
NOW, WE'D BEST BE GETTING TO GROOM LAKE BEFORE IT'S TOO LATE.
YAY, ARCHIBALD IS BACK! JUST IN TIME FOR HAPPY-FUN ALIEN INVASION HOUR!
ZVR

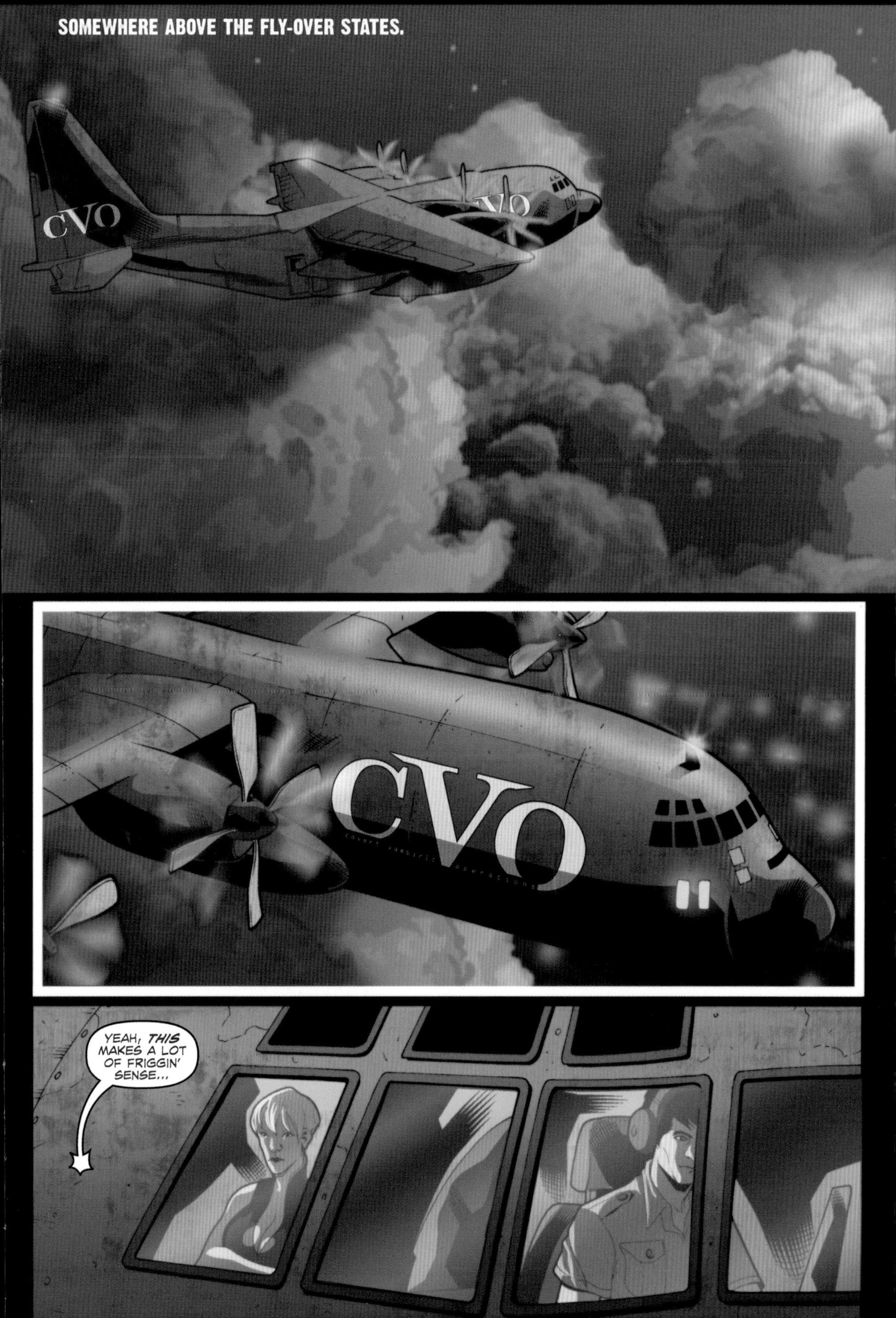
SOMEWHERE ABOVE THE FLY-OVER STATES.
CVO
CVO
covert vampiric operations
YEAH, *THIS* MAKES A LOT OF FRIGGIN' SENSE...

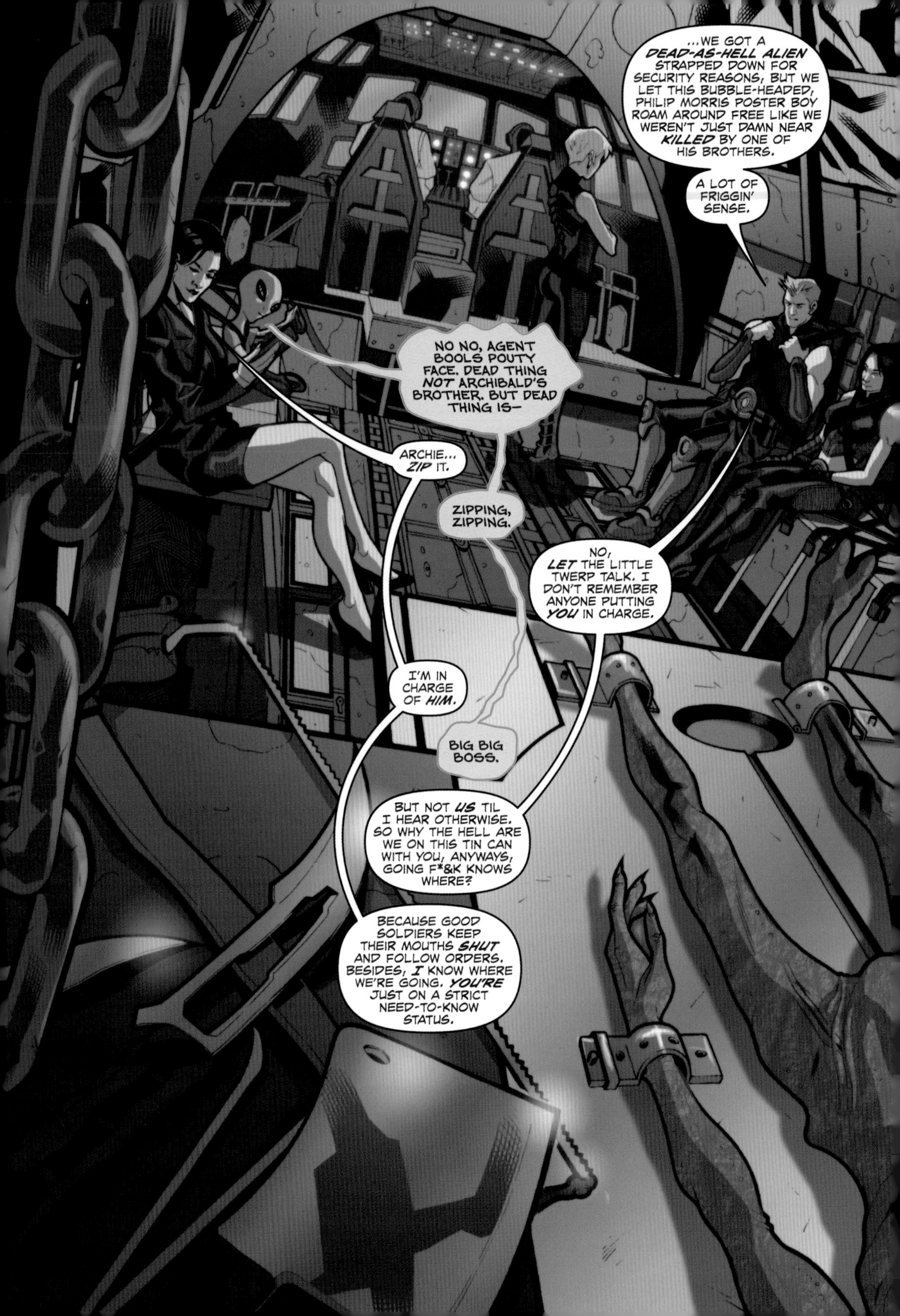
...WE GOT A DEAD-AS-HELL ALIEN STRAPPED DOWN FOR SECURITY REASONS, BUT WE LET THIS BUBBLE-HEADED, PHILIP MORRIS POSTER BOY ROAM AROUND FREE LIKE WE WEREN'T JUST DAMN NEAR KILLED BY ONE OF HIS BROTHERS.
A LOT OF FRIGGIN' SENSE.
NO NO, AGENT BOOLS POUTY FACE. DEAD THING NOT ARCHIBALD'S BROTHER. BUT DEAD THING IS—
ARCHIE... ZIP IT.
ZIPPING, ZIPPING.
NO, LET THE LITTLE TWERP TALK. I DON'T REMEMBER ANYONE PUTTING YOU IN CHARGE.
I'M IN CHARGE OF HIM.
BIG BIG BOSS.
BUT NOT US TIL I HEAR OTHERWISE. SO WHY THE HELL ARE WE ON THIS TIN CAN WITH YOU, ANYWAYS, GOING F*&K KNOWS WHERE?
BECAUSE GOOD SOLDIERS KEEP THEIR MOUTHS SHUT AND FOLLOW ORDERS. BESIDES, I KNOW WHERE WE'RE GOING. YOU'RE JUST ON A STRICT NEED-TO-KNOW STATUS.

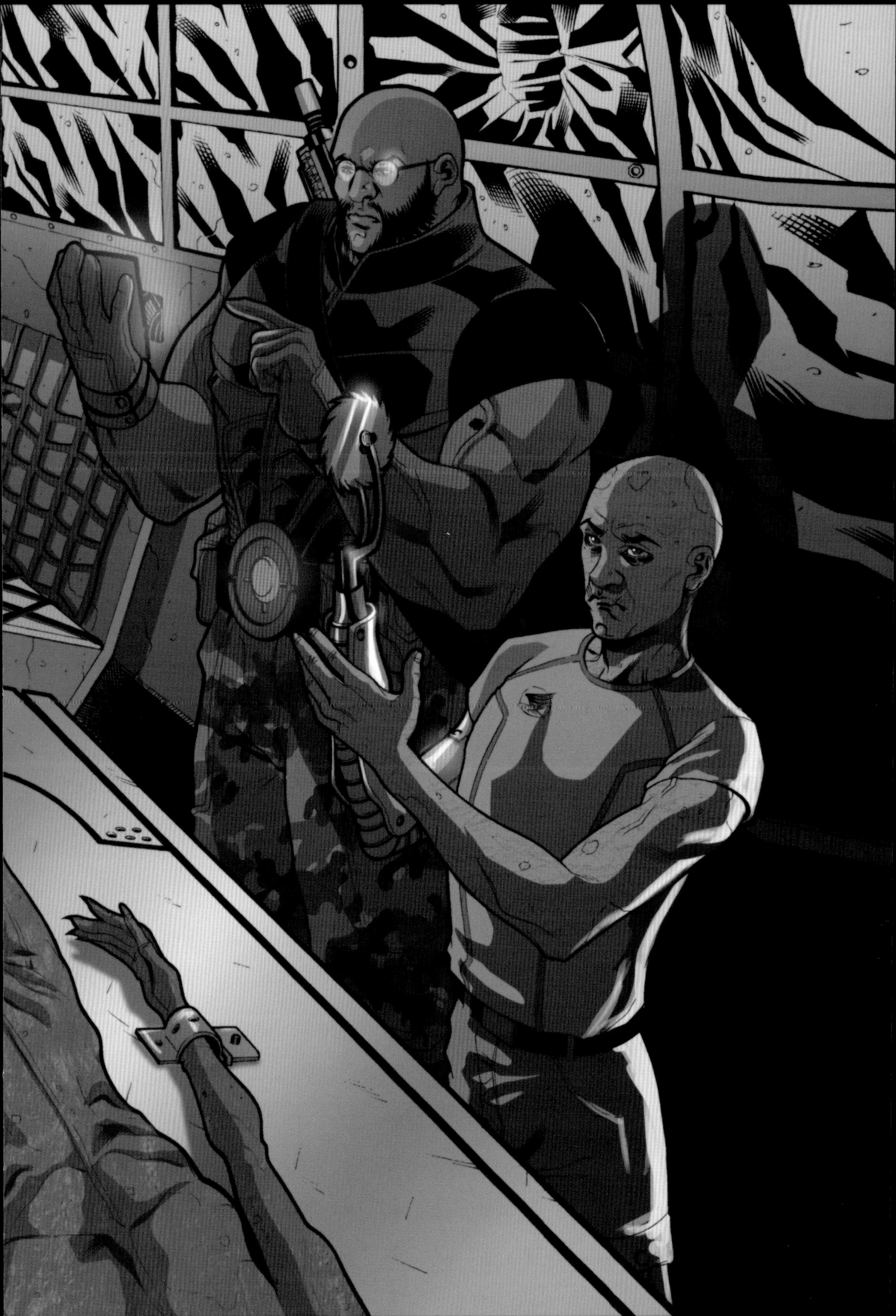

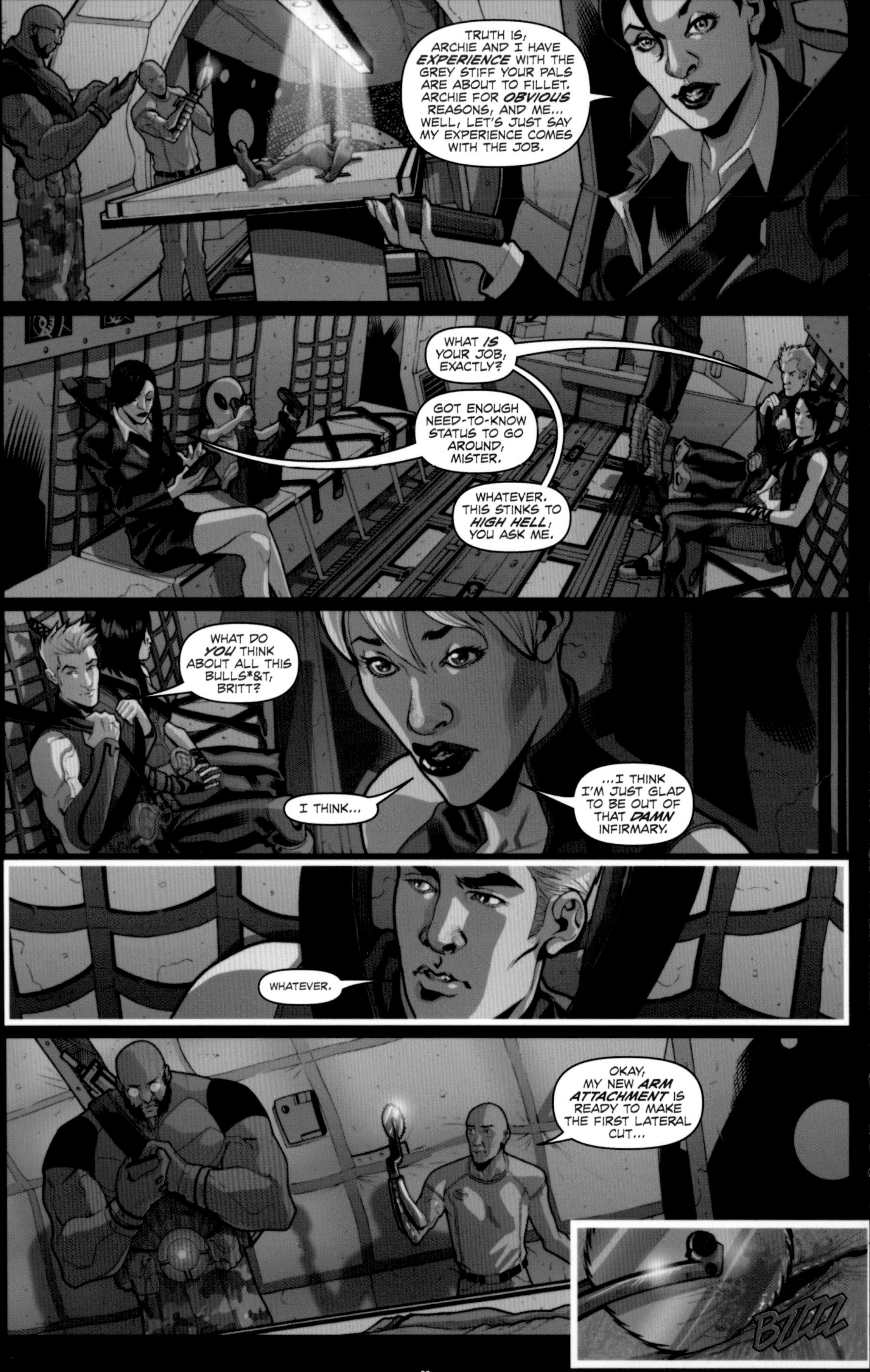
TRUTH IS, ARCHIE AND I HAVE EXPERIENCE WITH THE GREY STIFF YOUR PALS ARE ABOUT TO FILLET. ARCHIE FOR OBVIOUS REASONS, AND ME... WELL, LET'S JUST SAY MY EXPERIENCE COMES WITH THE JOB.
WHAT IS YOUR JOB, EXACTLY?
GOT ENOUGH NEED-TO-KNOW STATUS TO GO AROUND, MISTER.
WHATEVER. THIS STINKS TO HIGH HELL, YOU ASK ME.
WHAT DO YOU THINK ABOUT ALL THIS BULLS*&T, BRITT?
I THINK...
...I THINK I'M JUST GLAD TO BE OUT OF THAT DAMN INFIRMARY.
WHATEVER.
OKAY, MY NEW ARM ATTACHMENT IS READY TO MAKE THE FIRST LATERAL CUT...
BZZZ

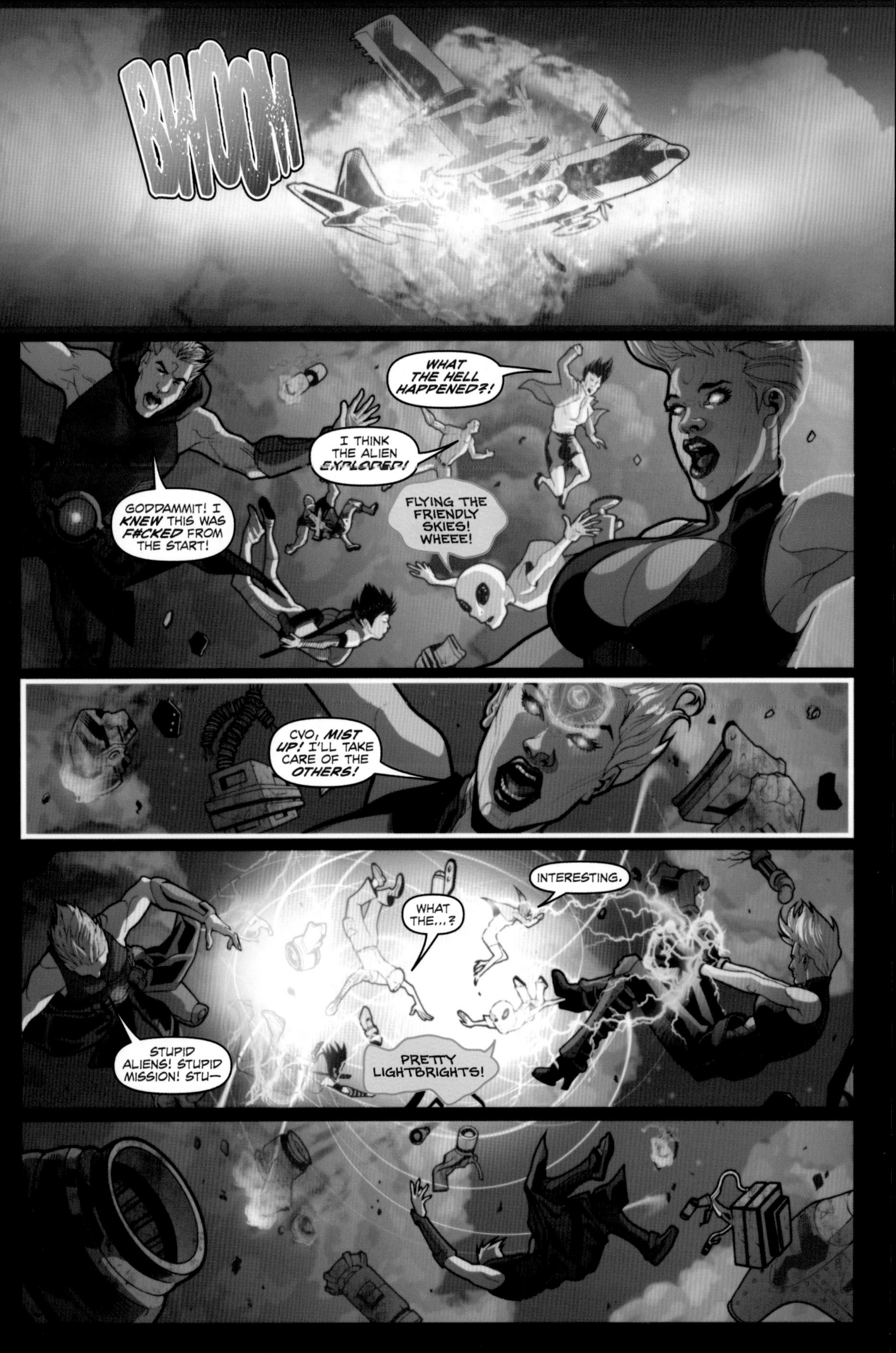
BWOOM
WHAT THE HELL HAPPENED?!
I THINK THE ALIEN EXPLODED!
GODDAMMIT! I KNEW THIS WAS F#CKED FROM THE START!
FLYING THE FRIENDLY SKIES! WHEEE!
CVO, MIST UP! I'LL TAKE CARE OF THE OTHERS!
INTERESTING.
WHAT THE...?
STUPID ALIENS! STUPID MISSION! STU—
PRETTY LIGHTBRIGHTS!

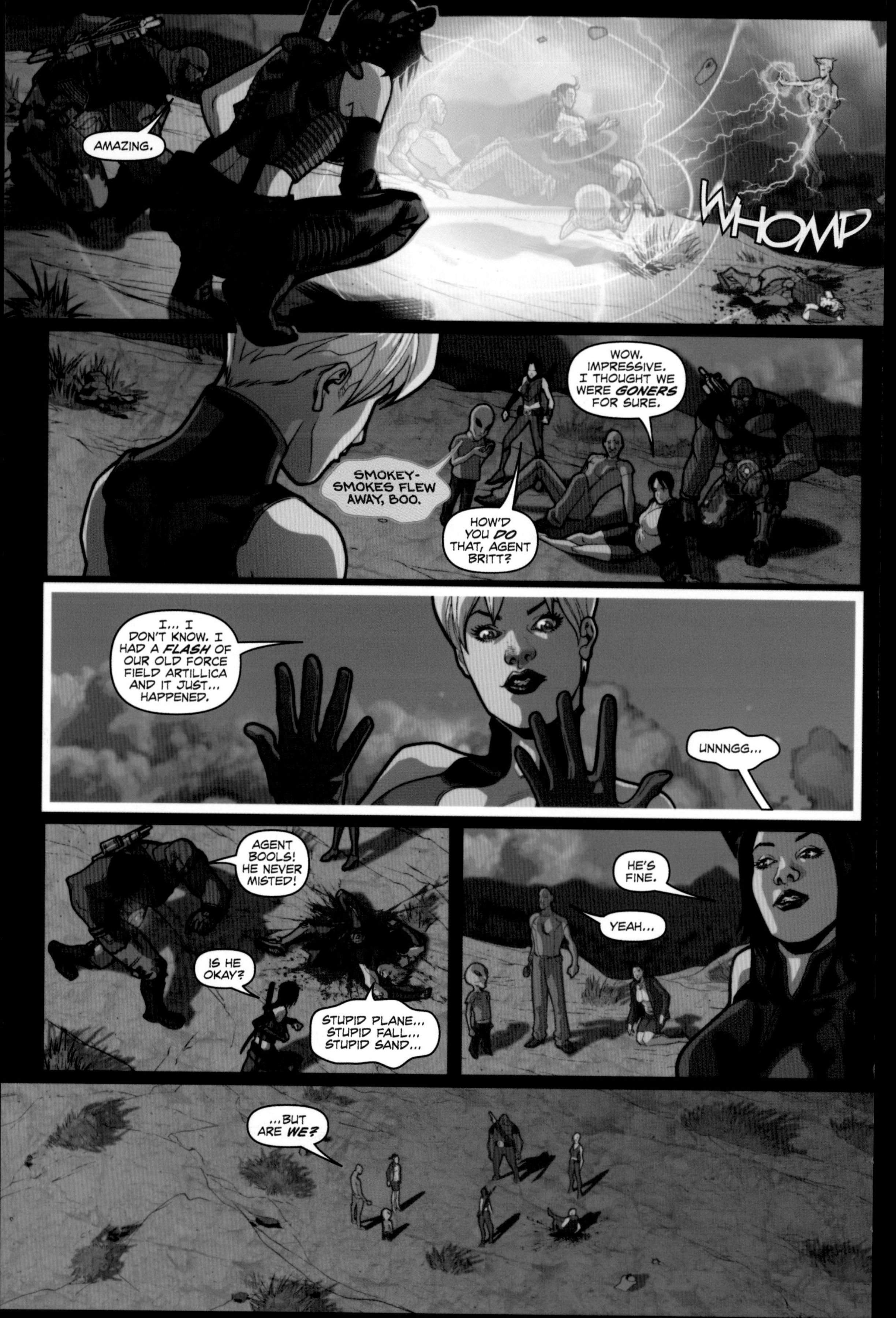
AMAZING.
WHOMP
WOW. IMPRESSIVE. I THOUGHT WE WERE GONERS FOR SURE.
SMOKEY-SMOKES FLEW AWAY, BOO.
HOW'D YOU DO THAT, AGENT BRITT?
I... I DON'T KNOW. I HAD A FLASH OF OUR OLD FORCE FIELD ARTILLICA AND IT JUST... HAPPENED.
UNNNGG...
AGENT BOOLS! HE NEVER MISTED!
IS HE OKAY?
STUPID PLANE... STUPID FALL... STUPID SAND...
HE'S FINE.
YEAH...
...BUT ARE WE?

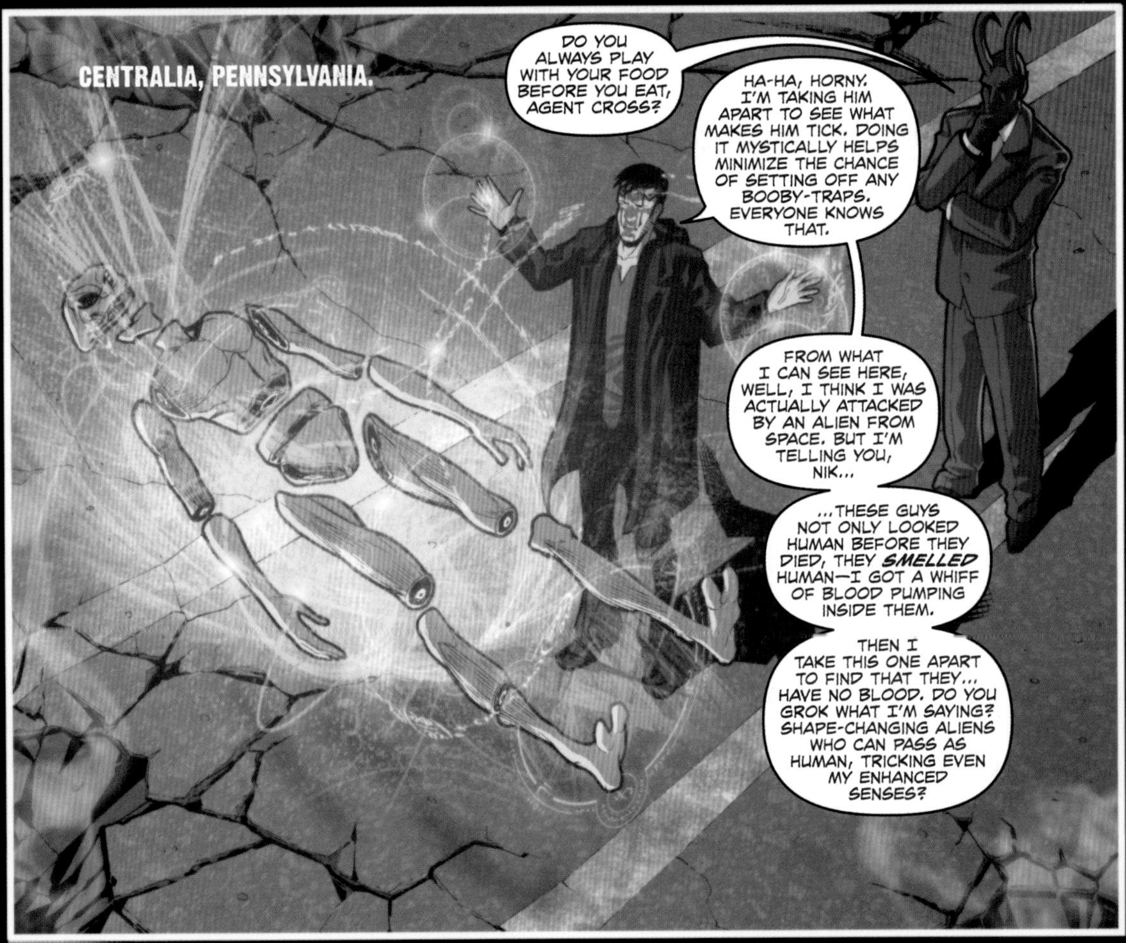
CENTRALIA, PENNSYLVANIA.
DO YOU ALWAYS PLAY WITH YOUR FOOD BEFORE YOU EAT, AGENT CROSS?
HA-HA, HORNY. I'M TAKING HIM APART TO SEE WHAT MAKES HIM TICK. DOING IT MYSTICALLY HELPS MINIMIZE THE CHANCE OF SETTING OFF ANY BOOBY-TRAPS. EVERYONE KNOWS THAT.
FROM WHAT I CAN SEE HERE, WELL, I THINK I WAS ACTUALLY ATTACKED BY AN ALIEN FROM SPACE. BUT I'M TELLING YOU, NIK...
...THESE GUYS NOT ONLY LOOKED HUMAN BEFORE THEY DIED, THEY SMELLED HUMAN—I GOT A WHIFF OF BLOOD PUMPING INSIDE THEM.
THEN I TAKE THIS ONE APART TO FIND THAT THEY... HAVE NO BLOOD. DO YOU GROK WHAT I'M SAYING? SHAPE-CHANGING ALIENS WHO CAN PASS AS HUMAN, TRICKING EVEN MY ENHANCED SENSES?

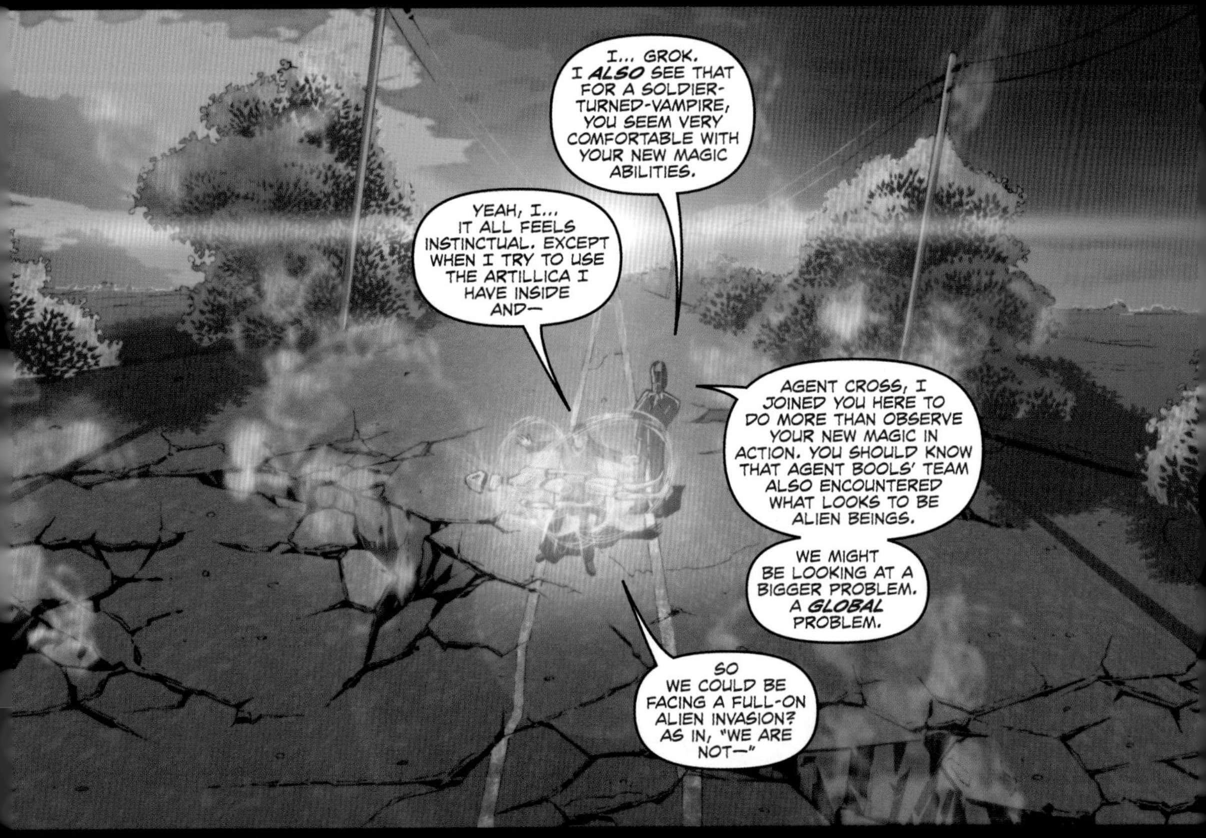
I... GROK. I ALSO SEE THAT FOR A SOLDIER-TURNED-VAMPIRE, YOU SEEM VERY COMFORTABLE WITH YOUR NEW MAGIC ABILITIES.
YEAH, I... IT ALL FEELS INSTINCTUAL. EXCEPT WHEN I TRY TO USE THE ARTILLICA I HAVE INSIDE AND—
AGENT CROSS, I JOINED YOU HERE TO DO MORE THAN OBSERVE YOUR NEW MAGIC IN ACTION. YOU SHOULD KNOW THAT AGENT BOOLS' TEAM ALSO ENCOUNTERED WHAT LOOKS TO BE ALIEN BEINGS.
WE MIGHT BE LOOKING AT A BIGGER PROBLEM. A GLOBAL PROBLEM.
SO WE COULD BE FACING A FULL-ON ALIEN INVASION? AS IN, "WE ARE NOT—"

"—ALONE?"

WHAT THE HELL—?

NIK, STAY CLOSE, I CAN GENERATE A SHIELD AND—

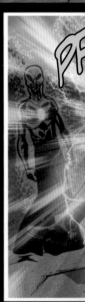

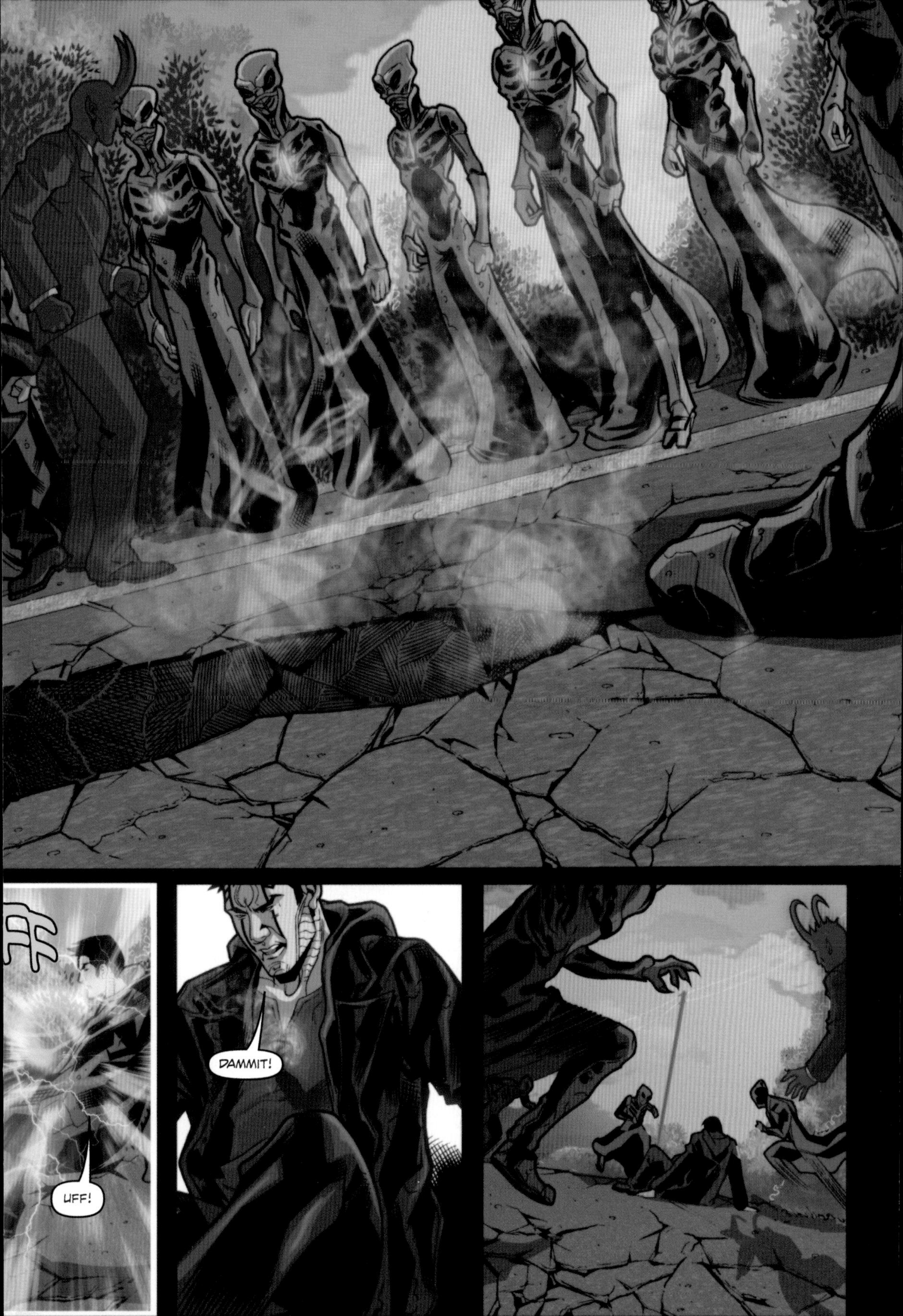
FF
UFF!
DAMMIT!

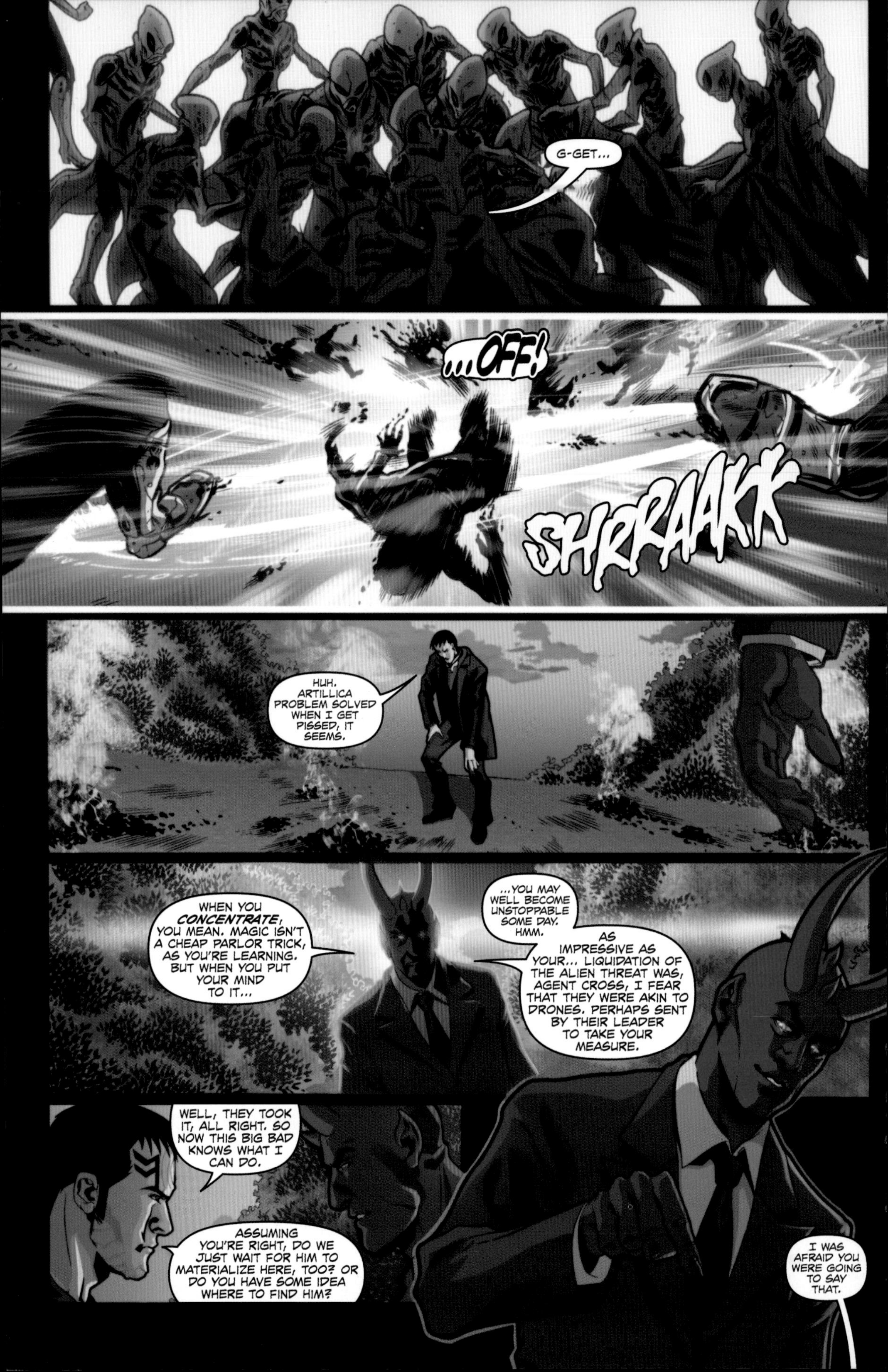
G-GET...
...OFF!
SHRRAAKK
HUH. ARTILLICA PROBLEM SOLVED WHEN I GET PISSED, IT SEEMS.
WHEN YOU *CONCENTRATE*, YOU MEAN. MAGIC ISN'T A CHEAP PARLOR TRICK, AS YOU'RE LEARNING. BUT WHEN YOU PUT YOUR MIND TO IT...
...YOU MAY WELL BECOME UNSTOPPABLE SOME DAY. HMM.
AS IMPRESSIVE AS YOUR... LIQUIDATION OF THE ALIEN THREAT WAS, AGENT CROSS, I FEAR THAT THEY WERE AKIN TO DRONES. PERHAPS SENT BY THEIR LEADER TO TAKE YOUR MEASURE.
WELL, THEY TOOK IT, ALL RIGHT. SO NOW THIS BIG BAD KNOWS WHAT I CAN DO.
ASSUMING YOU'RE RIGHT, DO WE JUST WAIT FOR HIM TO MATERIALIZE HERE, TOO? OR DO YOU HAVE SOME IDEA WHERE TO FIND HIM?
I WAS AFRAID YOU WERE GOING TO SAY THAT.

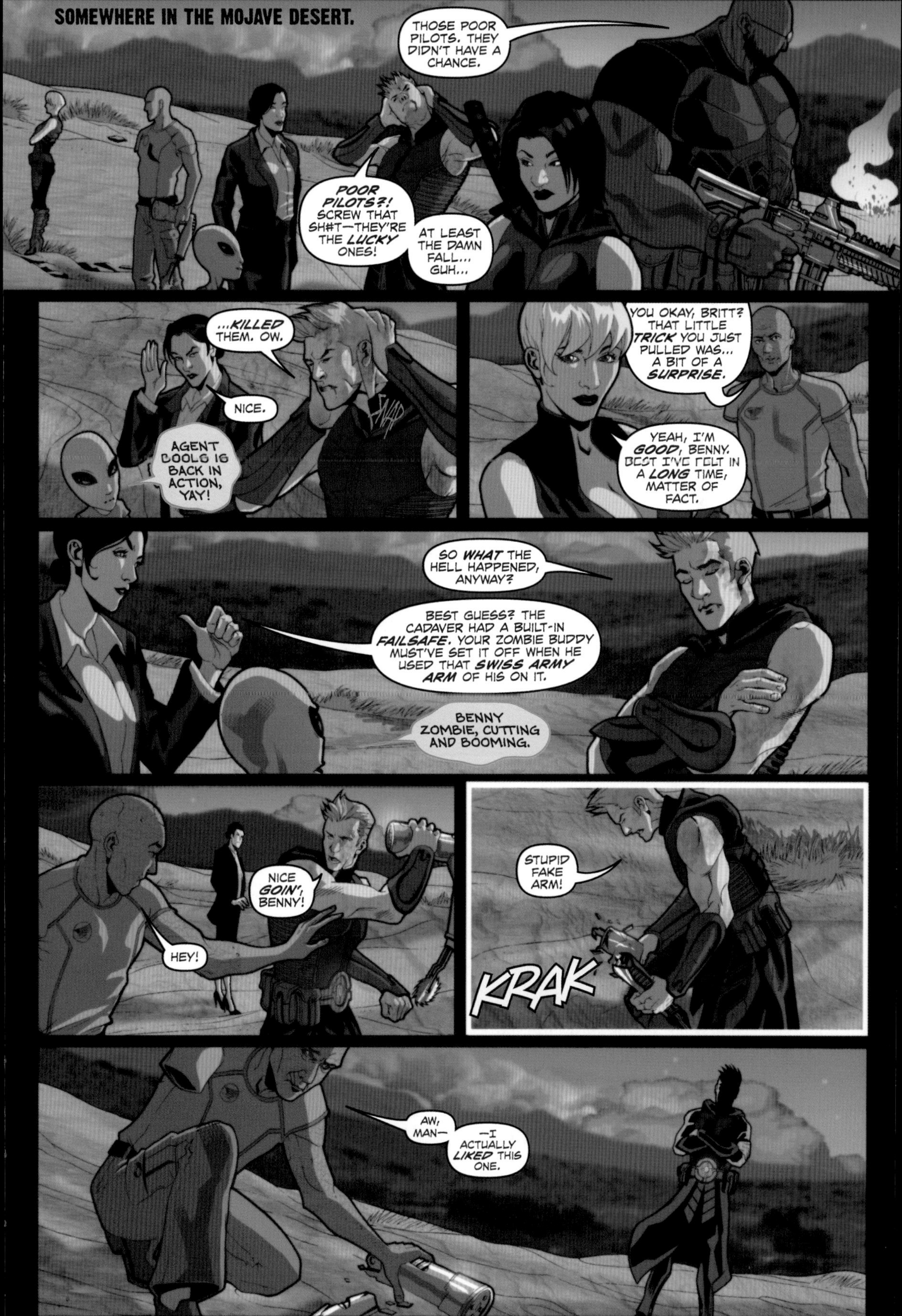
SOMEWHERE IN THE MOJAVE DESERT.
THOSE POOR PILOTS. THEY DIDN'T HAVE A CHANCE.
POOR PILOTS?! SCREW THAT SH#T—THEY'RE THE LUCKY ONES!
AT LEAST THE DAMN FALL... GUH...
...KILLED THEM. OW.
NICE.
AGENT BOOLS IS BACK IN ACTION, YAY!
YOU OKAY, BRITT? THAT LITTLE TRICK YOU JUST PULLED WAS... A BIT OF A SURPRISE.
YEAH, I'M GOOD, BENNY. BEST I'VE FELT IN A LONG TIME, MATTER OF FACT.
SO WHAT THE HELL HAPPENED, ANYWAY?
BEST GUESS? THE CADAVER HAD A BUILT-IN FAILSAFE. YOUR ZOMBIE BUDDY MUST'VE SET IT OFF WHEN HE USED THAT SWISS ARMY ARM OF HIS ON IT.
BENNY ZOMBIE, CUTTING AND BOOMING.
NICE GOIN', BENNY!
HEY!
STUPID FAKE ARM!
KRAK
AW, MAN—
—I ACTUALLY LIKED THIS ONE.

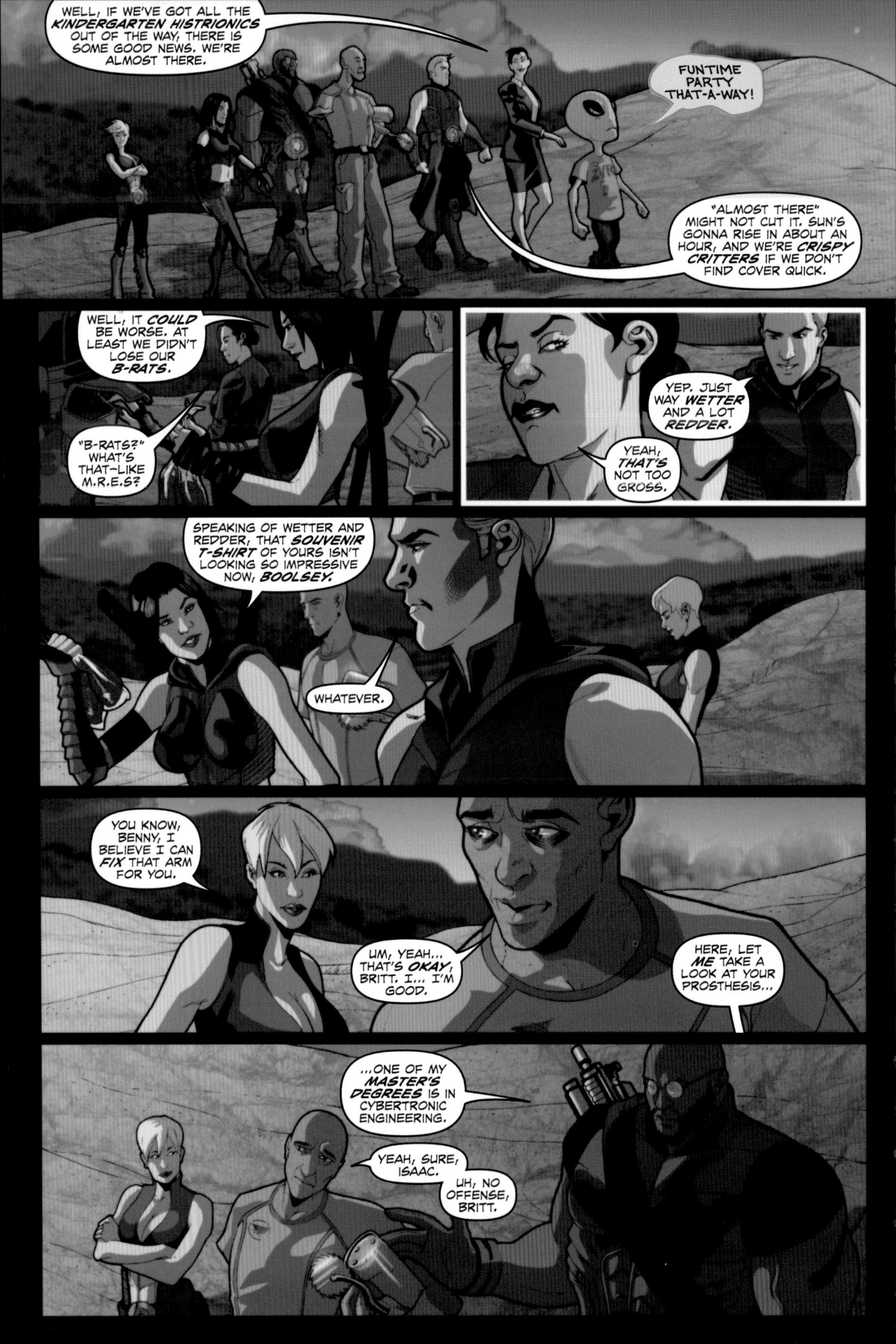
WELL, IF WE'VE GOT ALL THE KINDERGARTEN HISTRIONICS OUT OF THE WAY, THERE IS SOME GOOD NEWS. WE'RE ALMOST THERE.
FUNTIME PARTY THAT-A-WAY!
"ALMOST THERE" MIGHT NOT CUT IT. SUN'S GONNA RISE IN ABOUT AN HOUR, AND WE'RE CRISPY CRITTERS IF WE DON'T FIND COVER QUICK.
WELL, IT COULD BE WORSE. AT LEAST WE DIDN'T LOSE OUR B-RATS.
"B-RATS?" WHAT'S THAT–LIKE M.R.E.S?
YEP. JUST WAY WETTER AND A LOT REDDER.
YEAH, THAT'S NOT TOO GROSS.
SPEAKING OF WETTER AND REDDER, THAT SOUVENIR T-SHIRT OF YOURS ISN'T LOOKING SO IMPRESSIVE NOW, BOOLSEY.
WHATEVER.
YOU KNOW, BENNY, I BELIEVE I CAN FIX THAT ARM FOR YOU.
UM, YEAH... THAT'S OKAY, BRITT. I... I'M GOOD.
HERE, LET ME TAKE A LOOK AT YOUR PROSTHESIS...
...ONE OF MY MASTER'S DEGREES IS IN CYBERTRONIC ENGINEERING.
YEAH, SURE, ISAAC.
UH, NO OFFENSE, BRITT.

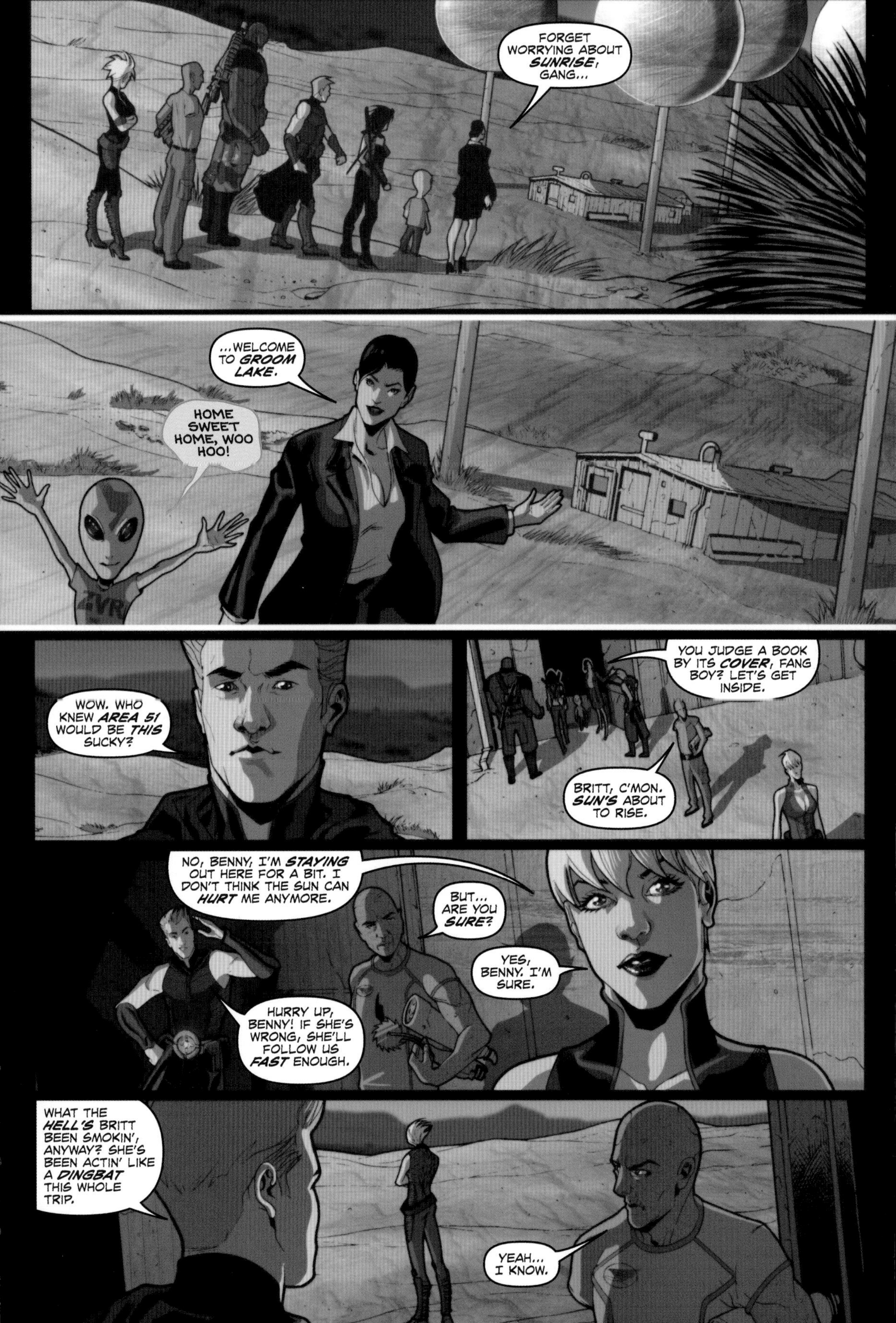
FORGET WORRYING ABOUT SUNRISE, GANG...
...WELCOME TO GROOM LAKE.
HOME SWEET HOME, WOO HOO!
WOW. WHO KNEW AREA 51 WOULD BE THIS SUCKY?
YOU JUDGE A BOOK BY ITS COVER, FANG BOY? LET'S GET INSIDE.
BRITT, C'MON. SUN'S ABOUT TO RISE.
NO, BENNY, I'M STAYING OUT HERE FOR A BIT. I DON'T THINK THE SUN CAN HURT ME ANYMORE.
BUT... ARE YOU SURE?
YES, BENNY. I'M SURE.
HURRY UP, BENNY! IF SHE'S WRONG, SHE'LL FOLLOW US FAST ENOUGH.
WHAT THE HELL'S BRITT BEEN SMOKIN', ANYWAY? SHE'S BEEN ACTIN' LIKE A DINGBAT THIS WHOLE TRIP.
YEAH... I KNOW.

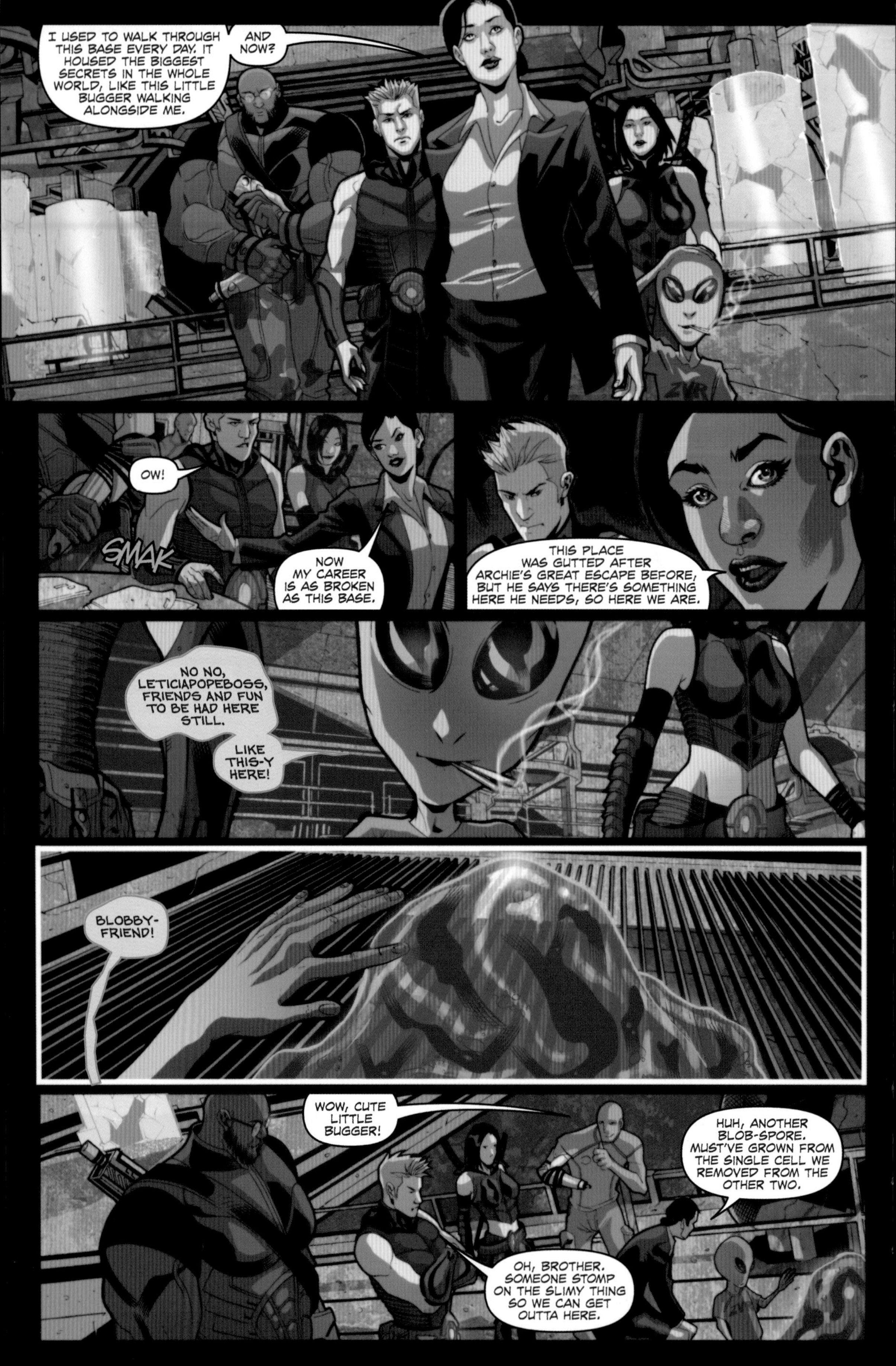
I USED TO WALK THROUGH THIS BASE EVERY DAY. IT HOUSED THE BIGGEST SECRETS IN THE WHOLE WORLD, LIKE THIS LITTLE BUGGER WALKING ALONGSIDE ME.
AND NOW?
OW!
SMAK
NOW MY CAREER IS AS BROKEN AS THIS BASE.
THIS PLACE WAS GUTTED AFTER ARCHIE'S GREAT ESCAPE BEFORE, BUT HE SAYS THERE'S SOMETHING HERE HE NEEDS, SO HERE WE ARE.
NO NO, LETICIAPOPEBOSS, FRIENDS AND FUN TO BE HAD HERE STILL.
LIKE THIS-Y HERE!
BLOBBY-FRIEND!
WOW, CUTE LITTLE BUGGER!
HUH, ANOTHER BLOB-SPORE. MUST'VE GROWN FROM THE SINGLE CELL WE REMOVED FROM THE OTHER TWO.
OH, BROTHER. SOMEONE STOMP ON THE SLIMY THING SO WE CAN GET OUTTA HERE.

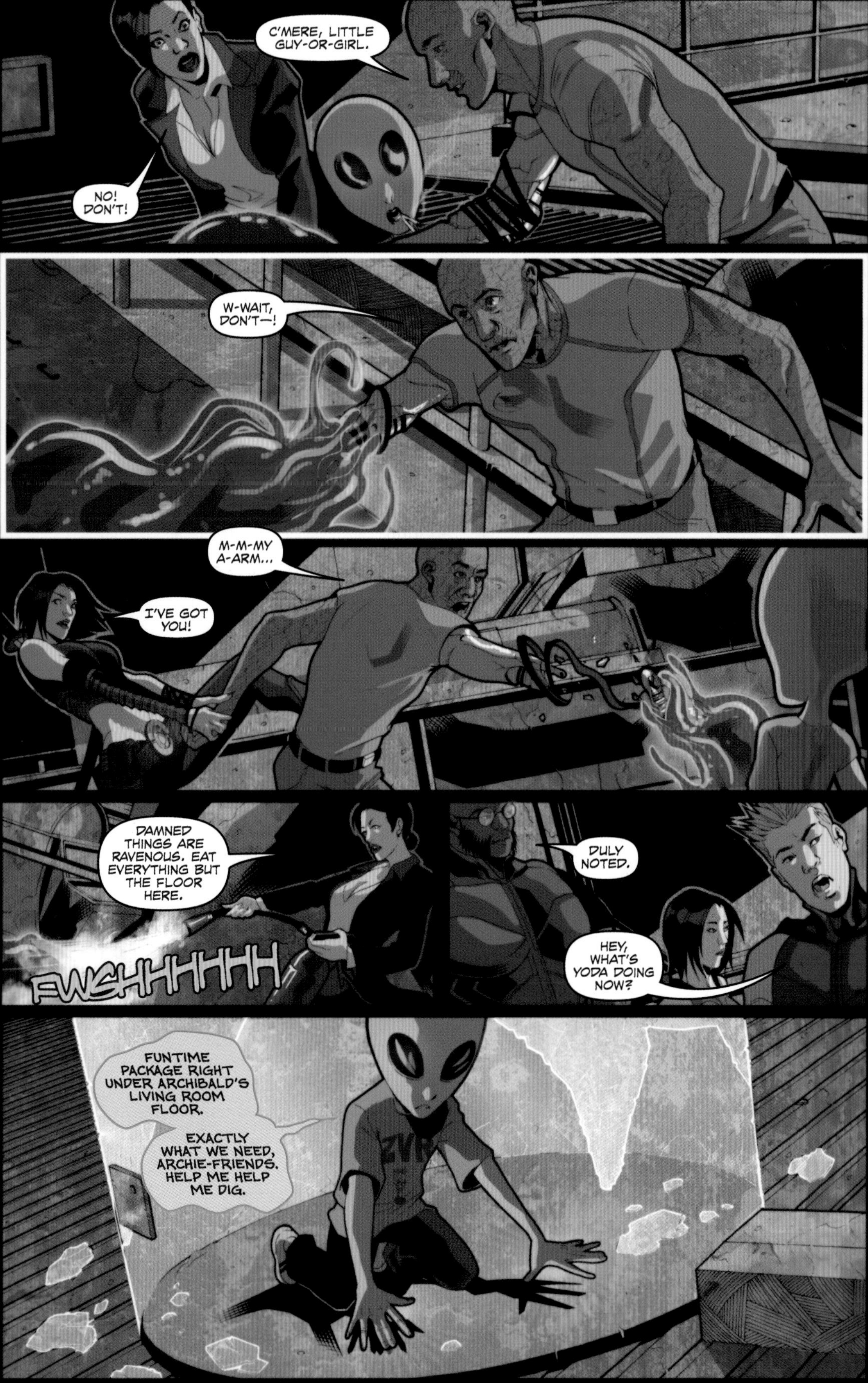
C'MERE, LITTLE GUY-OR-GIRL.
NO! DON'T!
W-WAIT, DON'T—!
M-M-MY A-ARM...
I'VE GOT YOU!
DAMNED THINGS ARE RAVENOUS. EAT EVERYTHING BUT THE FLOOR HERE.
FWSHHHHHH
DULY NOTED.
HEY, WHAT'S YODA DOING NOW?
FUNTIME PACKAGE RIGHT UNDER ARCHIBALD'S LIVING ROOM FLOOR.
EXACTLY WHAT WE NEED, ARCHIE-FRIENDS. HELP ME HELP ME DIG.

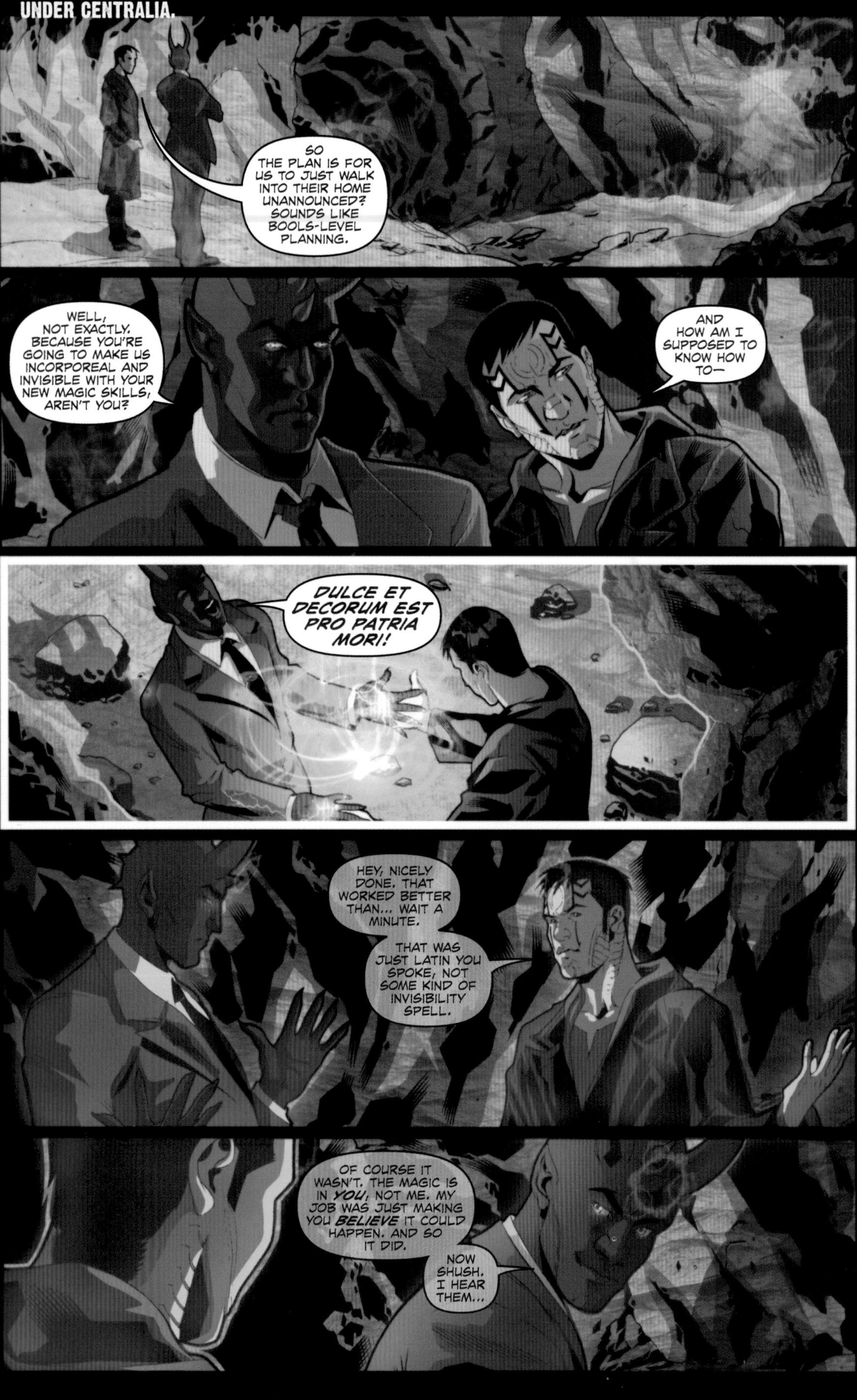
UNDER CENTRALIA.
SO THE PLAN IS FOR US TO JUST WALK INTO THEIR HOME UNANNOUNCED? SOUNDS LIKE BOOLS-LEVEL PLANNING.
WELL, NOT EXACTLY. BECAUSE YOU'RE GOING TO MAKE US INCORPOREAL AND INVISIBLE WITH YOUR NEW MAGIC SKILLS, AREN'T YOU?
AND HOW AM I SUPPOSED TO KNOW HOW TO—
DULCE ET DECORUM EST PRO PATRIA MORI!
HEY, NICELY DONE. THAT WORKED BETTER THAN... WAIT A MINUTE.
THAT WAS JUST LATIN YOU SPOKE, NOT SOME KIND OF INVISIBILITY SPELL.
OF COURSE IT WASN'T. THE MAGIC IS IN YOU, NOT ME. MY JOB WAS JUST MAKING YOU BELIEVE IT COULD HAPPEN. AND SO IT DID.
NOW SHUSH. I HEAR THEM...

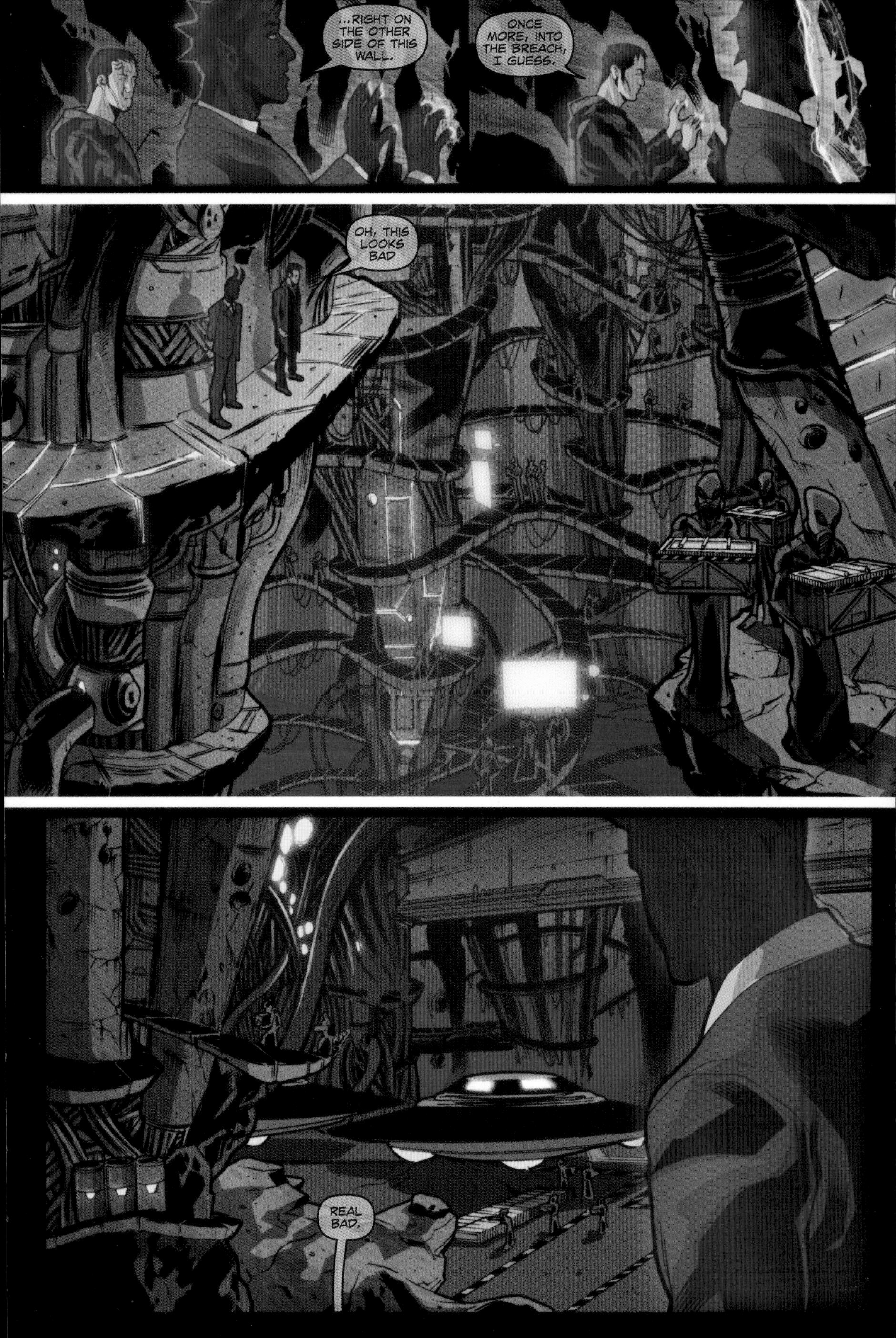
...RIGHT ON THE OTHER SIDE OF THIS WALL.
ONCE MORE, INTO THE BREACH, I GUESS.
OH, THIS LOOKS BAD
REAL BAD.

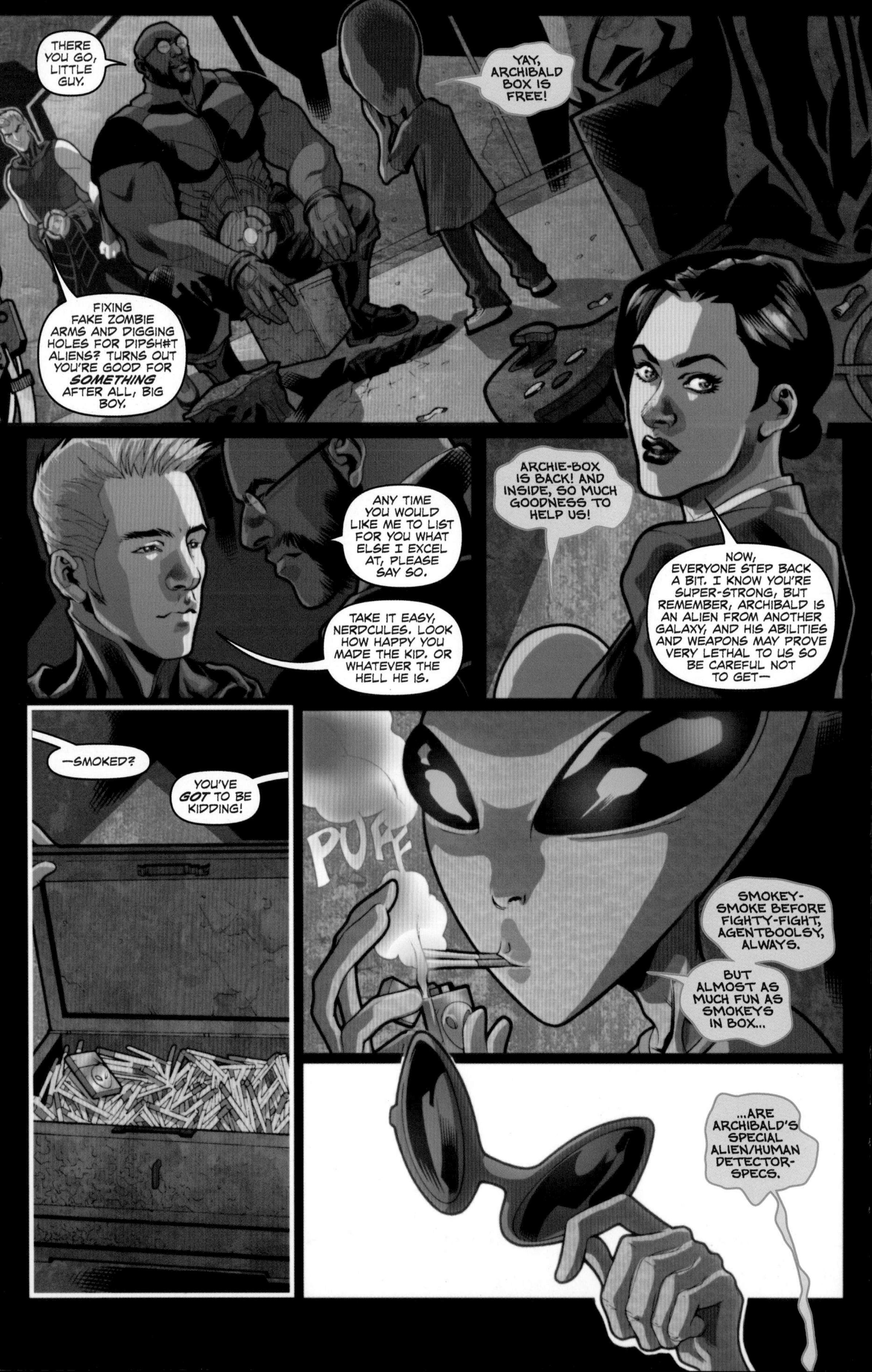
THERE YOU GO, LITTLE GUY.
YAY, ARCHIBALD BOX IS FREE!
FIXING FAKE ZOMBIE ARMS AND DIGGING HOLES FOR DIPSH#T ALIENS? TURNS OUT YOU'RE GOOD FOR SOMETHING AFTER ALL, BIG BOY.
ANY TIME YOU WOULD LIKE ME TO LIST FOR YOU WHAT ELSE I EXCEL AT, PLEASE SAY SO.
TAKE IT EASY, NERDCULES. LOOK HOW HAPPY YOU MADE THE KID. OR WHATEVER THE HELL HE IS.
ARCHIE-BOX IS BACK! AND INSIDE, SO MUCH GOODNESS TO HELP US!
NOW, EVERYONE STEP BACK A BIT. I KNOW YOU'RE SUPER-STRONG, BUT REMEMBER, ARCHIBALD IS AN ALIEN FROM ANOTHER GALAXY, AND HIS ABILITIES AND WEAPONS MAY PROVE VERY LETHAL TO US SO BE CAREFUL NOT TO GET—
—SMOKED?
YOU'VE GOT TO BE KIDDING!
PUFF
SMOKEY-SMOKE BEFORE FIGHTY-FIGHT, AGENTBOOLSY, ALWAYS.
BUT ALMOST AS MUCH FUN AS SMOKEYS IN BOX...
...ARE ARCHIBALD'S SPECIAL ALIEN/HUMAN DETECTOR-SPECS.

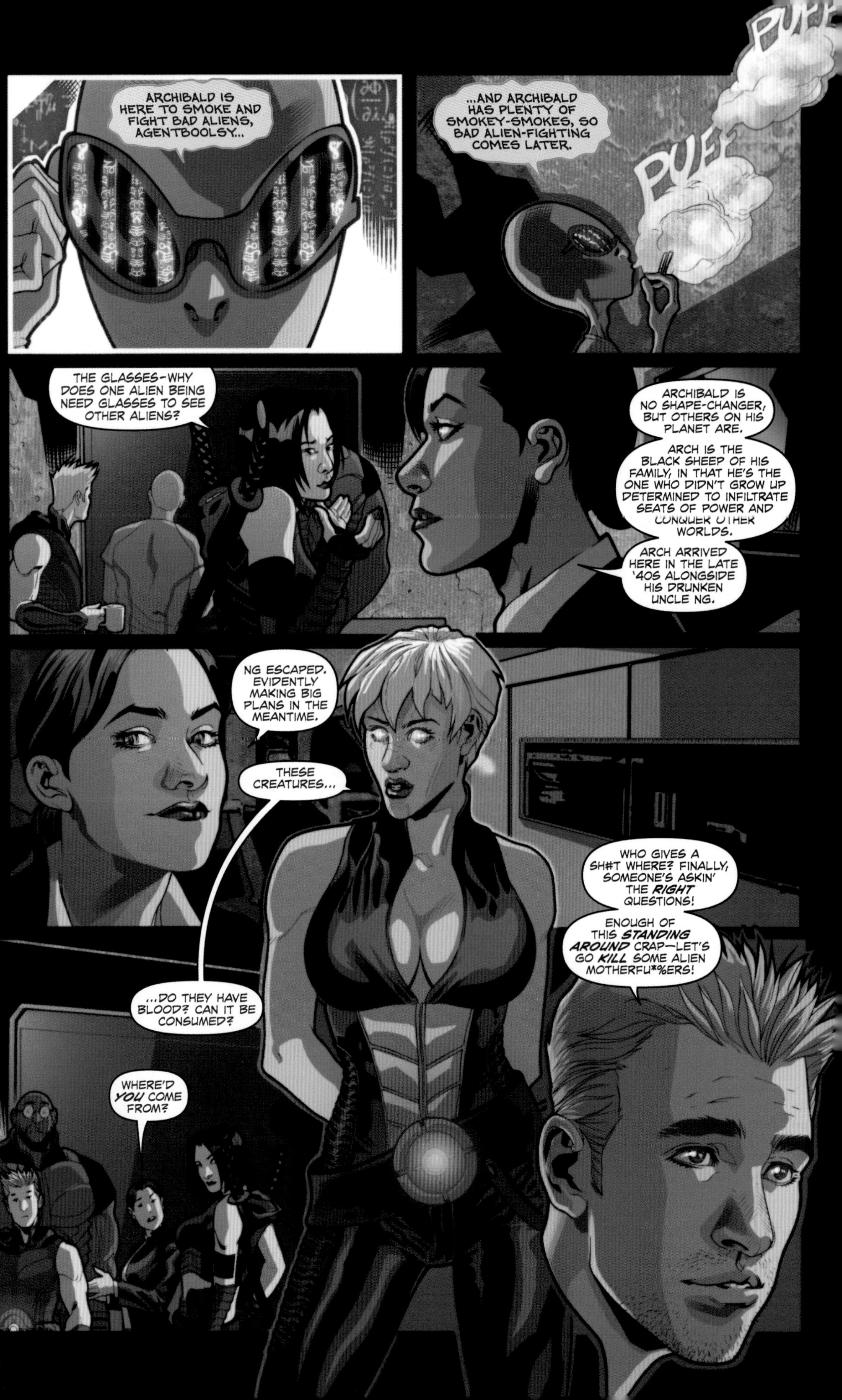
PUFF
ARCHIBALD IS HERE TO SMOKE AND FIGHT BAD ALIENS, AGENTBOOLSY...
...AND ARCHIBALD HAS PLENTY OF SMOKEY-SMOKES, SO BAD ALIEN-FIGHTING COMES LATER.
PUFF
THE GLASSES—WHY DOES ONE ALIEN BEING NEED GLASSES TO SEE OTHER ALIENS?
ARCHIBALD IS NO SHAPE-CHANGER, BUT OTHERS ON HIS PLANET ARE.
ARCH IS THE BLACK SHEEP OF HIS FAMILY, IN THAT HE'S THE ONE WHO DIDN'T GROW UP DETERMINED TO INFILTRATE SEATS OF POWER AND CONQUER OTHER WORLDS.
ARCH ARRIVED HERE IN THE LATE '40S ALONGSIDE HIS DRUNKEN UNCLE NG.
NG ESCAPED. EVIDENTLY MAKING BIG PLANS IN THE MEANTIME.
THESE CREATURES...
...DO THEY HAVE BLOOD? CAN IT BE CONSUMED?
WHO GIVES A SH#T WHERE? FINALLY, SOMEONE'S ASKIN' THE *RIGHT* QUESTIONS!
ENOUGH OF THIS *STANDING AROUND* CRAP—LET'S GO *KILL* SOME ALIEN MOTHERFU*%ERS!
WHERE'D *YOU* COME FROM?

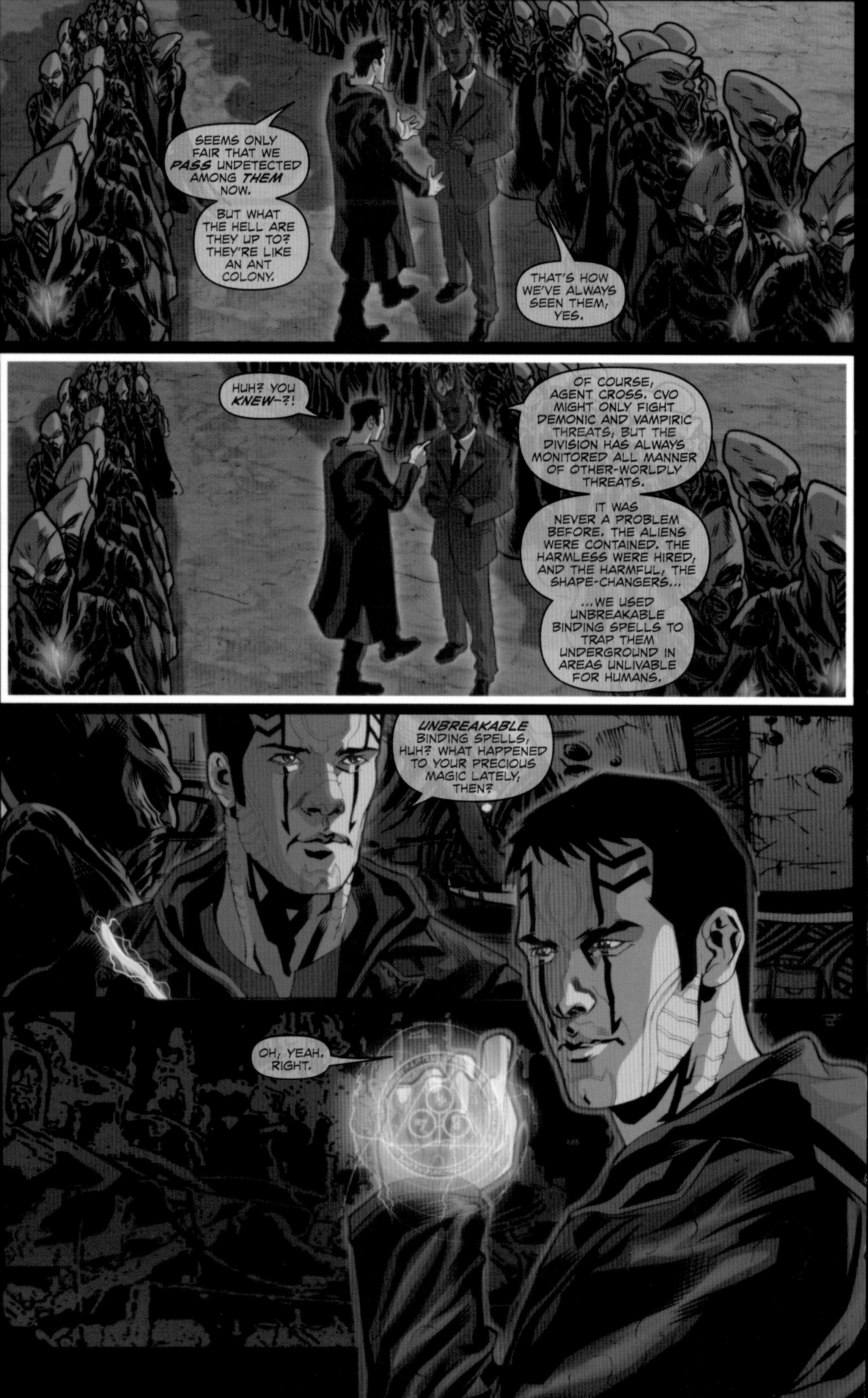
SEEMS ONLY FAIR THAT WE PASS UNDETECTED AMONG THEM NOW.
BUT WHAT THE HELL ARE THEY UP TO? THEY'RE LIKE AN ANT COLONY.
THAT'S HOW WE'VE ALWAYS SEEN THEM, YES.
HUH? YOU KNEW--?!
OF COURSE, AGENT CROSS. CVO MIGHT ONLY FIGHT DEMONIC AND VAMPIRIC THREATS, BUT THE DIVISION HAS ALWAYS MONITORED ALL MANNER OF OTHER-WORLDLY THREATS.
IT WAS NEVER A PROBLEM BEFORE. THE ALIENS WERE CONTAINED. THE HARMLESS WERE HIRED, AND THE HARMFUL, THE SHAPE-CHANGERS...
...WE USED UNBREAKABLE BINDING SPELLS TO TRAP THEM UNDERGROUND IN AREAS UNLIVABLE FOR HUMANS.
UNBREAKABLE BINDING SPELLS, HUH? WHAT HAPPENED TO YOUR PRECIOUS MAGIC LATELY, THEN?
OH, YEAH. RIGHT.

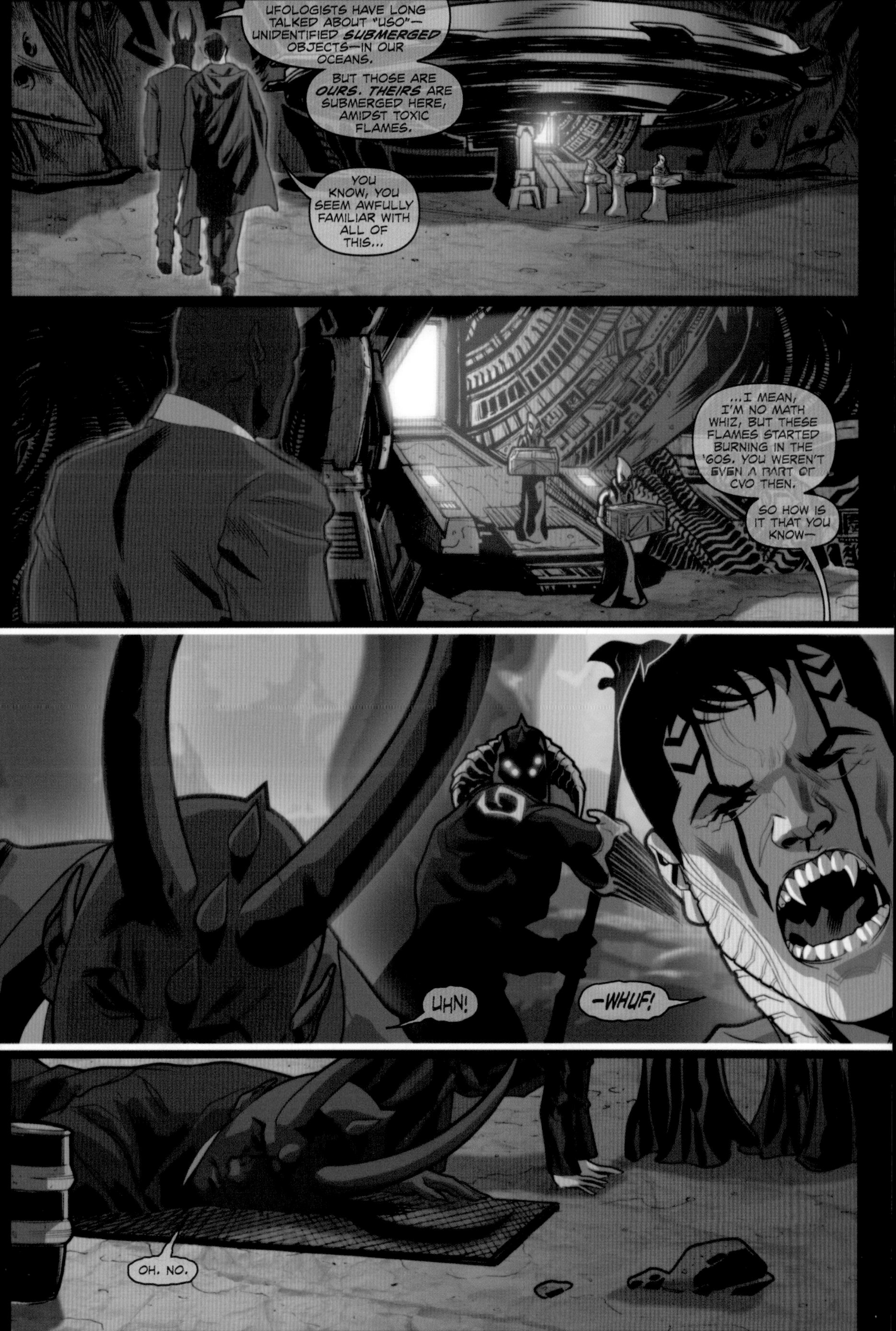
UFOLOGISTS HAVE LONG TALKED ABOUT "USO"—UNIDENTIFIED SUBMERGED OBJECTS—IN OUR OCEANS.
BUT THOSE ARE OURS. THEIRS ARE SUBMERGED HERE, AMIDST TOXIC FLAMES.
YOU KNOW, YOU SEEM AWFULLY FAMILIAR WITH ALL OF THIS...
...I MEAN, I'M NO MATH WHIZ, BUT THESE FLAMES STARTED BURNING IN THE '60S. YOU WEREN'T EVEN A PART OF CVO THEN.
SO HOW IS IT THAT YOU KNOW—
UHN!
-WHUF!
OH. NO.

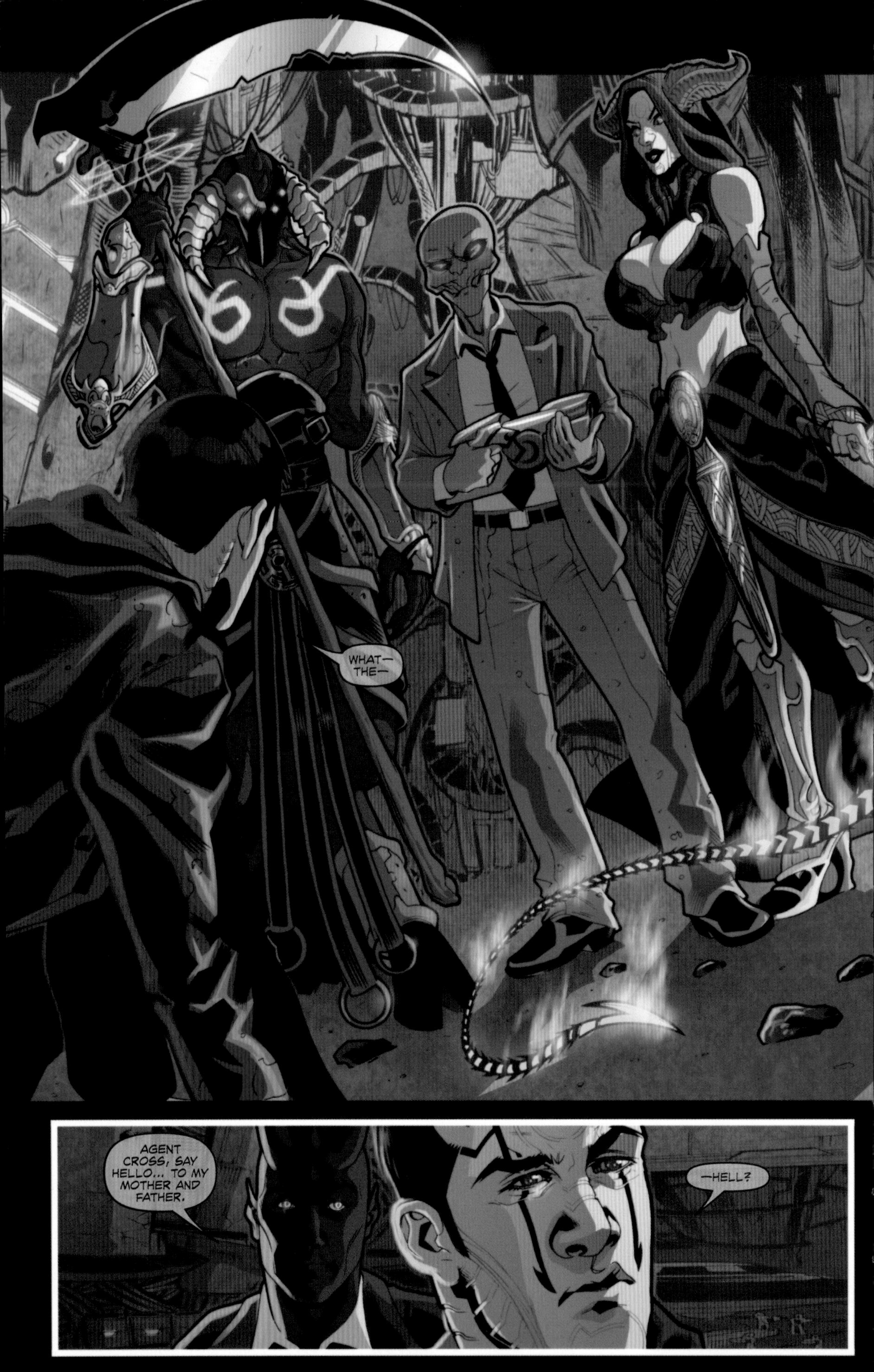
WHAT—
THE—
AGENT CROSS, SAY HELLO... TO MY MOTHER AND FATHER.
—HELL?

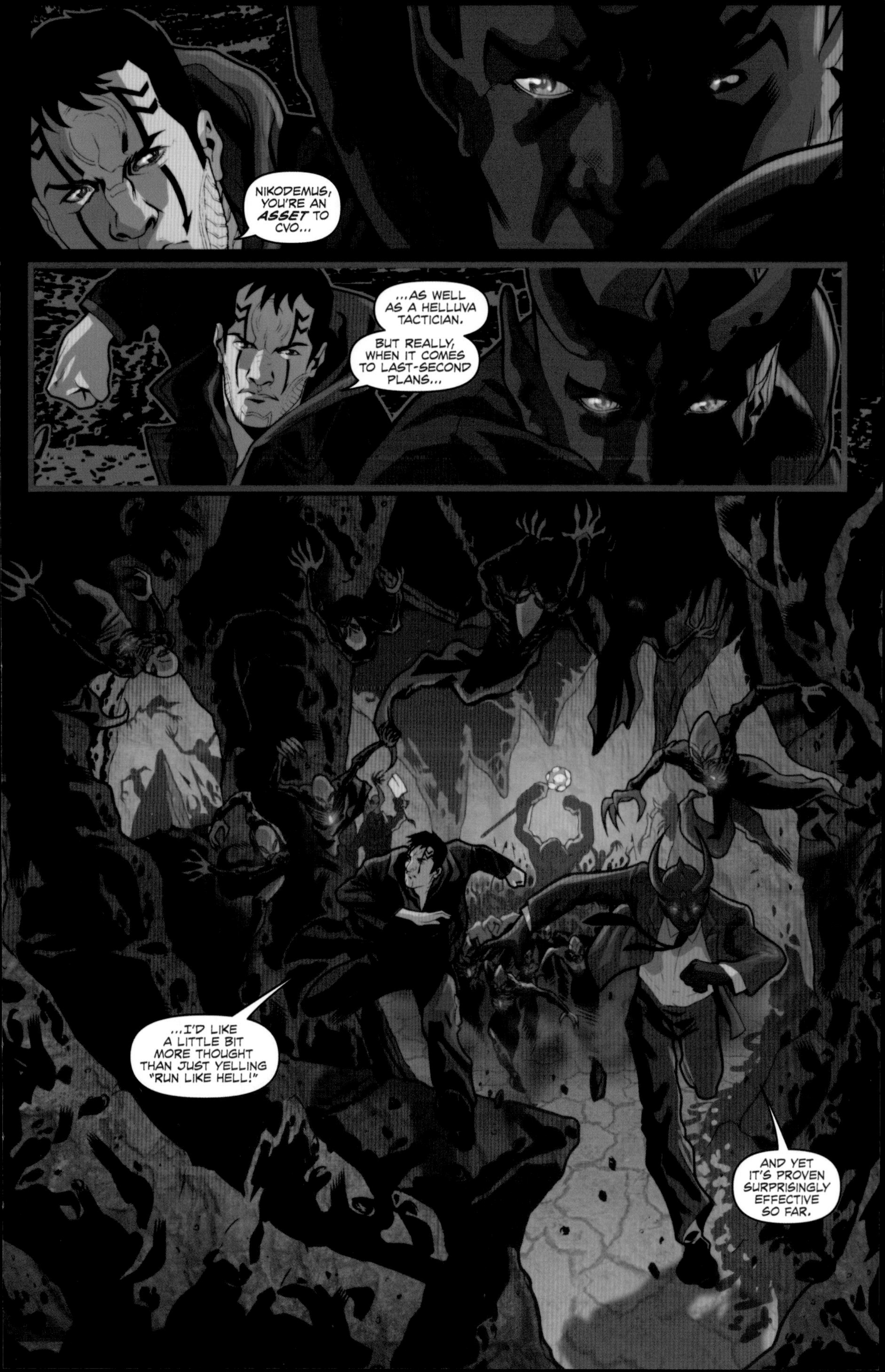
NIKODEMUS, YOU'RE AN *ASSET* TO CVO...
...AS WELL AS A HELLUVA TACTICIAN.
BUT REALLY, WHEN IT COMES TO LAST-SECOND PLANS...
...I'D LIKE A LITTLE BIT MORE THOUGHT THAN JUST YELLING "RUN LIKE HELL!"
AND YET IT'S PROVEN SURPRISINGLY EFFECTIVE SO FAR.

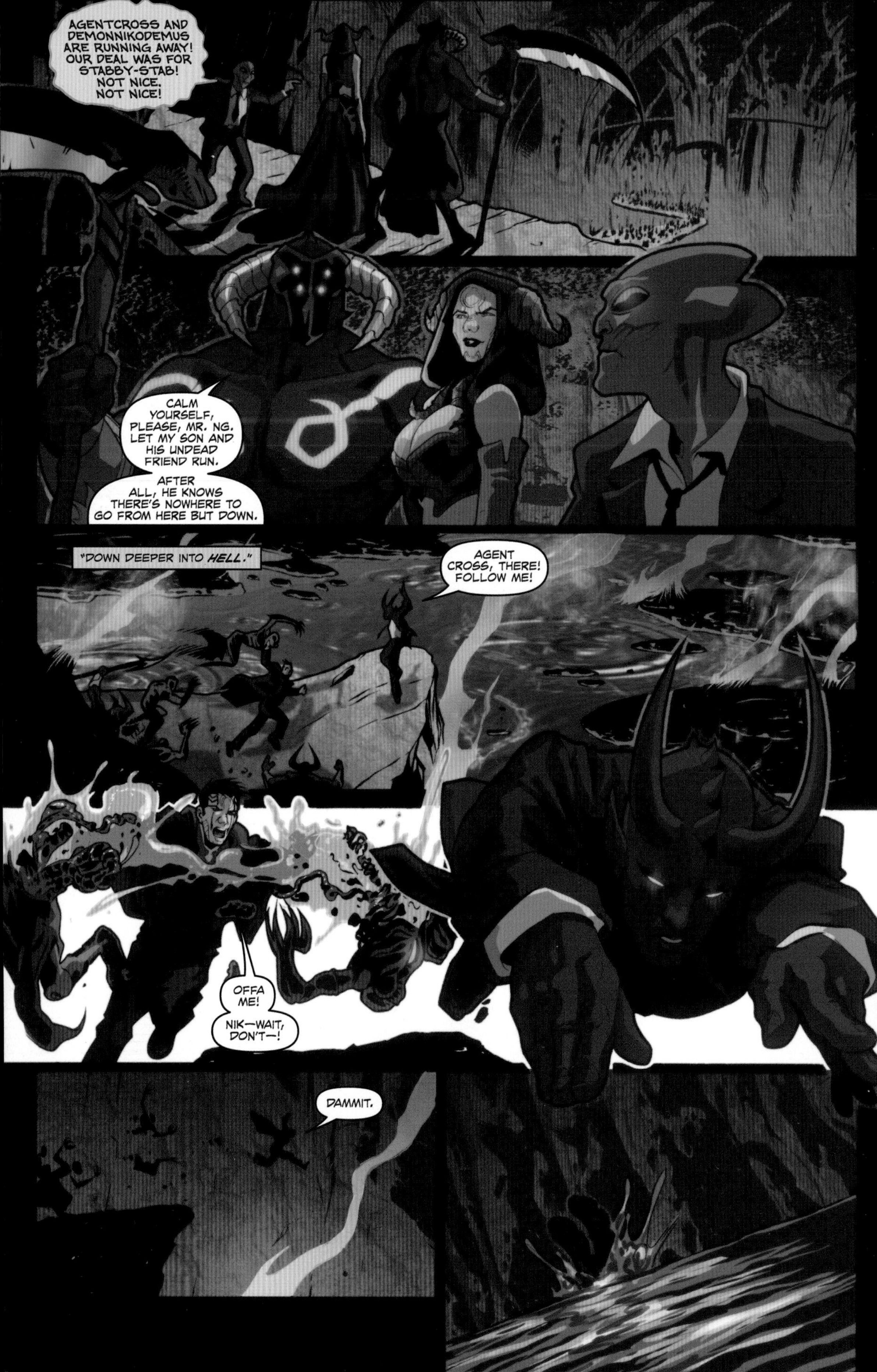

AGENTCROSS AND DEMONNIKODEMUS ARE RUNNING AWAY! OUR DEAL WAS FOR STABBY-STAB! NOT NICE. NOT NICE!
CALM YOURSELF, PLEASE, MR. NG. LET MY SON AND HIS UNDEAD FRIEND RUN.
AFTER ALL, HE KNOWS THERE'S NOWHERE TO GO FROM HERE BUT DOWN.
"DOWN DEEPER INTO *HELL*."
AGENT CROSS, THERE! FOLLOW ME!
OFFA ME!
NIK—WAIT, DON'T—!
DAMMIT.

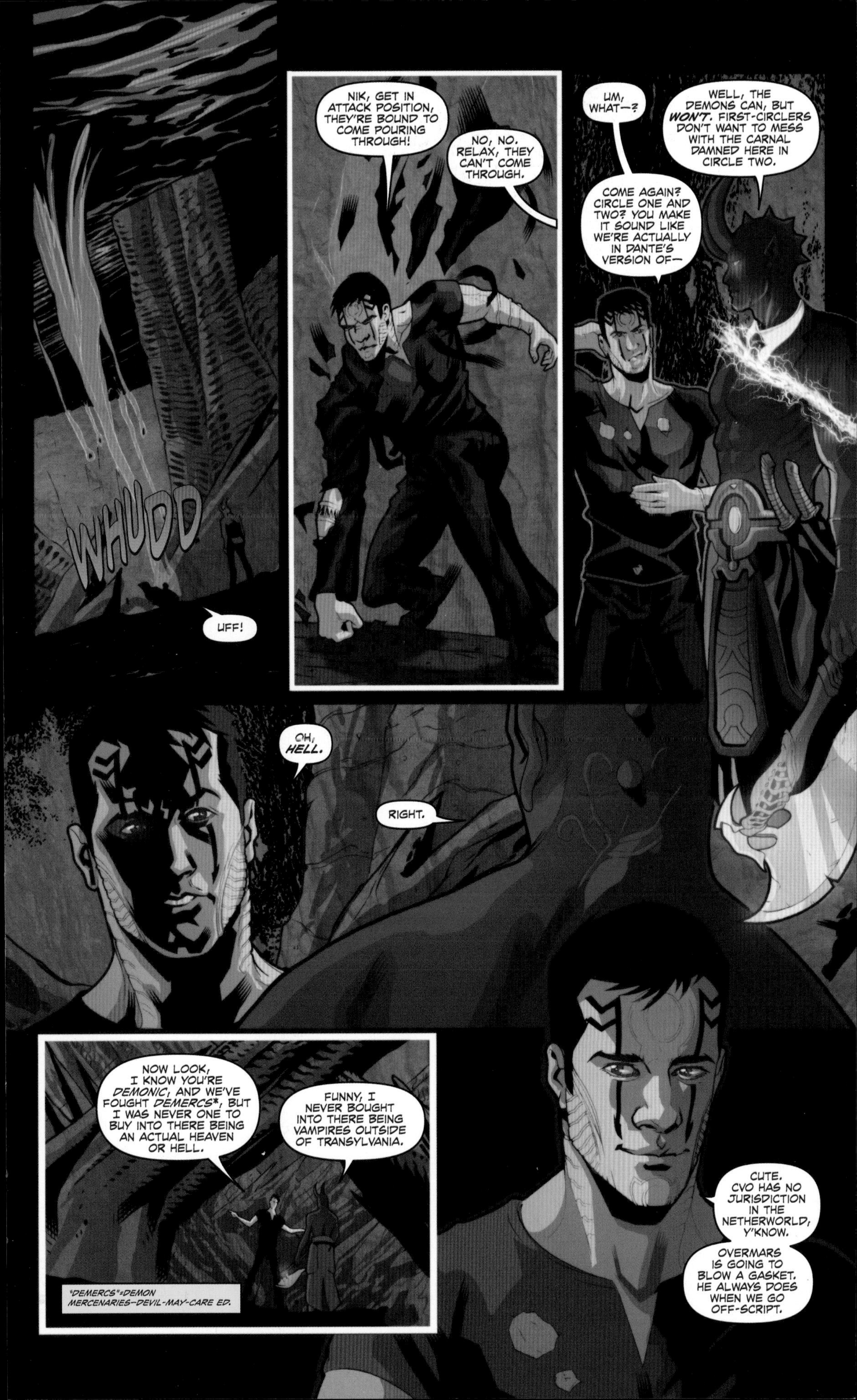
WHUDD
UFF!
NIK, GET IN ATTACK POSITION, THEY'RE BOUND TO COME POURING THROUGH!
NO, NO. RELAX, THEY CAN'T COME THROUGH.
UM, WHAT—?
WELL, THE DEMONS CAN, BUT WON'T. FIRST-CIRCLERS DON'T WANT TO MESS WITH THE CARNAL DAMNED HERE IN CIRCLE TWO.
COME AGAIN? CIRCLE ONE AND TWO? YOU MAKE IT SOUND LIKE WE'RE ACTUALLY IN DANTE'S VERSION OF—
OH, HELL.
RIGHT.
NOW LOOK, I KNOW YOU'RE DEMONIC, AND WE'VE FOUGHT DEMERCS*, BUT I WAS NEVER ONE TO BUY INTO THERE BEING AN ACTUAL HEAVEN OR HELL.
FUNNY, I NEVER BOUGHT INTO THERE BEING VAMPIRES OUTSIDE OF TRANSYLVANIA.
"DEMERCS"=DEMON MERCENARIES—DEVIL-MAY-CARE ED.
CUTE. CVO HAS NO JURISDICTION IN THE NETHERWORLD, Y'KNOW.
OVERMARS IS GOING TO BLOW A GASKET. HE ALWAYS DOES WHEN WE GO OFF-SCRIPT.

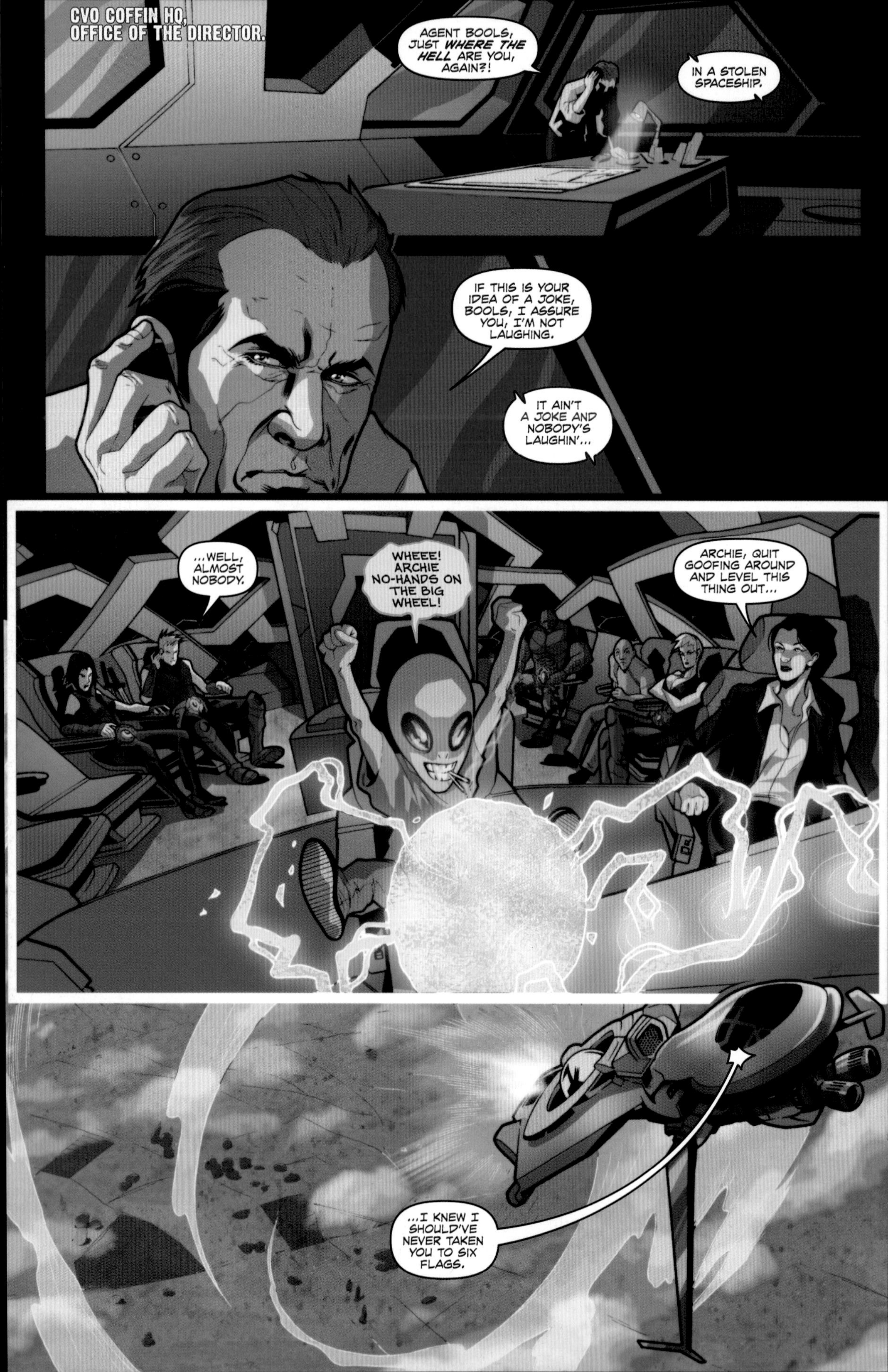
CVO COFFIN HQ, OFFICE OF THE DIRECTOR.
AGENT BOOLS, JUST WHERE THE HELL ARE YOU, AGAIN?!
IN A STOLEN SPACESHIP.
IF THIS IS YOUR IDEA OF A JOKE, BOOLS, I ASSURE YOU, I'M NOT LAUGHING.
IT AIN'T A JOKE AND NOBODY'S LAUGHIN'...
...WELL, ALMOST NOBODY.
WHEEE! ARCHIE NO-HANDS ON THE BIG WHEEL!
ARCHIE, QUIT GOOFING AROUND AND LEVEL THIS THING OUT...
...I KNEW I SHOULD'VE NEVER TAKEN YOU TO SIX FLAGS.

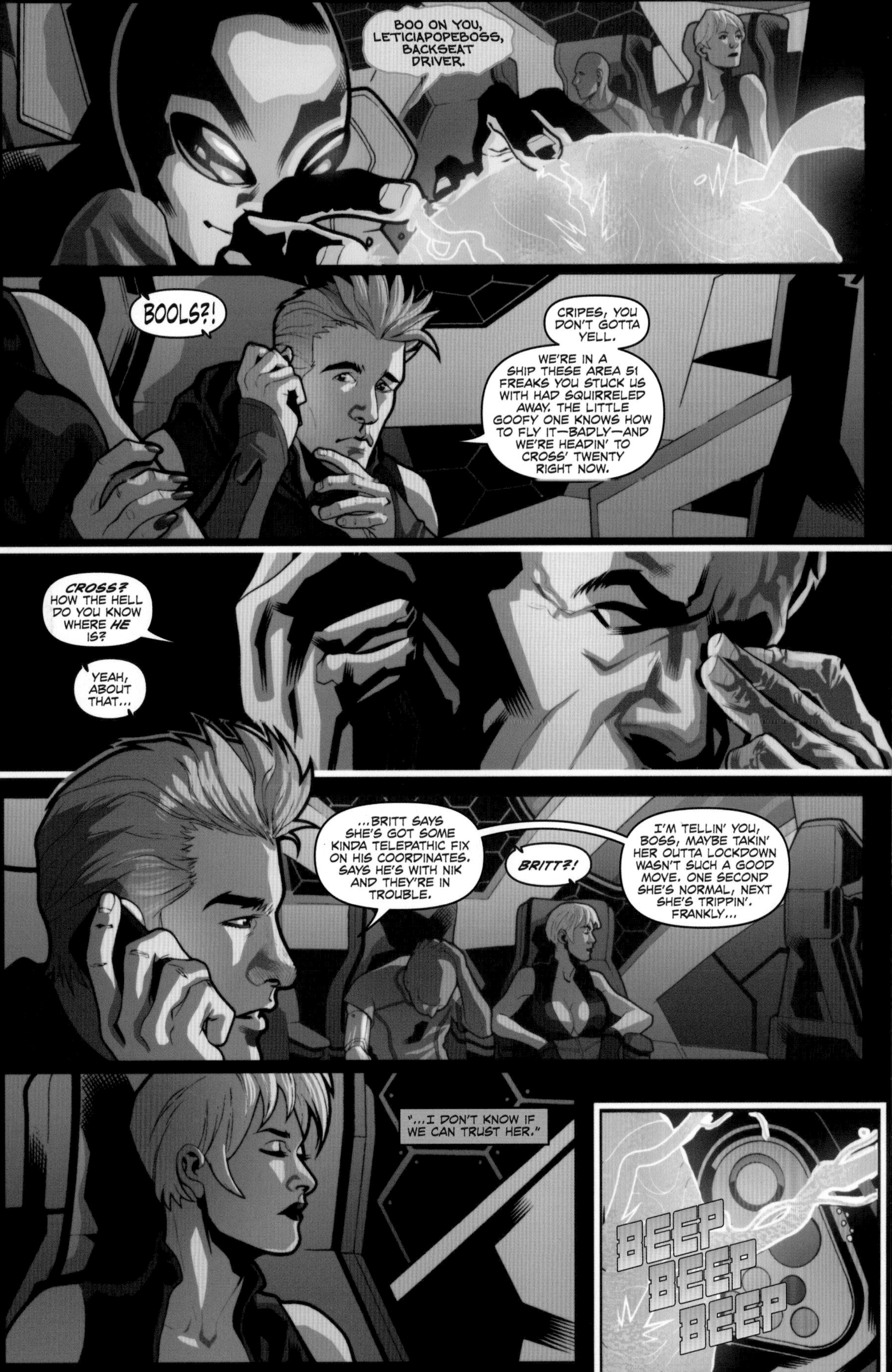
BOO ON YOU, LETICIAPOPEBOSS, BACKSEAT DRIVER.
BOOLS?!
CRIPES, YOU DON'T GOTTA YELL.
WE'RE IN A SHIP THESE AREA 51 FREAKS YOU STUCK US WITH HAD SQUIRRELED AWAY. THE LITTLE GOOFY ONE KNOWS HOW TO FLY IT—BADLY—AND WE'RE HEADIN' TO CROSS' TWENTY RIGHT NOW.
CROSS? HOW THE HELL DO YOU KNOW WHERE HE IS?
YEAH, ABOUT THAT...
...BRITT SAYS SHE'S GOT SOME KINDA TELEPATHIC FIX ON HIS COORDINATES. SAYS HE'S WITH NIK AND THEY'RE IN TROUBLE.
BRITT?!
I'M TELLIN' YOU, BOSS, MAYBE TAKIN' HER OUTTA LOCKDOWN WASN'T SUCH A GOOD MOVE. ONE SECOND SHE'S NORMAL, NEXT SHE'S TRIPPIN'. FRANKLY...
"...I DON'T KNOW IF WE CAN TRUST HER."
BEEP BEEP BEEP

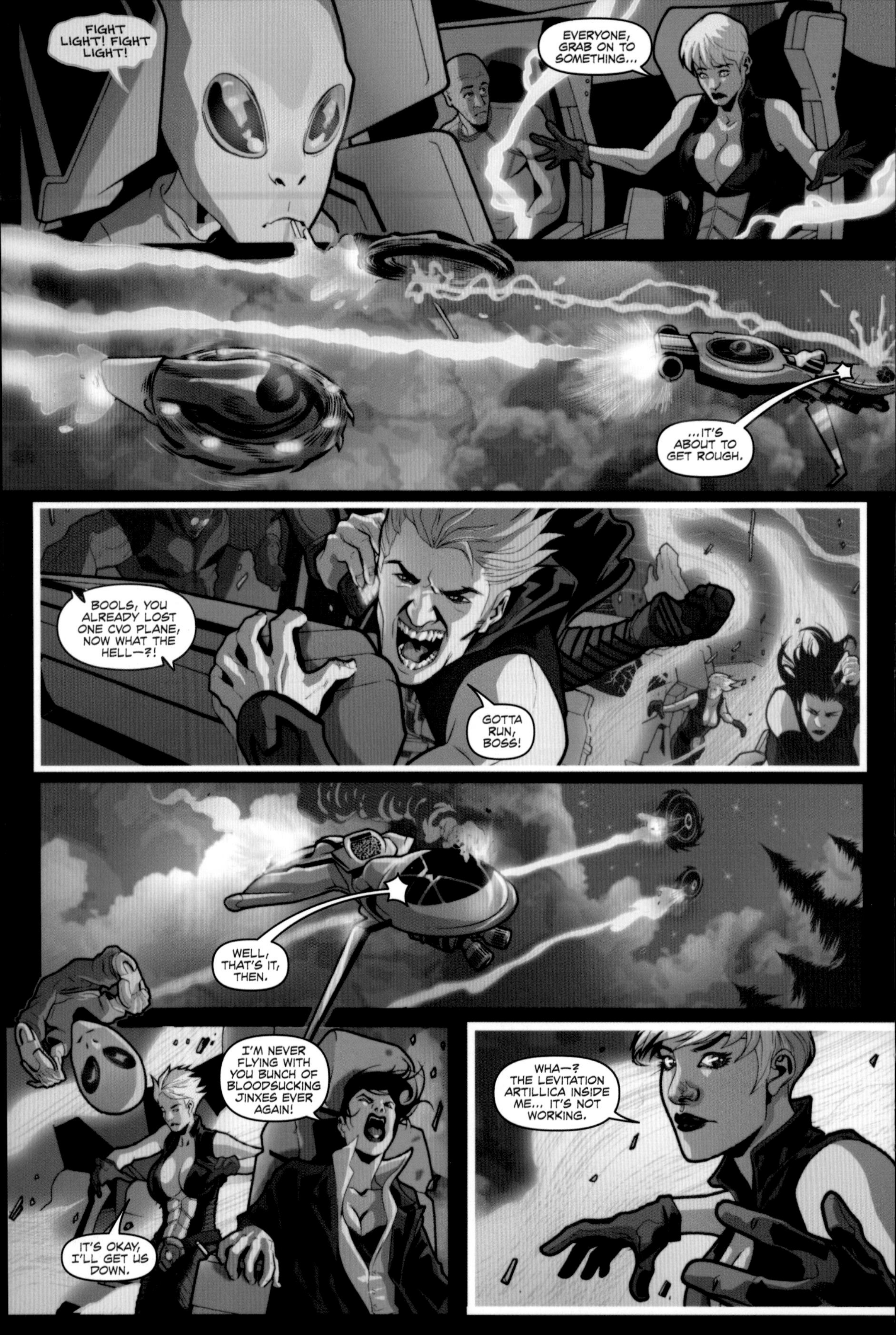
FIGHT LIGHT! FIGHT LIGHT!
EVERYONE, GRAB ON TO SOMETHING...
...IT'S ABOUT TO GET ROUGH.
BOOLS, YOU ALREADY LOST ONE CVO PLANE, NOW WHAT THE HELL—?!
GOTTA RUN, BOSS!
WELL, THAT'S IT, THEN.
I'M NEVER FLYING WITH YOU BUNCH OF BLOODSUCKING JINXES EVER AGAIN!
IT'S OKAY, I'LL GET US DOWN.
WHA—? THE LEVITATION ARTILLICA INSIDE ME... IT'S NOT WORKING.

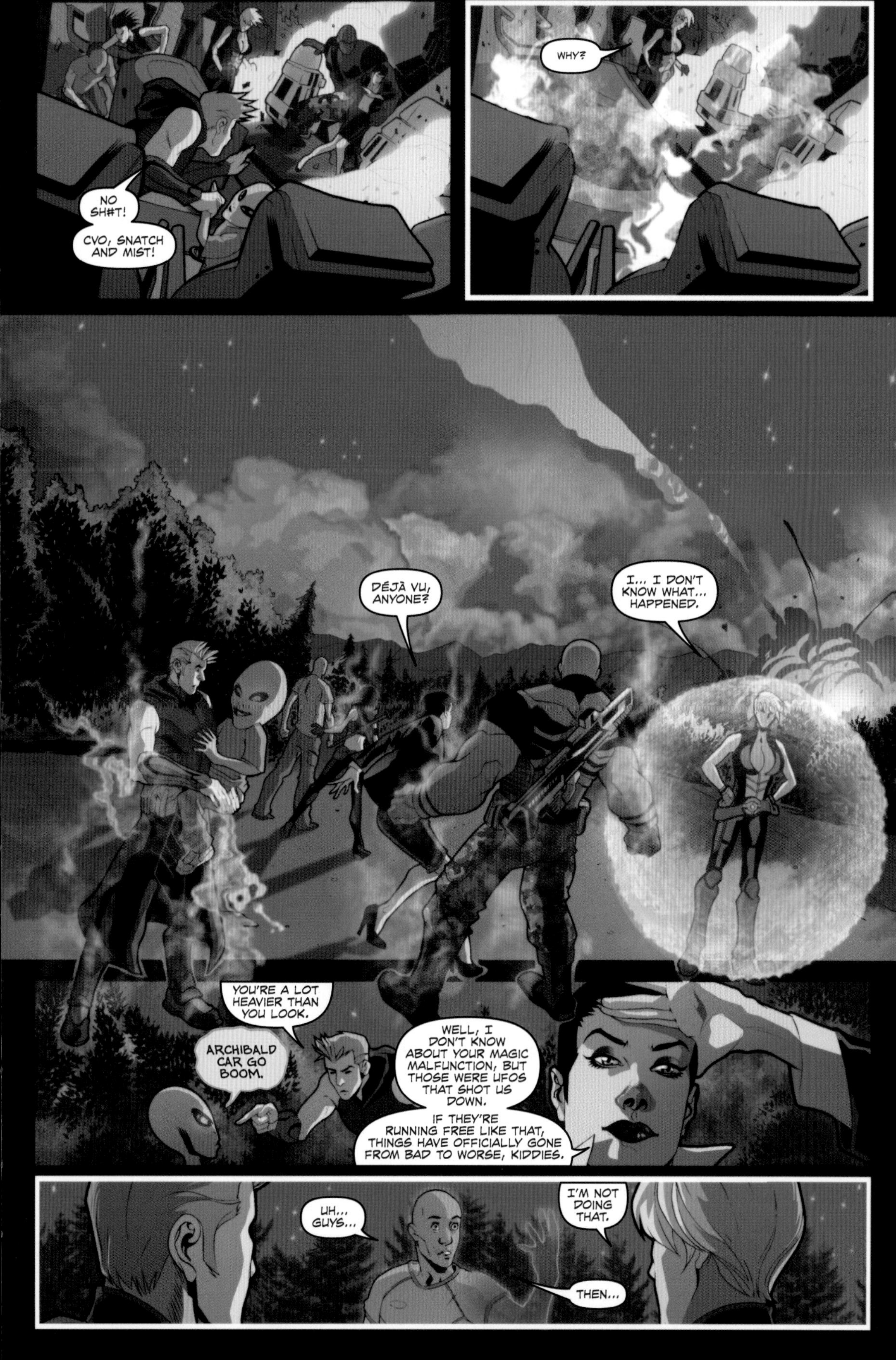
NO SH#T!
CVO, SNATCH AND MIST!
WHY?
DÉJÀ VU, ANYONE?
I... I DON'T KNOW WHAT... HAPPENED.
YOU'RE A LOT HEAVIER THAN YOU LOOK.
ARCHIBALD CAR GO BOOM.
WELL, I DON'T KNOW ABOUT YOUR MAGIC MALFUNCTION, BUT THOSE WERE UFOS THAT SHOT US DOWN.
IF THEY'RE RUNNING FREE LIKE THAT, THINGS HAVE OFFICIALLY GONE FROM BAD TO WORSE, KIDDIES.
UH... GUYS...
I'M NOT DOING THAT.
THEN...

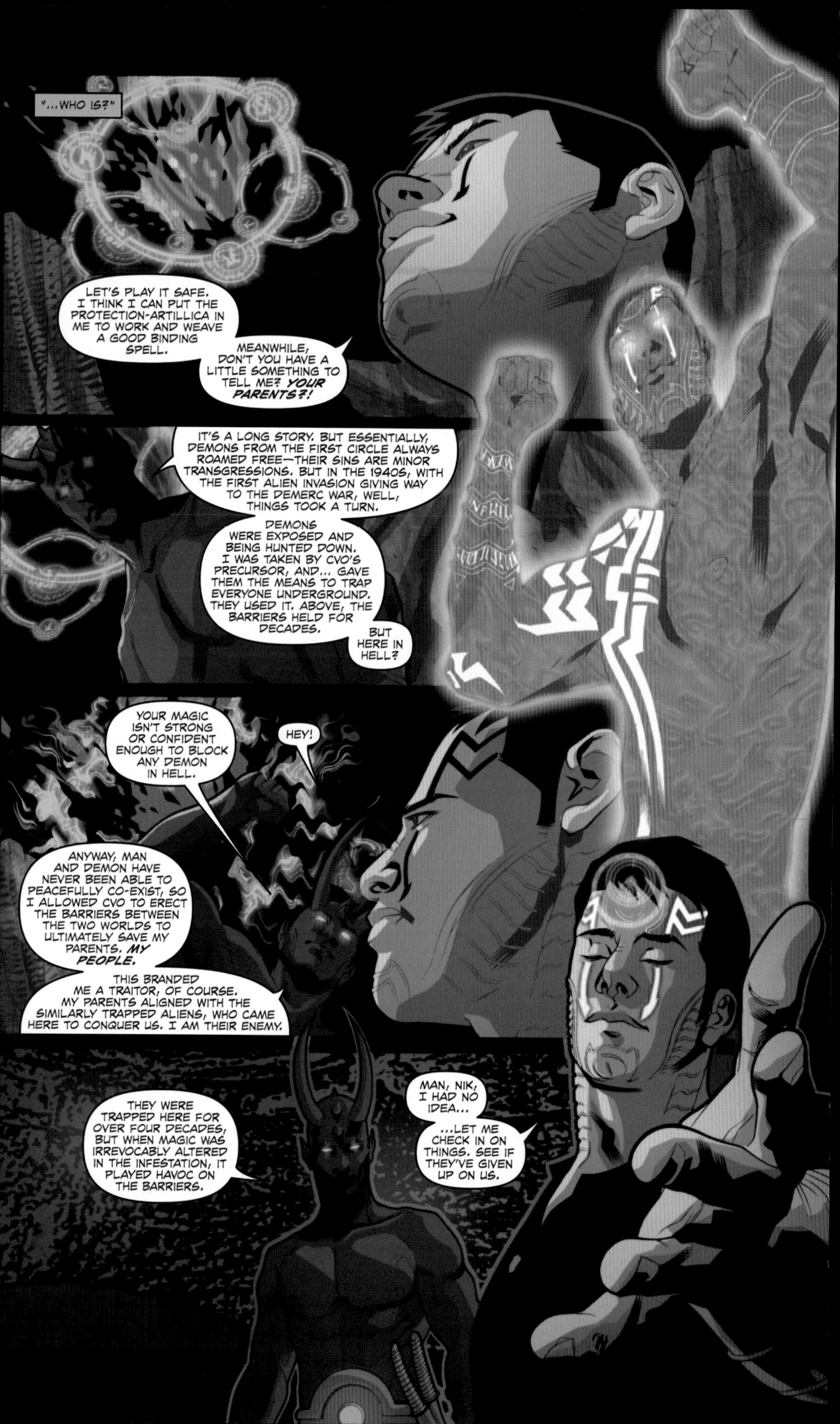
"...WHO IS?"
LET'S PLAY IT SAFE. I THINK I CAN PUT THE PROTECTION-ARTILLICA IN ME TO WORK AND WEAVE A GOOD BINDING SPELL.
MEANWHILE, DON'T YOU HAVE A LITTLE SOMETHING TO TELL ME? YOUR PARENTS?!
IT'S A LONG STORY. BUT ESSENTIALLY, DEMONS FROM THE FIRST CIRCLE ALWAYS ROAMED FREE—THEIR SINS ARE MINOR TRANSGRESSIONS. BUT IN THE 1940S, WITH THE FIRST ALIEN INVASION GIVING WAY TO THE DEMERC WAR, WELL, THINGS TOOK A TURN.
DEMONS WERE EXPOSED AND BEING HUNTED DOWN. I WAS TAKEN BY CVO'S PRECURSOR, AND... GAVE THEM THE MEANS TO TRAP EVERYONE UNDERGROUND. THEY USED IT. ABOVE, THE BARRIERS HELD FOR DECADES.
BUT HERE IN HELL?
YOUR MAGIC ISN'T STRONG OR CONFIDENT ENOUGH TO BLOCK ANY DEMON IN HELL.
HEY!
ANYWAY, MAN AND DEMON HAVE NEVER BEEN ABLE TO PEACEFULLY CO-EXIST, SO I ALLOWED CVO TO ERECT THE BARRIERS BETWEEN THE TWO WORLDS TO ULTIMATELY SAVE MY PARENTS. MY PEOPLE.
THIS BRANDED ME A TRAITOR, OF COURSE. MY PARENTS ALIGNED WITH THE SIMILARLY TRAPPED ALIENS, WHO CAME HERE TO CONQUER US. I AM THEIR ENEMY.
THEY WERE TRAPPED HERE FOR OVER FOUR DECADES, BUT WHEN MAGIC WAS IRREVOCABLY ALTERED IN THE INFESTATION, IT PLAYED HAVOC ON THE BARRIERS.
MAN, NIK, I HAD NO IDEA...
...LET ME CHECK IN ON THINGS. SEE IF THEY'VE GIVEN UP ON US.

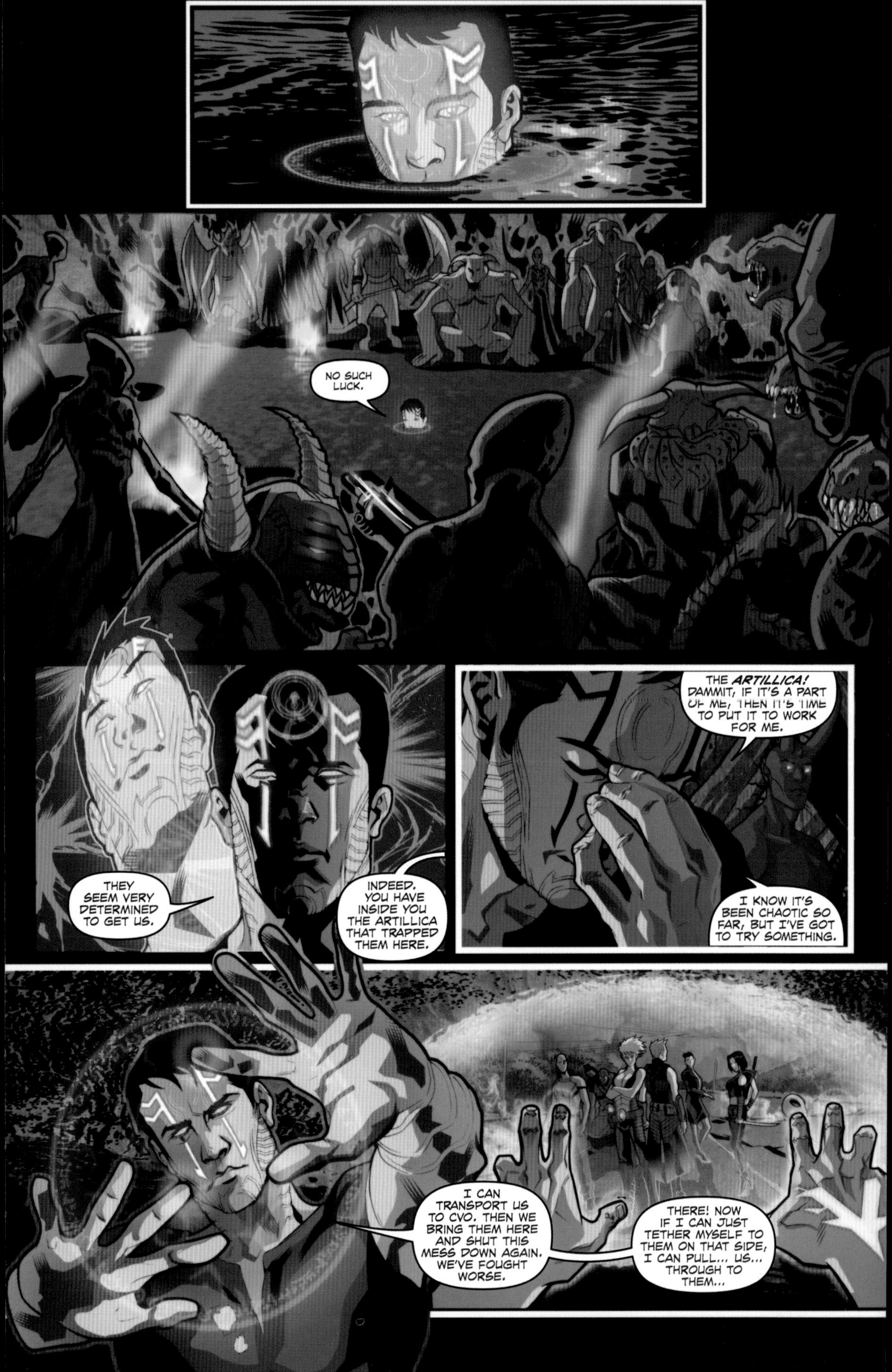
NO SUCH LUCK.
THEY SEEM VERY DETERMINED TO GET US.
INDEED. YOU HAVE INSIDE YOU THE ARTILLICA THAT TRAPPED THEM HERE.
THE *ARTILLICA!* DAMMIT, IF IT'S A PART OF ME, THEN IT'S TIME TO PUT IT TO WORK FOR ME.
I KNOW IT'S BEEN CHAOTIC SO FAR, BUT I'VE GOT TO TRY SOMETHING.
I CAN TRANSPORT US TO CVO. THEN WE BRING THEM HERE AND SHUT THIS MESS DOWN AGAIN. WE'VE FOUGHT WORSE.
THERE! NOW IF I CAN JUST TETHER MYSELF TO THEM ON THAT SIDE, I CAN PULL... US... THROUGH TO THEM...

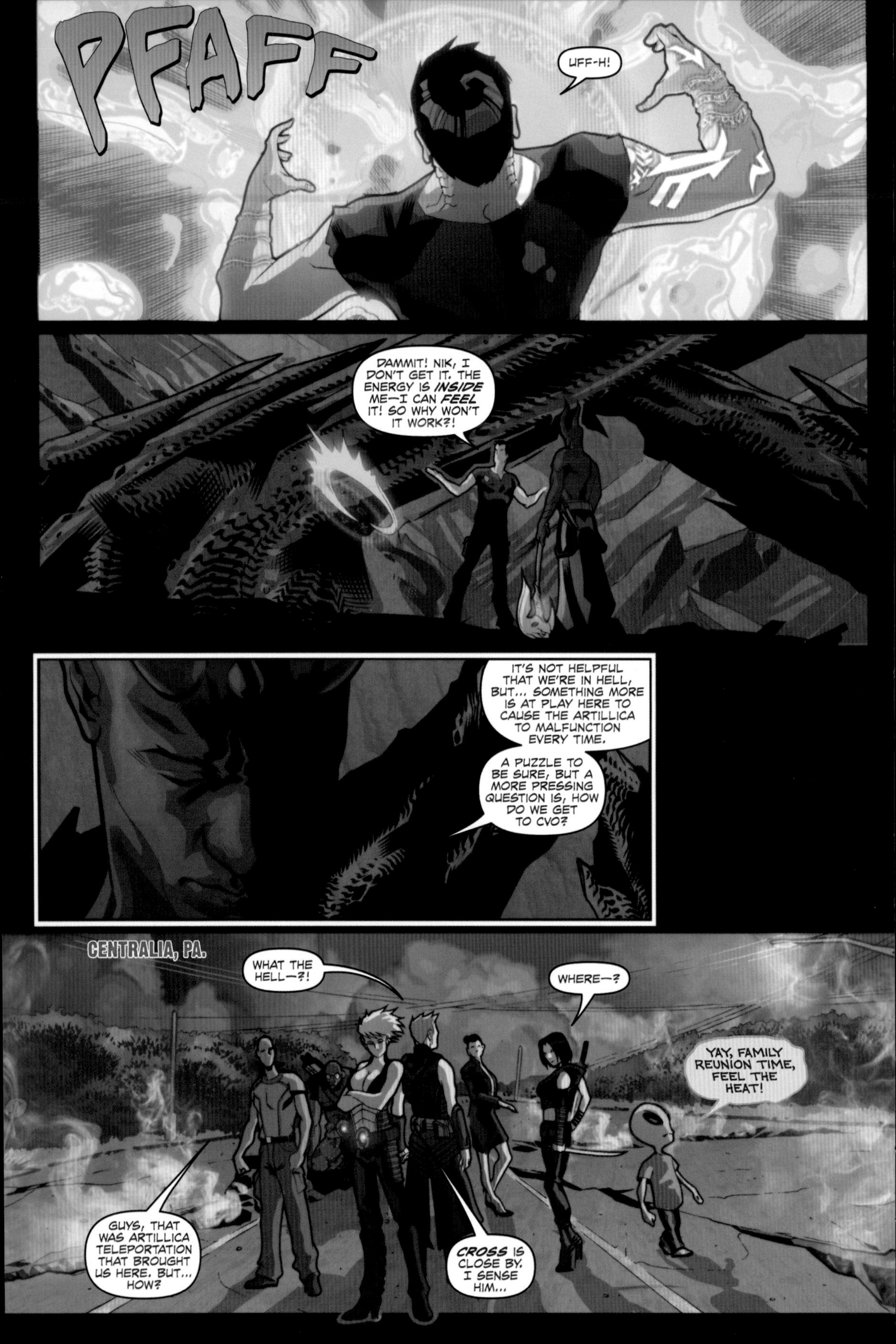
PFAFF
UFF-H!
DAMMIT! NIK, I DON'T GET IT. THE ENERGY IS *INSIDE* ME—I CAN *FEEL* IT! SO WHY WON'T IT WORK?!
IT'S NOT HELPFUL THAT WE'RE IN HELL, BUT... SOMETHING MORE IS AT PLAY HERE TO CAUSE THE ARTILLICA TO MALFUNCTION EVERY TIME.
A PUZZLE TO BE SURE, BUT A MORE PRESSING QUESTION IS, HOW DO WE GET TO CVO?
CENTRALIA, PA.
WHAT THE HELL—?!
WHERE—?
YAY, FAMILY REUNION TIME, FEEL THE HEAT!
GUYS, THAT WAS ARTILLICA TELEPORTATION THAT BROUGHT US HERE. BUT... HOW?
CROSS IS CLOSE BY. I SENSE HIM...

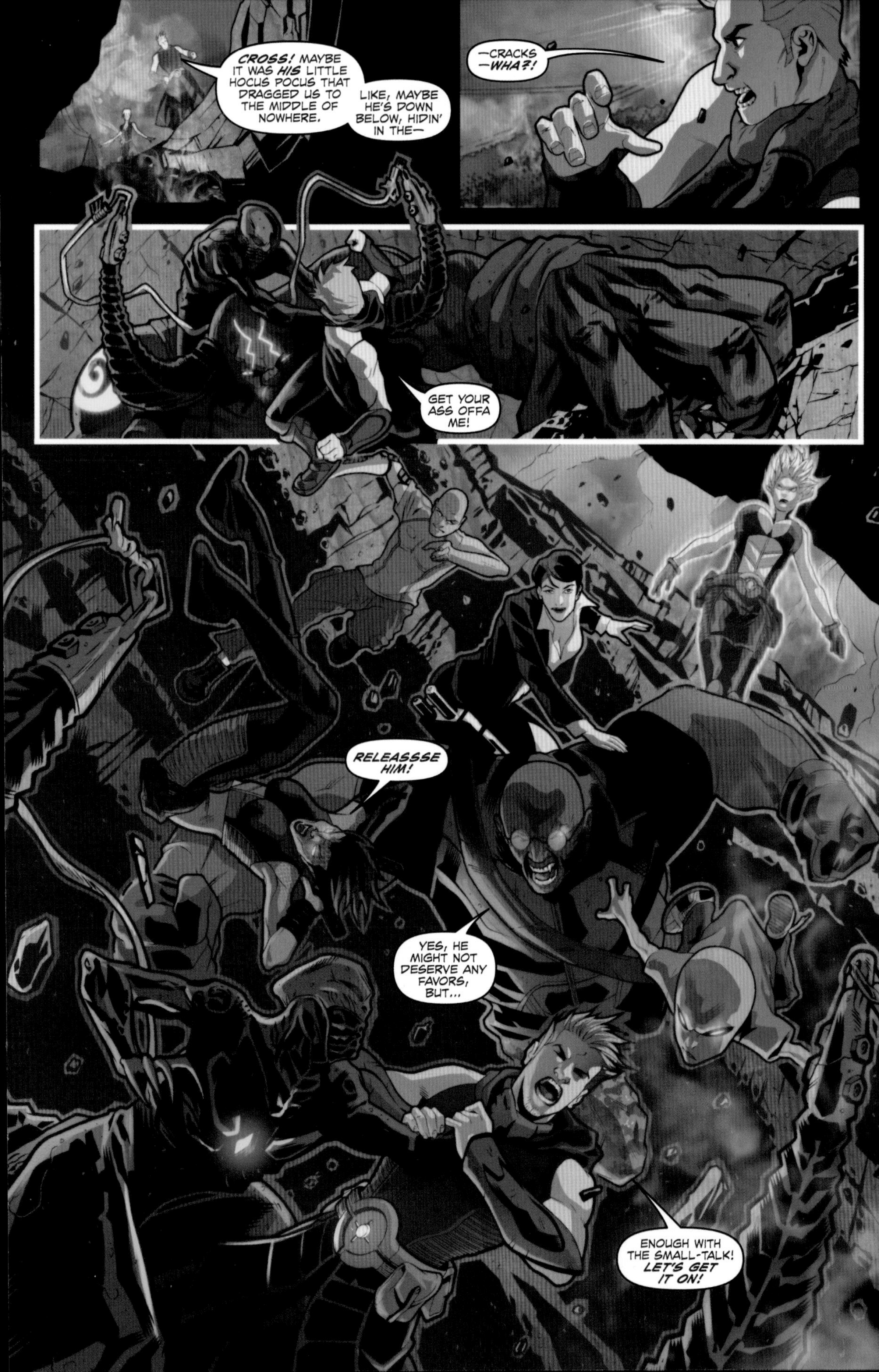

CROSS! MAYBE IT WAS HIS LITTLE HOCUS POCUS THAT DRAGGED US TO THE MIDDLE OF NOWHERE.
LIKE, MAYBE HE'S DOWN BELOW, HIDIN' IN THE—
—CRACKS —WHA?!
GET YOUR ASS OFFA ME!
RELEASSSE HIM!
YES, HE MIGHT NOT DESERVE ANY FAVORS, BUT...
ENOUGH WITH THE SMALL-TALK! LET'S GET IT ON!

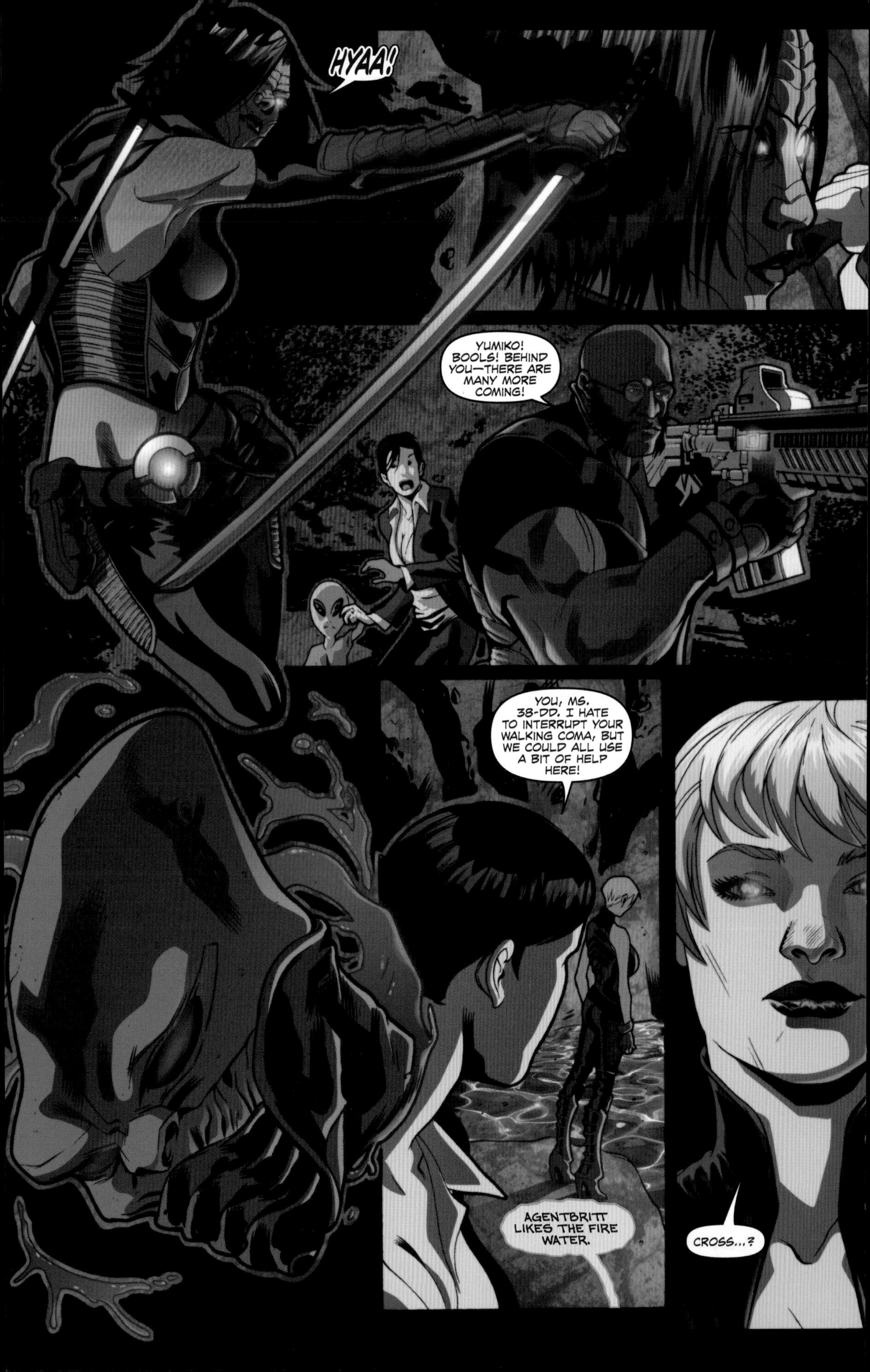
HYAA!
YUMIKO! BOOLS! BEHIND YOU—THERE ARE MANY MORE COMING!
YOU, MS. 38-DD. I HATE TO INTERRUPT YOUR WALKING COMA, BUT WE COULD ALL USE A BIT OF HELP HERE!
AGENTBRITT LIKES THE FIRE WATER.
CROSS...?

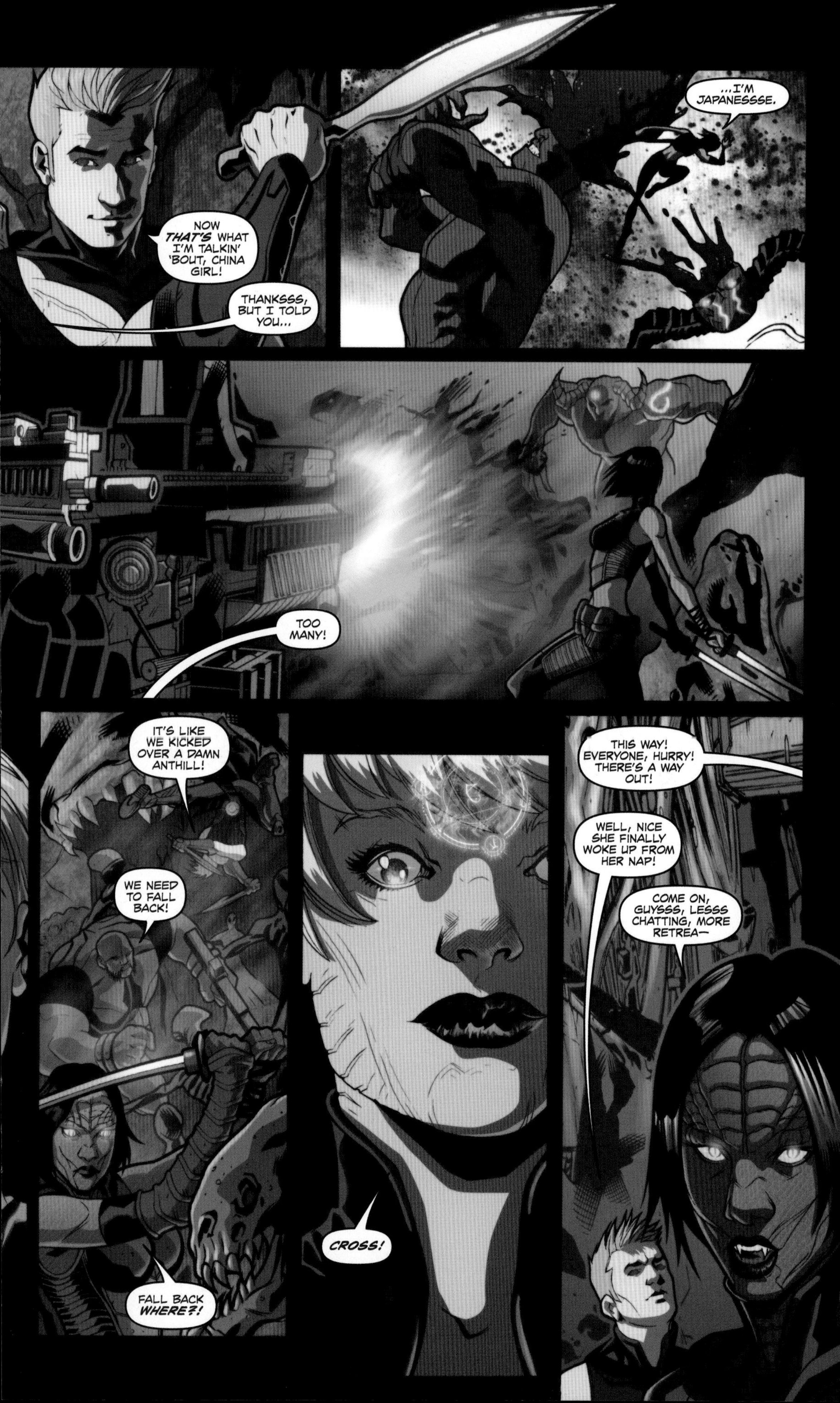
NOW THAT'S WHAT I'M TALKIN' 'BOUT, CHINA GIRL!
THANKSSS, BUT I TOLD YOU...
...I'M JAPANESSSE.
TOO MANY!
IT'S LIKE WE KICKED OVER A DAMN ANTHILL!
WE NEED TO FALL BACK!
FALL BACK WHERE?!
CROSS!
THIS WAY! EVERYONE, HURRY! THERE'S A WAY OUT!
WELL, NICE SHE FINALLY WOKE UP FROM HER NAP!
COME ON, GUYSSS, LESSS CHATTING, MORE RETREA—

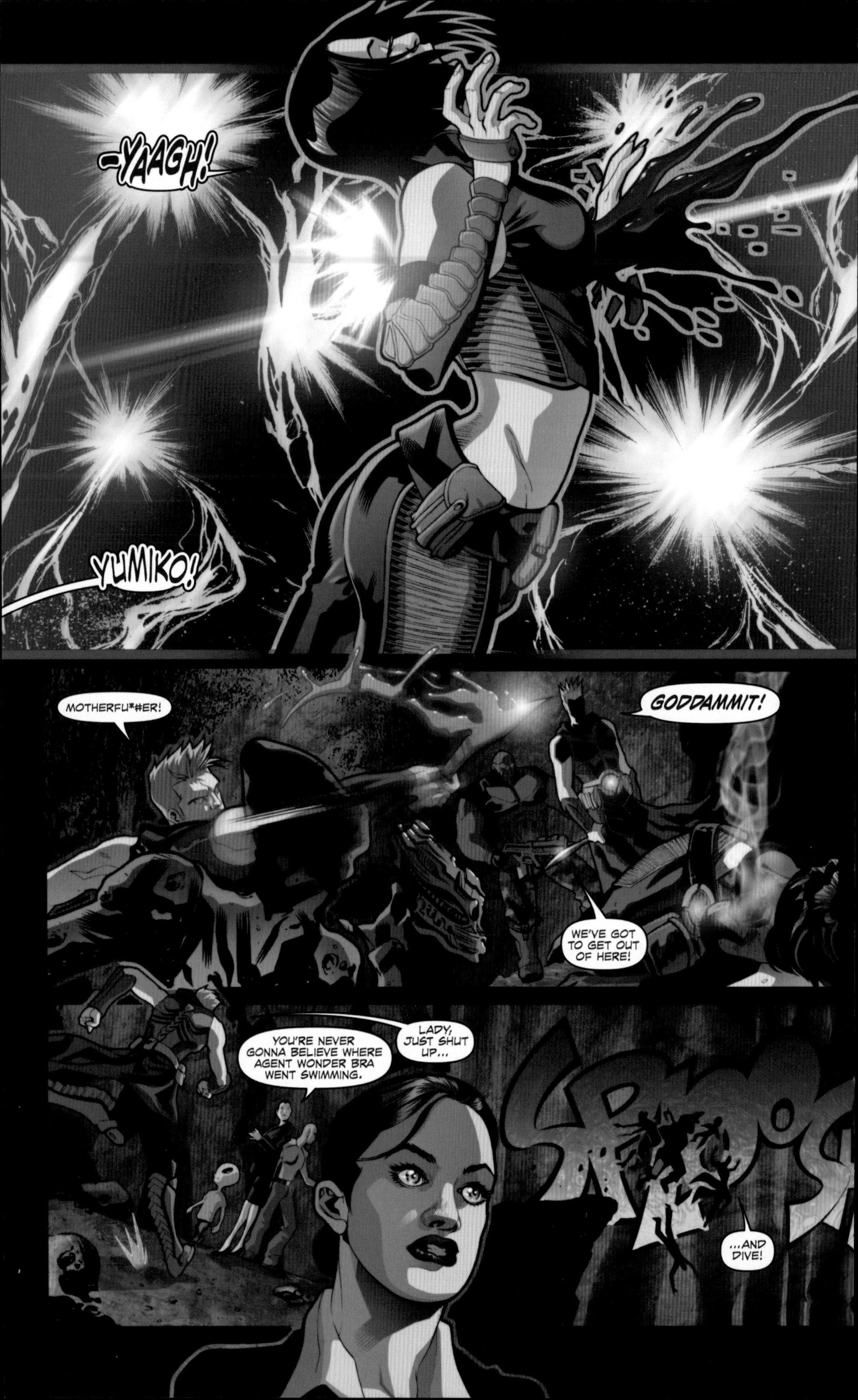

-YAAGH!
YUMIKO!
MOTHERFU*#ER!
GODDAMMIT!
WE'VE GOT TO GET OUT OF HERE!
YOU'RE NEVER GONNA BELIEVE WHERE AGENT WONDER BRA WENT SWIMMING.
LADY, JUST SHUT UP...
...AND DIVE!

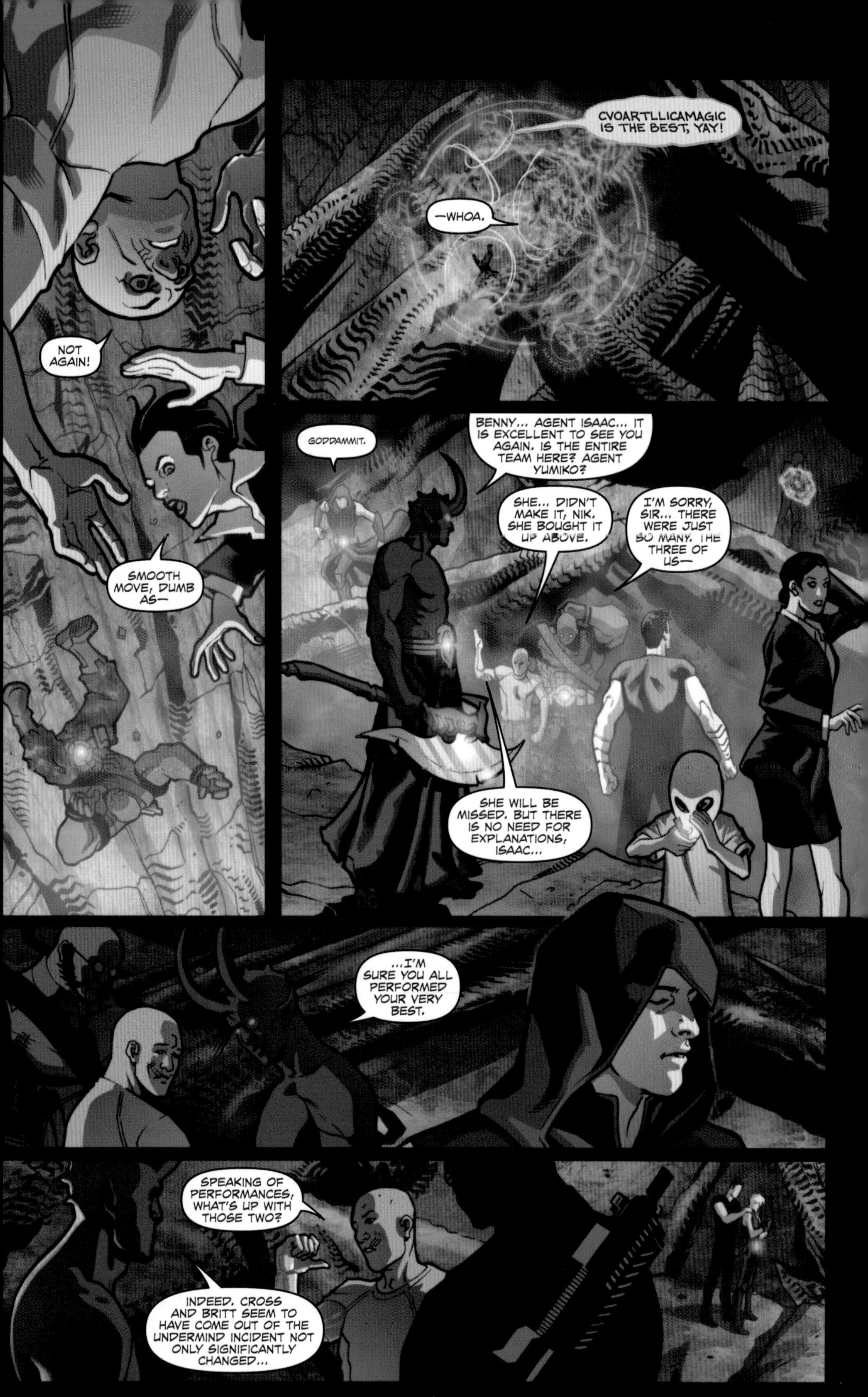
NOT AGAIN!
SMOOTH MOVE, DUMB AS—
CVOARTLLICAMAGIC IS THE BEST, YAY!
—WHOA.
GODDAMMIT.
BENNY... AGENT ISAAC... IT IS EXCELLENT TO SEE YOU AGAIN. IS THE ENTIRE TEAM HERE? AGENT YUMIKO?
SHE... DIDN'T MAKE IT, NIK. SHE BOUGHT IT UP ABOVE.
I'M SORRY, SIR... THERE WERE JUST SO MANY. THE THREE OF US—
SHE WILL BE MISSED. BUT THERE IS NO NEED FOR EXPLANATIONS, ISAAC...
...I'M SURE YOU ALL PERFORMED YOUR VERY BEST.
SPEAKING OF PERFORMANCES, WHAT'S UP WITH THOSE TWO?
INDEED. CROSS AND BRITT SEEM TO HAVE COME OUT OF THE UNDERMIND INCIDENT NOT ONLY SIGNIFICANTLY CHANGED...

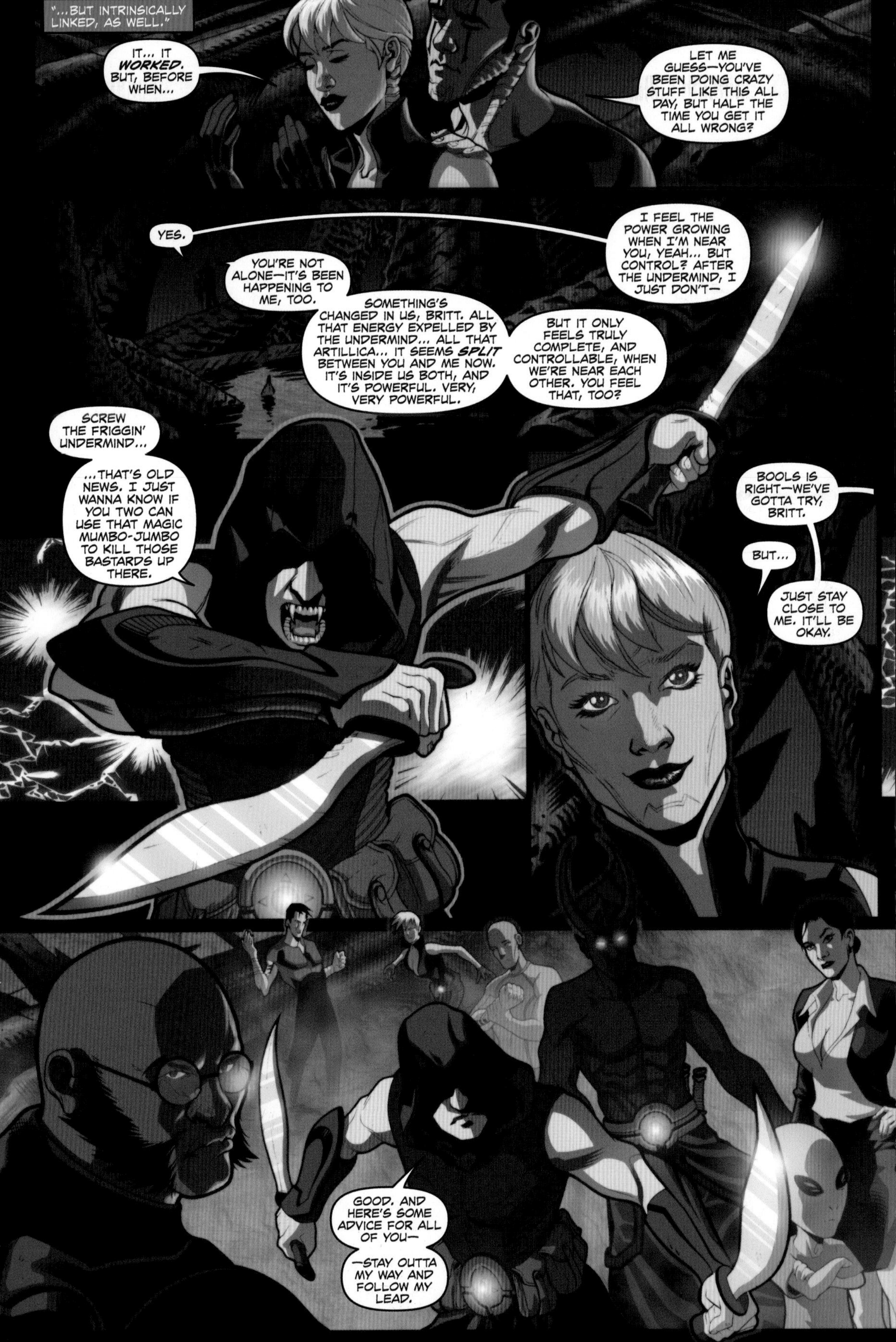
"...BUT INTRINSICALLY LINKED, AS WELL."
IT... IT ***WORKED***. BUT, BEFORE WHEN...
LET ME GUESS—YOU'VE BEEN DOING CRAZY STUFF LIKE THIS ALL DAY, BUT HALF THE TIME YOU GET IT ALL WRONG?
YES.
I FEEL THE POWER GROWING WHEN I'M NEAR YOU, YEAH... BUT CONTROL? AFTER THE UNDERMIND, I JUST DON'T—
YOU'RE NOT ALONE—IT'S BEEN HAPPENING TO ME, TOO.
SOMETHING'S CHANGED IN US, BRITT. ALL THAT ENERGY EXPELLED BY THE UNDERMIND... ALL THAT ARTILLICA... IT SEEMS ***SPLIT*** BETWEEN YOU AND ME NOW. IT'S INSIDE US BOTH, AND IT'S POWERFUL. VERY, VERY POWERFUL.
BUT IT ONLY FEELS TRULY COMPLETE, AND CONTROLLABLE, WHEN WE'RE NEAR EACH OTHER. YOU FEEL THAT, TOO?
SCREW THE FRIGGIN' UNDERMIND...
...THAT'S OLD NEWS. I JUST WANNA KNOW IF YOU TWO CAN USE THAT MAGIC MUMBO-JUMBO TO KILL THOSE BASTARDS UP THERE.
BOOLS IS RIGHT—WE'VE GOTTA TRY, BRITT.
BUT...
JUST STAY CLOSE TO ME. IT'LL BE OKAY.
GOOD. AND HERE'S SOME ADVICE FOR ALL OF YOU—
—STAY OUTTA MY WAY AND FOLLOW MY LEAD.

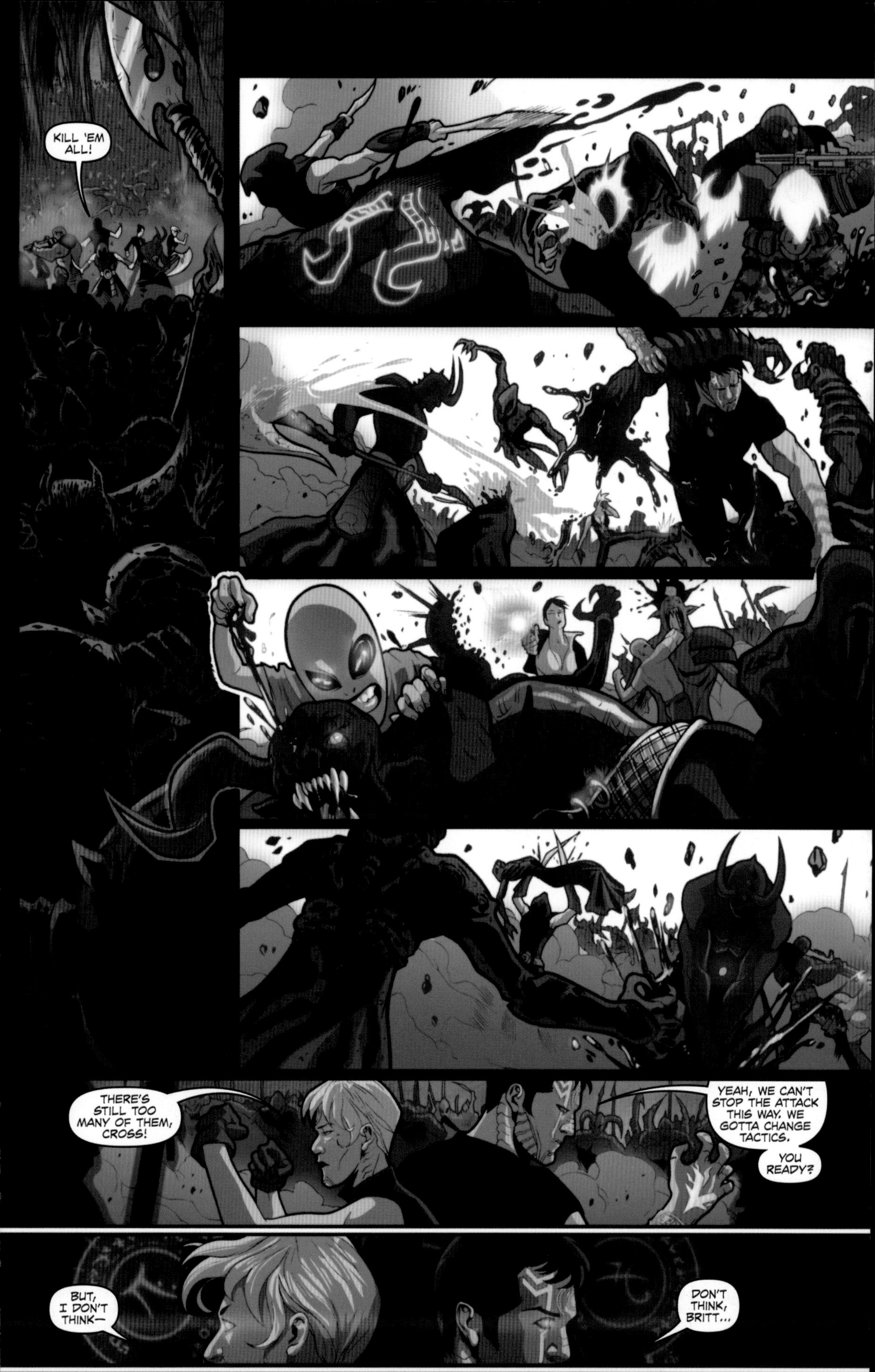
KILL 'EM ALL!
THERE'S STILL TOO MANY OF THEM, CROSS!
YEAH, WE CAN'T STOP THE ATTACK THIS WAY. WE GOTTA CHANGE TACTICS.
YOU READY?
BUT, I DON'T THINK—
DON'T THINK, BRITT...

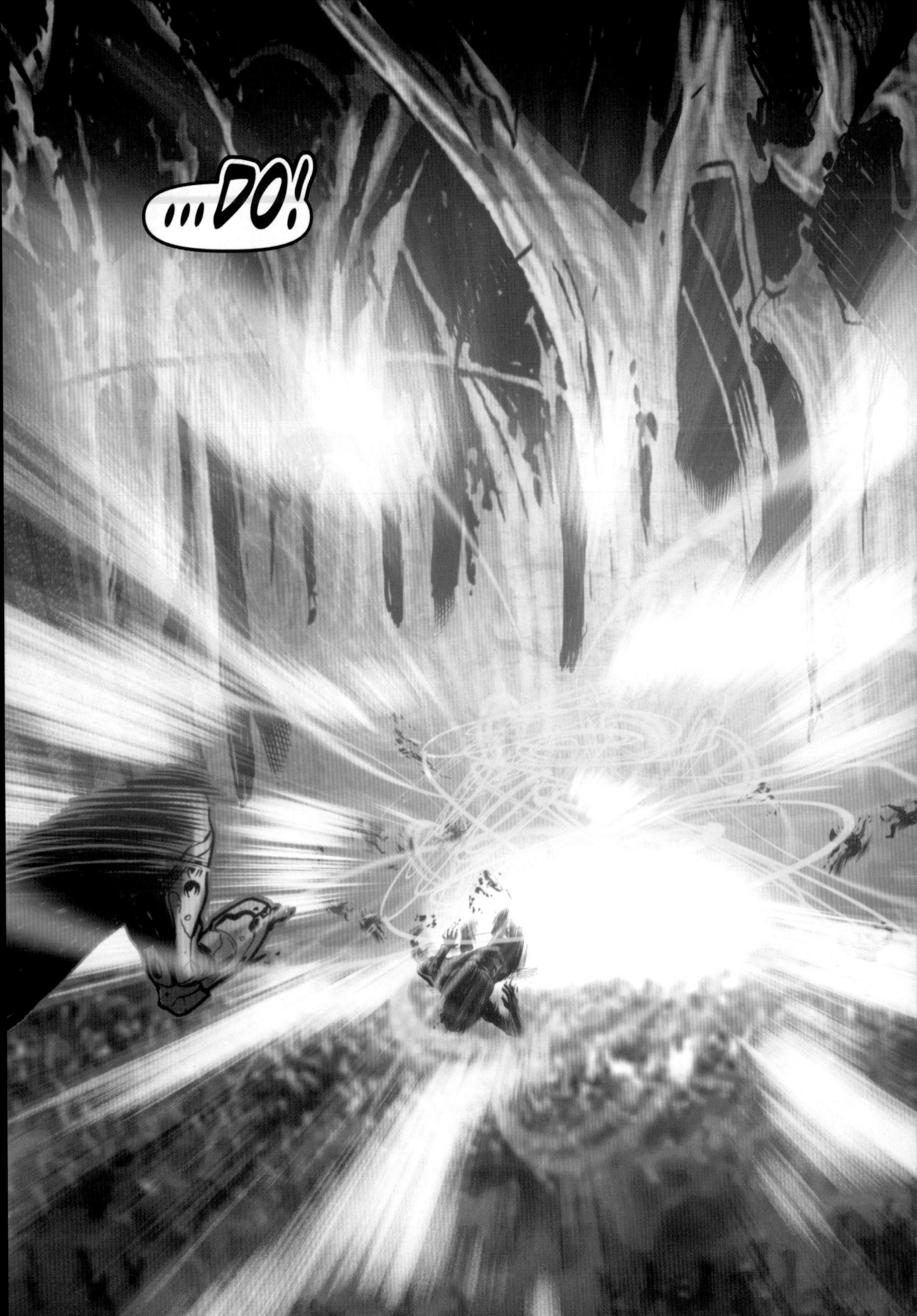
...DO!

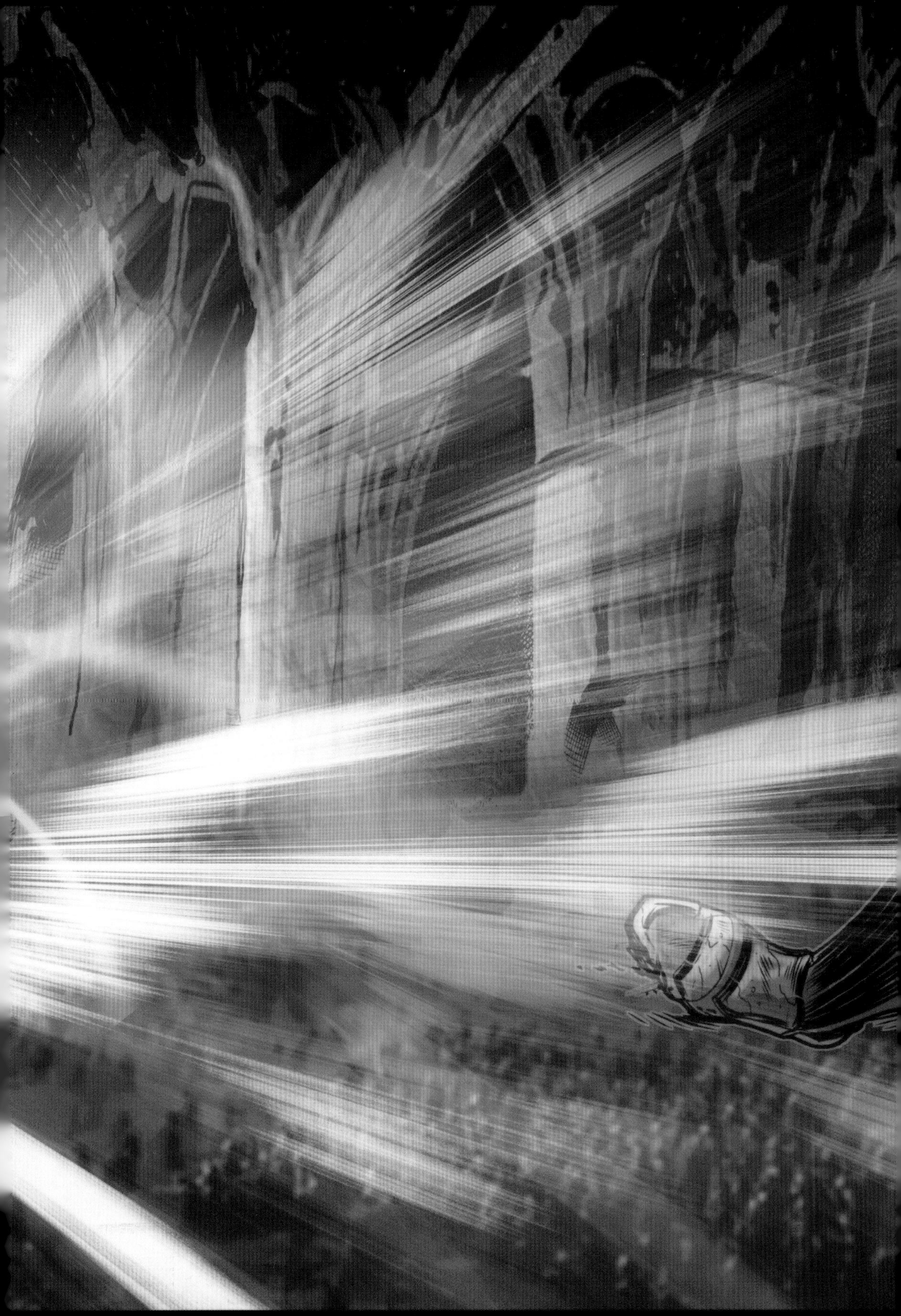

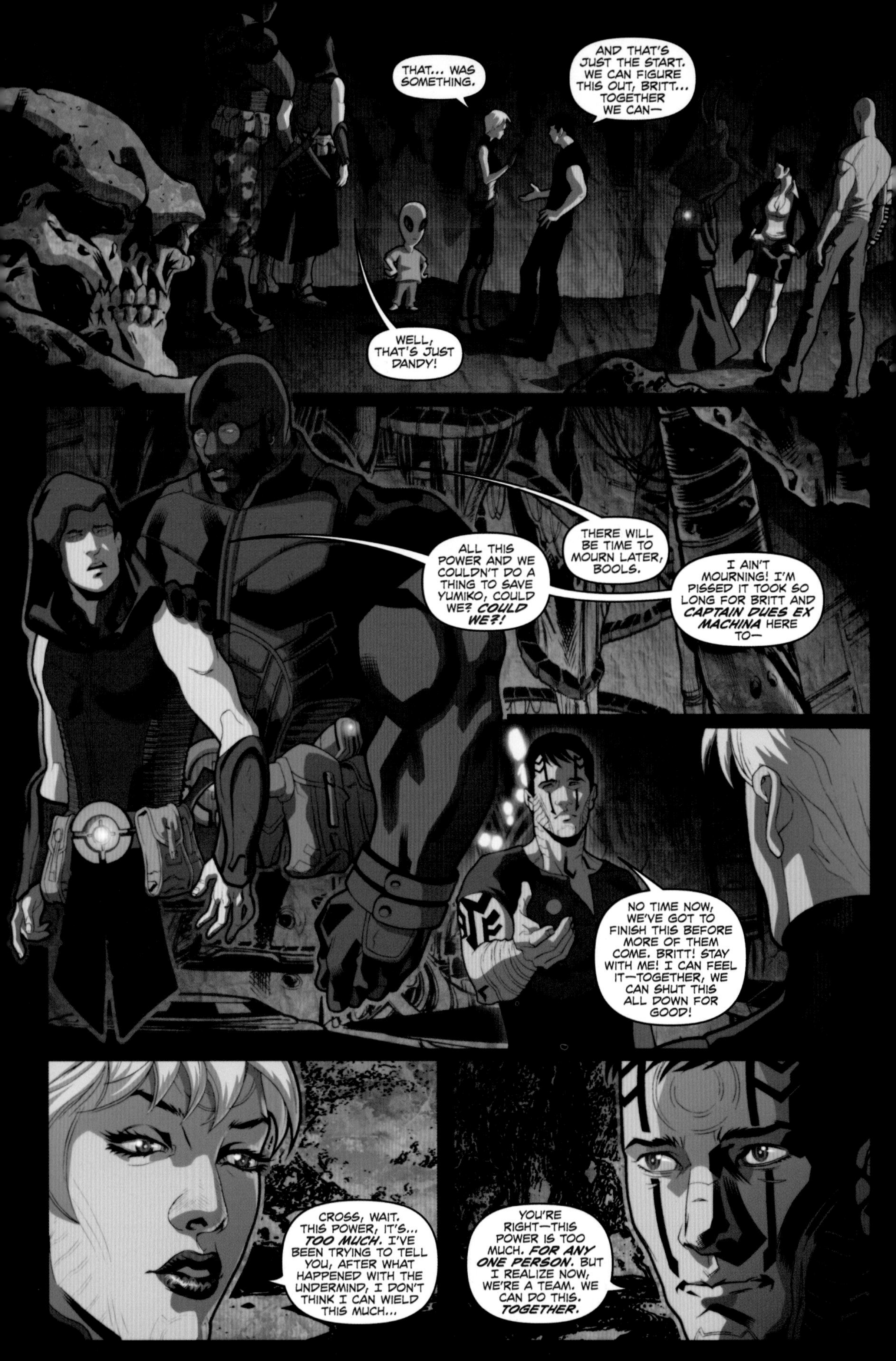

THAT... WAS SOMETHING.
AND THAT'S JUST THE START. WE CAN FIGURE THIS OUT, BRITT... TOGETHER WE CAN—
WELL, THAT'S JUST DANDY!
ALL THIS POWER AND WE COULDN'T DO A THING TO SAVE YUMIKO, COULD WE? *COULD WE?!*
THERE WILL BE TIME TO MOURN LATER, BOOLS.
I AIN'T MOURNING! I'M PISSED IT TOOK SO LONG FOR BRITT AND *CAPTAIN DUES EX MACHINA* HERE TO—
NO TIME NOW, WE'VE GOT TO FINISH THIS BEFORE MORE OF THEM COME. BRITT! STAY WITH ME! I CAN FEEL IT—TOGETHER, WE CAN SHUT THIS ALL DOWN FOR GOOD!
CROSS, WAIT. THIS POWER, IT'S... *TOO MUCH*. I'VE BEEN TRYING TO TELL YOU, AFTER WHAT HAPPENED WITH THE UNDERMIND, I DON'T THINK I CAN WIELD THIS MUCH...
YOU'RE RIGHT—THIS POWER IS TOO MUCH. *FOR ANY ONE PERSON*. BUT I REALIZE NOW, WE'RE A TEAM. WE CAN DO THIS. *TOGETHER*.

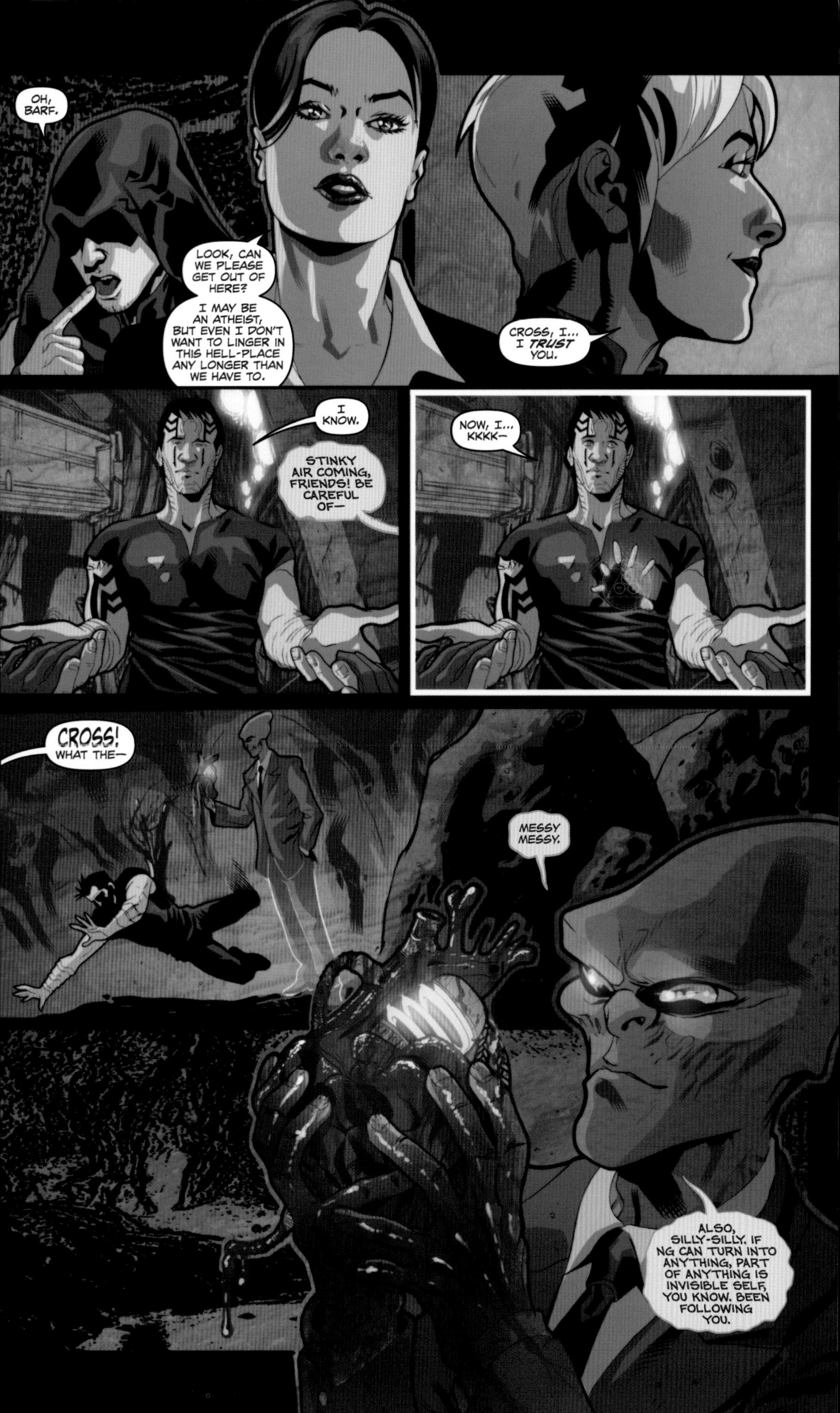
OH, BARF.
LOOK, CAN WE PLEASE GET OUT OF HERE?
I MAY BE AN ATHEIST, BUT EVEN I DON'T WANT TO LINGER IN THIS HELL-PLACE ANY LONGER THAN WE HAVE TO.
CROSS, I... I *TRUST* YOU.
I KNOW.
STINKY AIR COMING, FRIENDS! BE CAREFUL OF—
NOW, I... KKKK—
CROSS! WHAT THE—
MESSY MESSY.
ALSO, SILLY-SILLY. IF NG CAN TURN INTO ANYTHING, PART OF ANYTHING IS INVISIBLE SELF, YOU KNOW. BEEN FOLLOWING YOU.

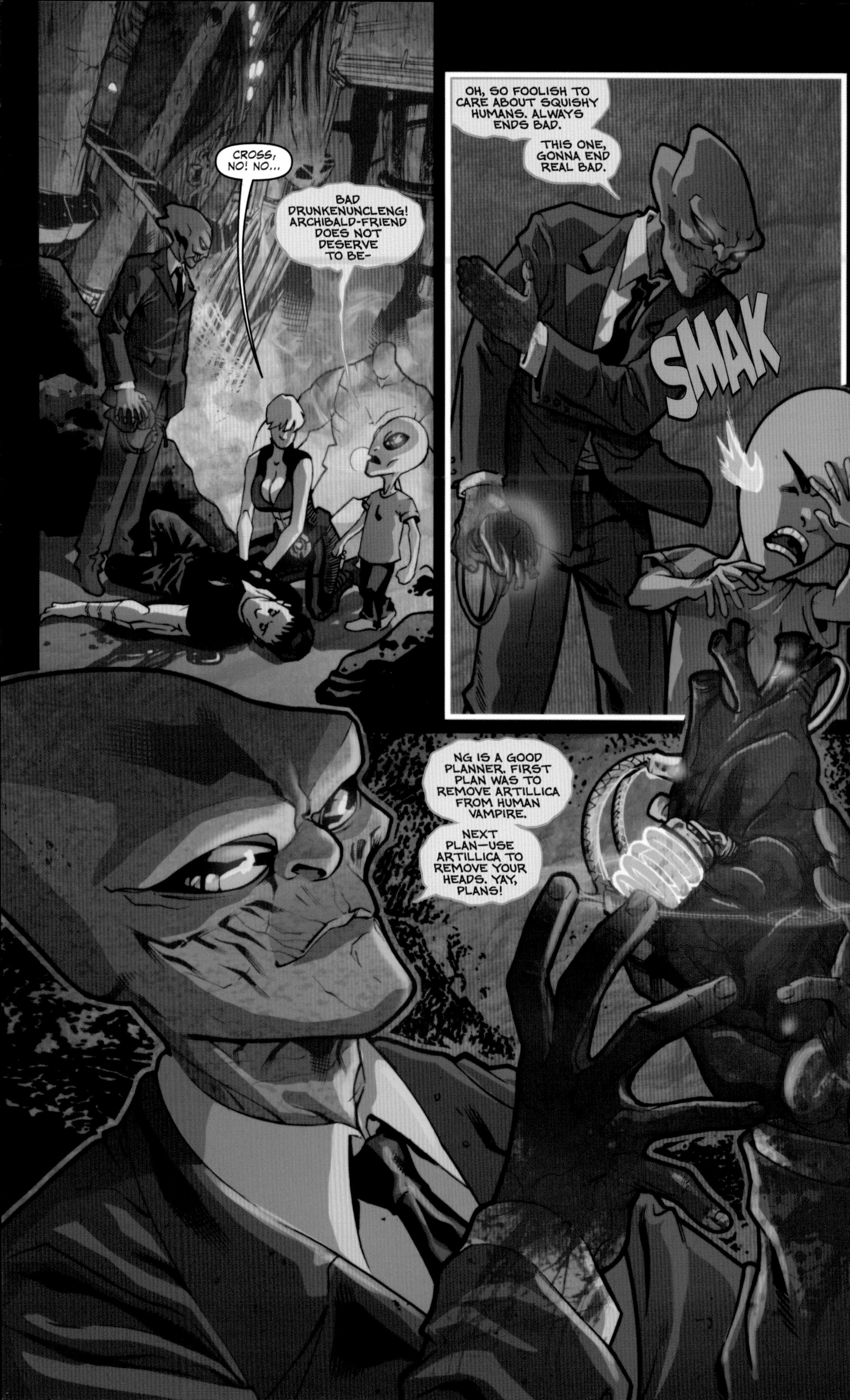
CROSS, NO! NO...
BAD DRUNKENUNCLENG! ARCHIBALD-FRIEND DOES NOT DESERVE TO BE-
OH, SO FOOLISH TO CARE ABOUT SQUISHY HUMANS. ALWAYS ENDS BAD.
THIS ONE, GONNA END REAL BAD.
SMAK
NG IS A GOOD PLANNER. FIRST PLAN WAS TO REMOVE ARTILLICA FROM HUMAN VAMPIRE.
NEXT PLAN—USE ARTILLICA TO REMOVE YOUR HEADS. YAY, PLANS!

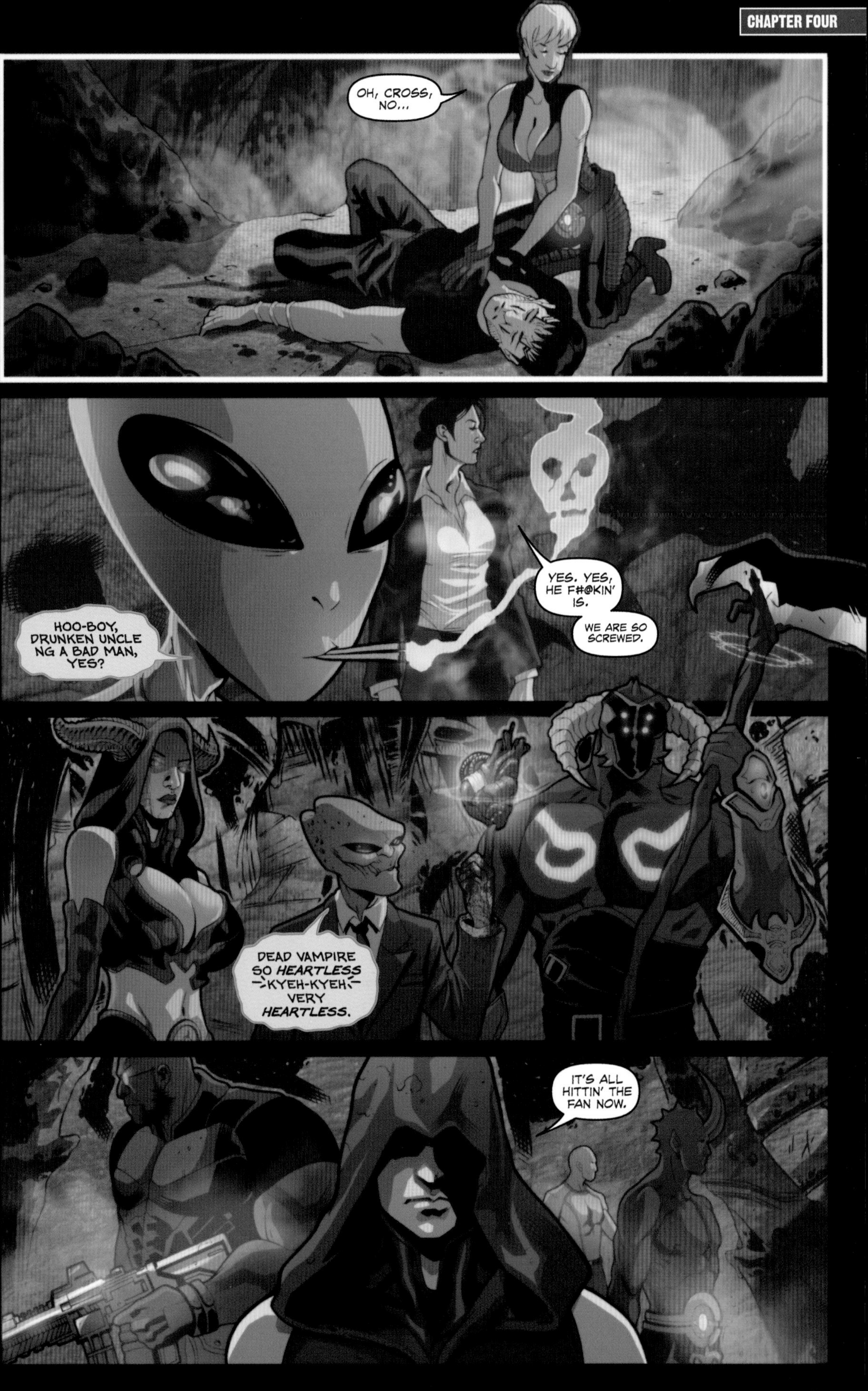
OH, CROSS, NO...
HOO-BOY, DRUNKEN UNCLE NG A BAD MAN, YES?
YES. YES, HE F#@KIN' IS.
WE ARE SO SCREWED.
DEAD VAMPIRE SO HEARTLESS -KYEH-KYEH- VERY HEARTLESS.
IT'S ALL HITTIN' THE FAN NOW.

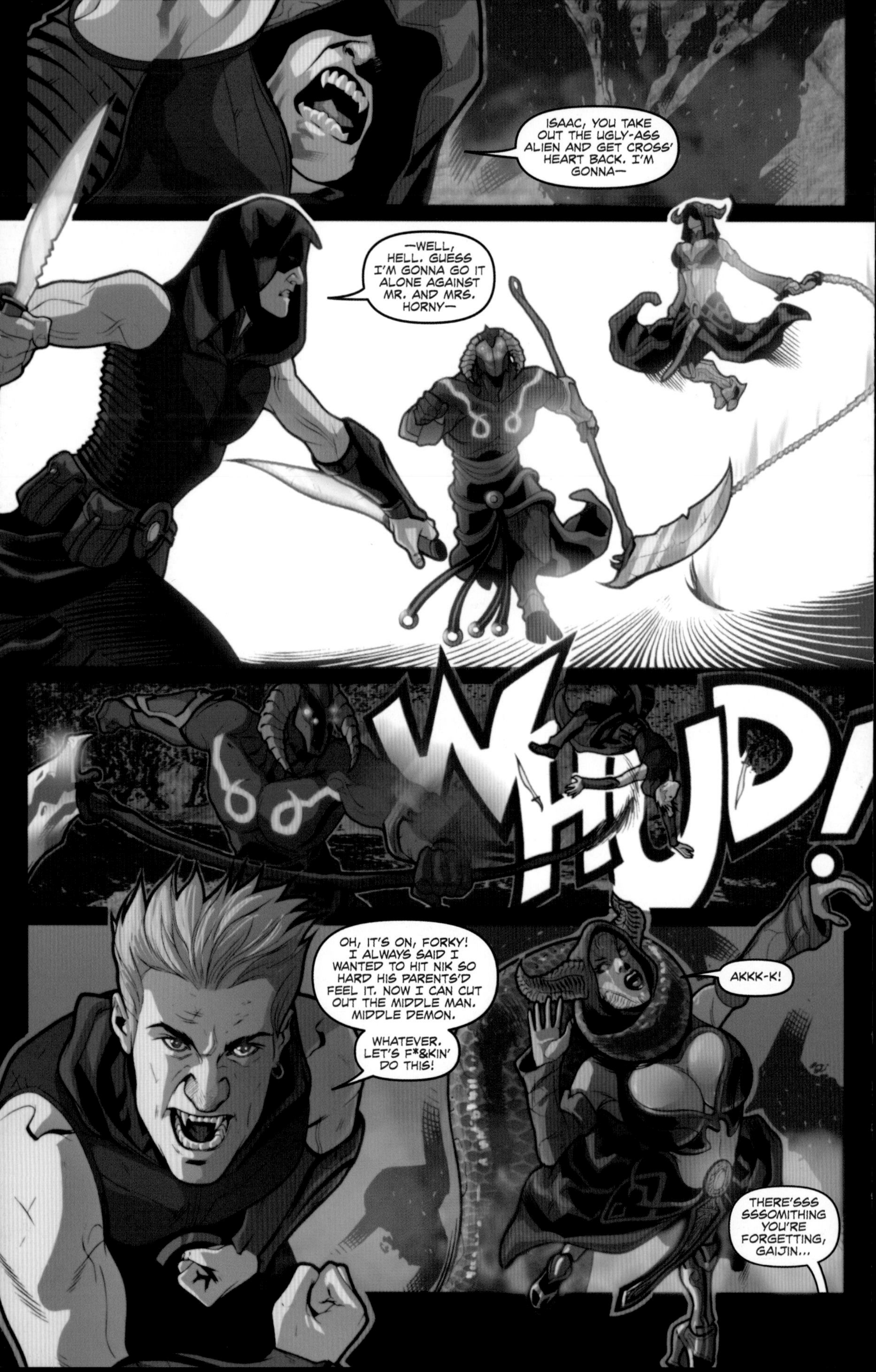
ISAAC, YOU TAKE OUT THE UGLY-ASS ALIEN AND GET CROSS' HEART BACK. I'M GONNA—
—WELL, HELL. GUESS I'M GONNA GO IT ALONE AGAINST MR. AND MRS. HORNY—
WHUD!
OH, IT'S ON, FORKY! I ALWAYS SAID I WANTED TO HIT NIK SO HARD HIS PARENTS'D FEEL IT. NOW I CAN CUT OUT THE MIDDLE MAN. MIDDLE DEMON.
WHATEVER. LET'S F*&KIN' DO THIS!
AKKK-K!
THERE'SSS SSSOMITHING YOU'RE FORGETTING, GAIJIN...

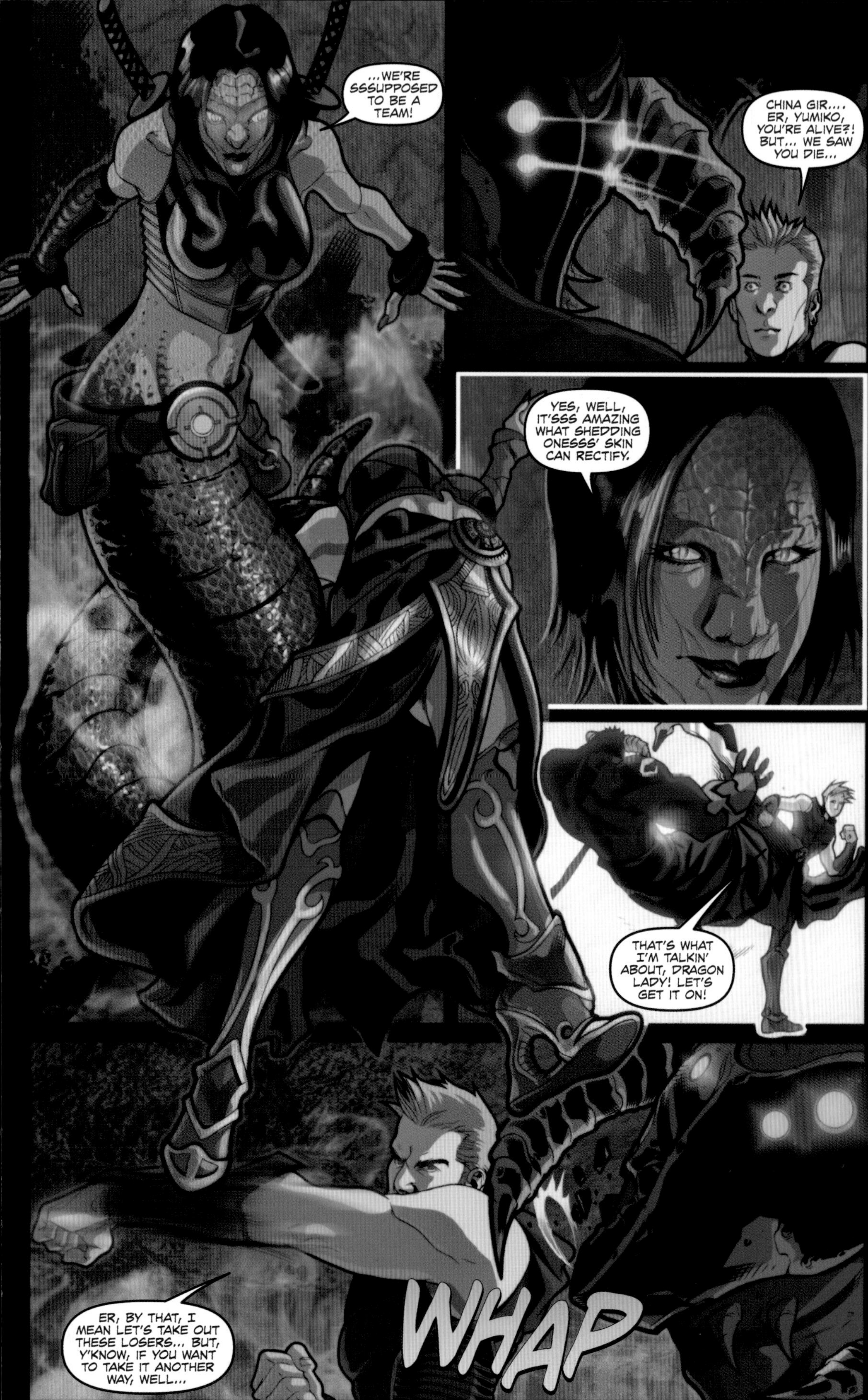
...WE'RE SSSUPPOSED TO BE A TEAM!
CHINA GIR.... ER, YUMIKO, YOU'RE ALIVE?! BUT... WE SAW YOU DIE...
YES, WELL, IT'SSS AMAZING WHAT SHEDDING ONESSS' SKIN CAN RECTIFY.
THAT'S WHAT I'M TALKIN' ABOUT, DRAGON LADY! LET'S GET IT ON!
ER, BY THAT, I MEAN LET'S TAKE OUT THESE LOSERS... BUT, Y'KNOW, IF YOU WANT TO TAKE IT ANOTHER WAY, WELL...
WHAP

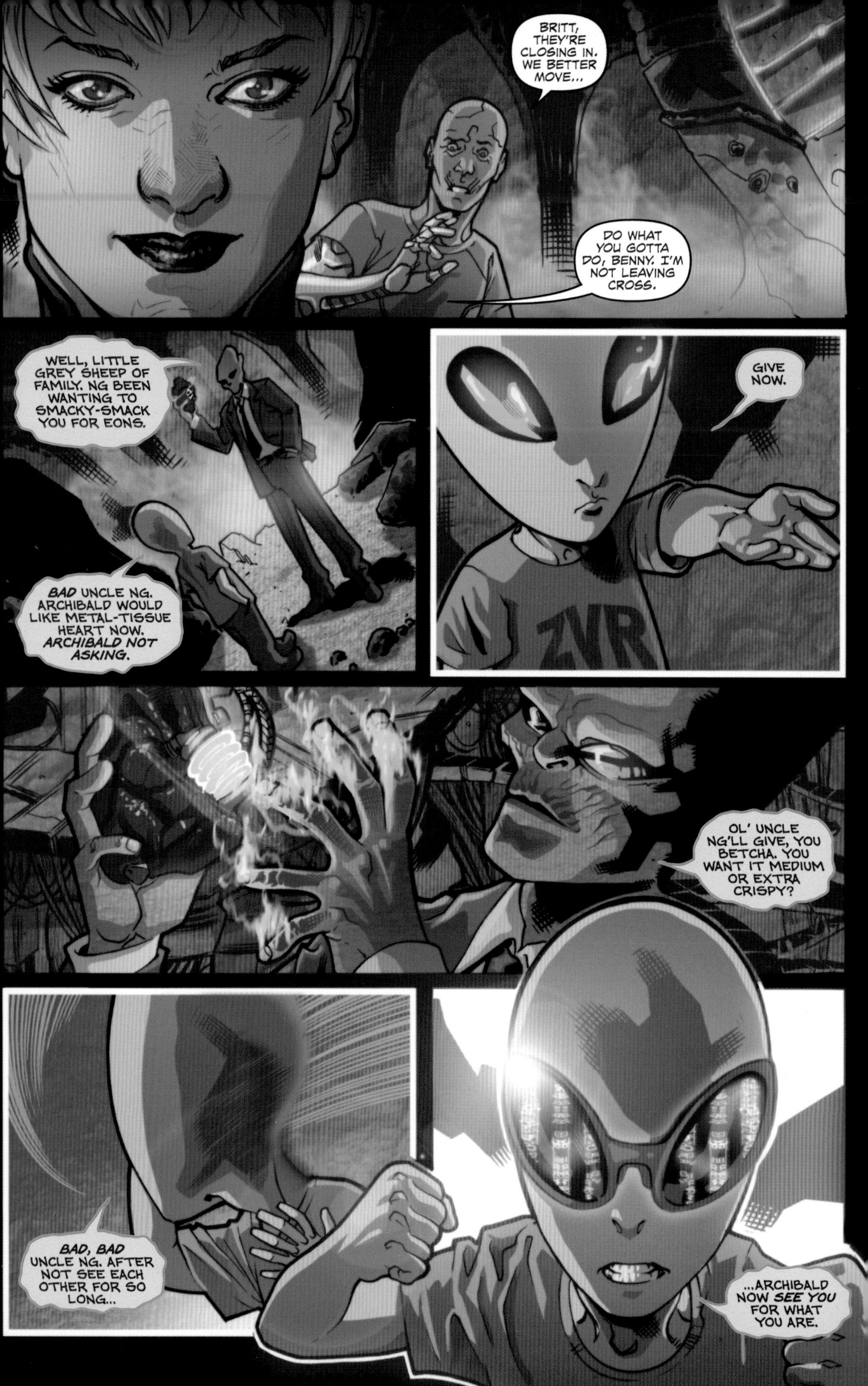
BRITT, THEY'RE CLOSING IN. WE BETTER MOVE...
DO WHAT YOU GOTTA DO, BENNY. I'M NOT LEAVING CROSS.
WELL, LITTLE GREY SHEEP OF FAMILY. NG BEEN WANTING TO SMACKY-SMACK YOU FOR EONS.
BAD UNCLE NG. ARCHIBALD WOULD LIKE METAL-TISSUE HEART NOW. *ARCHIBALD NOT ASKING.*
GIVE NOW.
OL' UNCLE NG'LL GIVE, YOU BETCHA. YOU WANT IT MEDIUM OR EXTRA CRISPY?
BAD, BAD UNCLE NG. AFTER NOT SEE EACH OTHER FOR SO LONG...
...ARCHIBALD NOW *SEE YOU* FOR WHAT YOU ARE.
ZVR

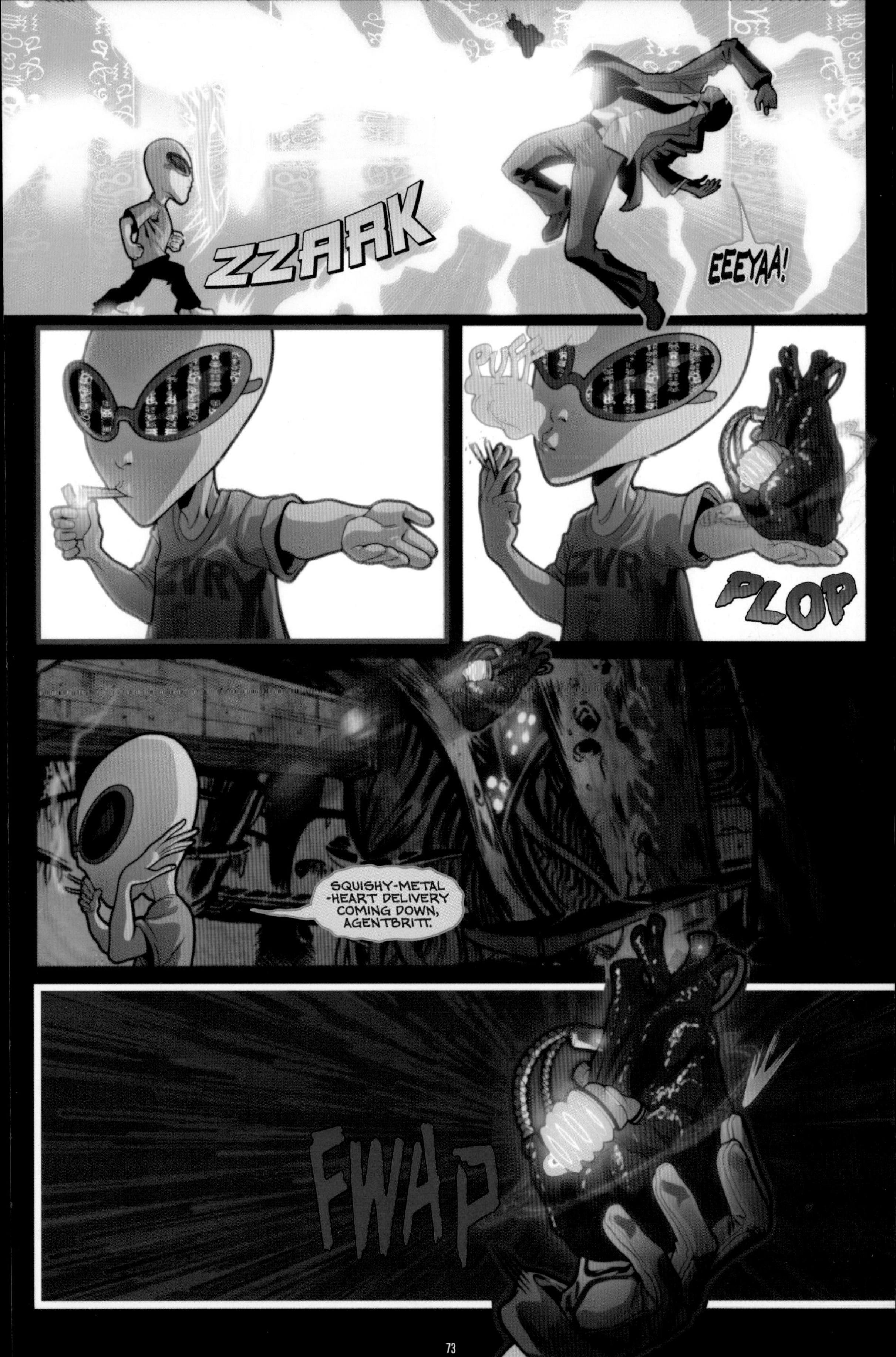
ZZAAK
EEEYAA!
PUFF
PLOP
SQUISHY-METAL -HEART DELIVERY COMING DOWN, AGENTBRITT.
FWAP

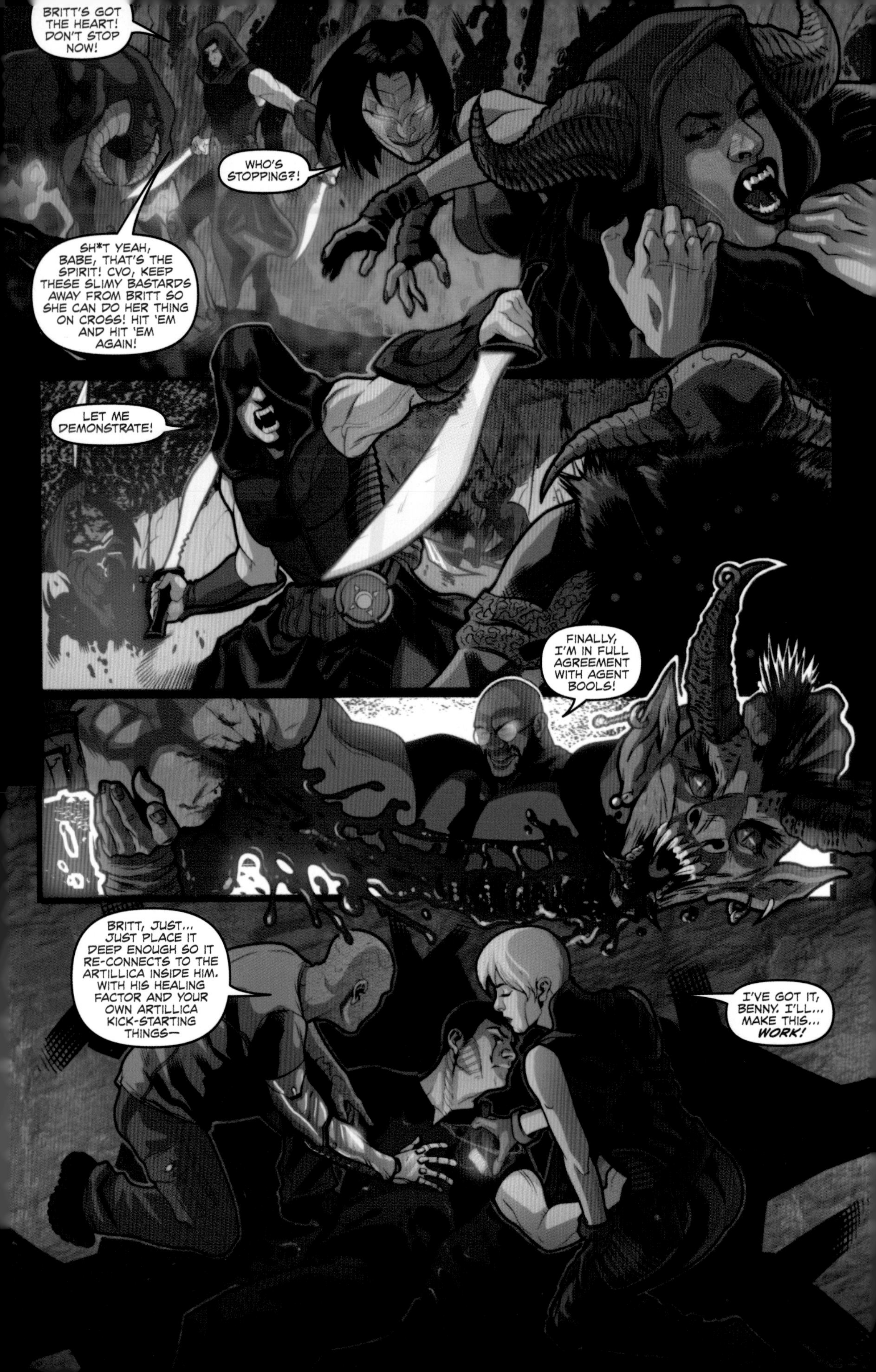
BRITT'S GOT THE HEART! DON'T STOP NOW!
WHO'S STOPPING?!
SH*T YEAH, BABE, THAT'S THE SPIRIT! CVO, KEEP THESE SLIMY BASTARDS AWAY FROM BRITT SO SHE CAN DO HER THING ON CROSS! HIT 'EM AND HIT 'EM AGAIN!
LET ME DEMONSTRATE!
FINALLY, I'M IN FULL AGREEMENT WITH AGENT BOOLS!
BRITT, JUST... JUST PLACE IT DEEP ENOUGH SO IT RE-CONNECTS TO THE ARTILLICA INSIDE HIM. WITH HIS HEALING FACTOR AND YOUR OWN ARTILLICA KICK-STARTING THINGS—
I'VE GOT IT, BENNY. I'LL... MAKE THIS... ***WORK!***

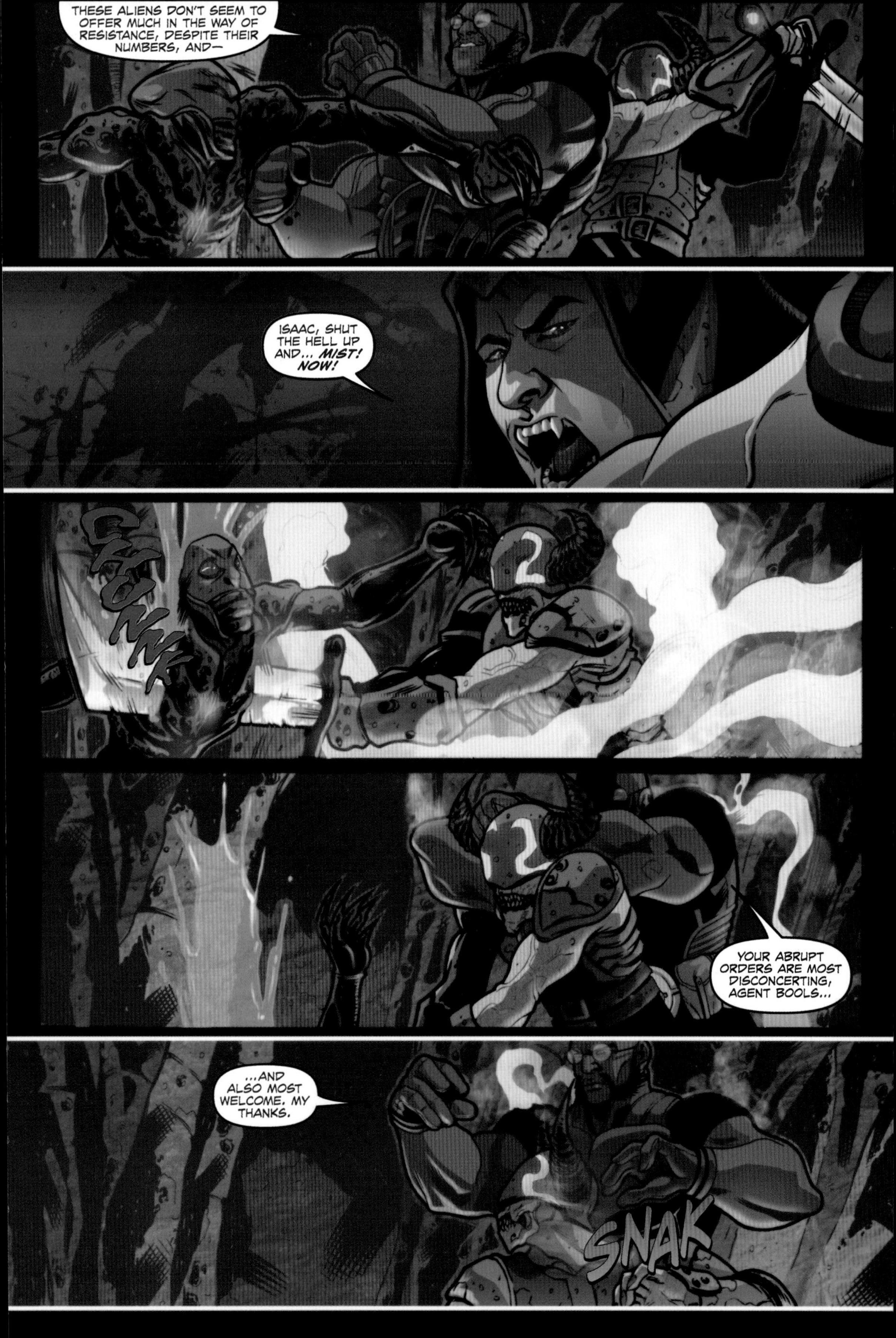

THESE ALIENS DON'T SEEM TO OFFER MUCH IN THE WAY OF RESISTANCE, DESPITE THEIR NUMBERS, AND—
ISAAC, SHUT THE HELL UP AND... MIST! NOW!
CHONNK
YOUR ABRUPT ORDERS ARE MOST DISCONCERTING, AGENT BOOLS...
...AND ALSO MOST WELCOME. MY THANKS.
SNAK

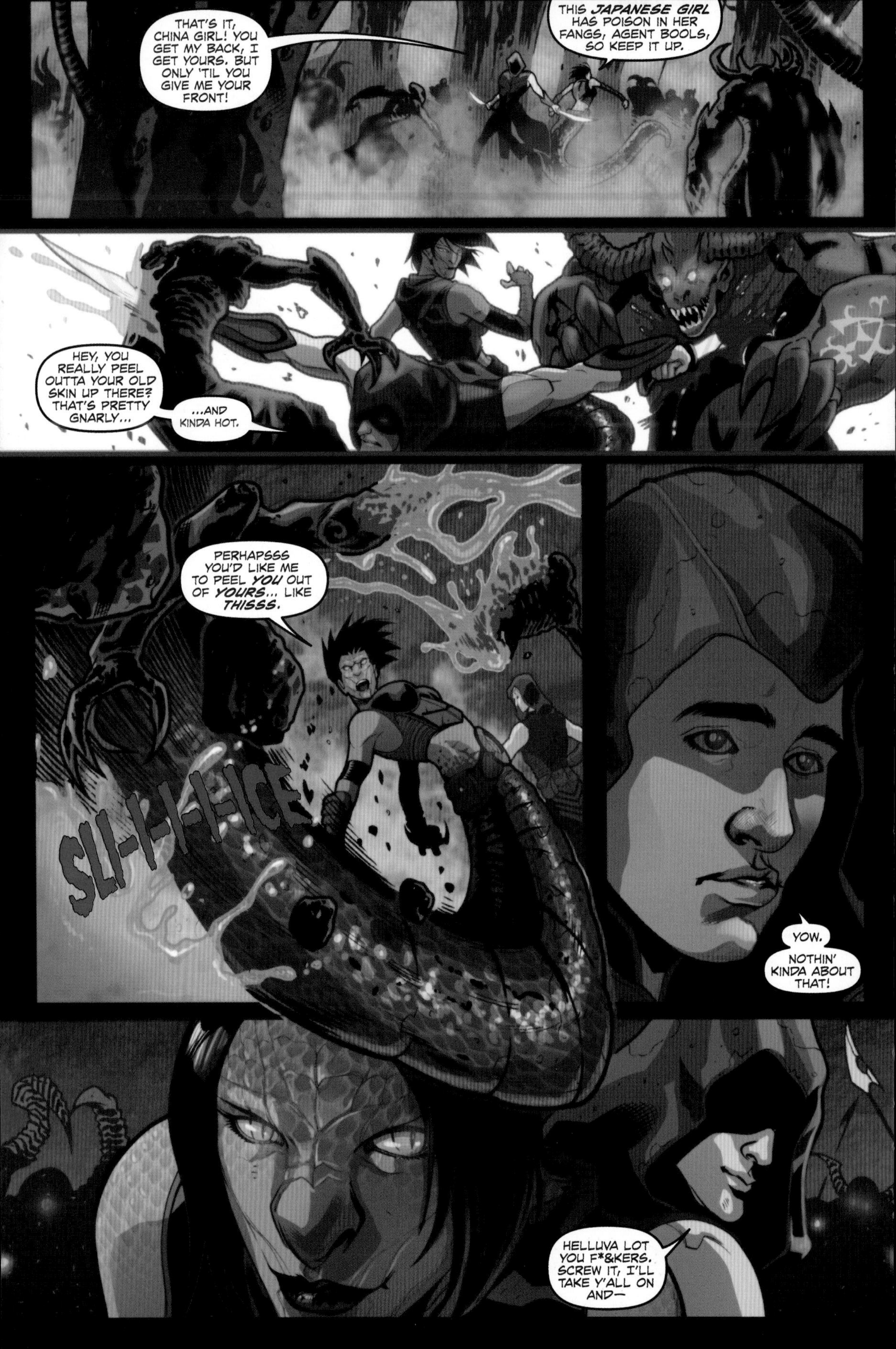
THAT'S IT, CHINA GIRL! YOU GET MY BACK, I GET YOURS. BUT ONLY 'TIL YOU GIVE ME YOUR FRONT!
THIS JAPANESE GIRL HAS POISON IN HER FANGS, AGENT BOOLS, SO KEEP IT UP.
HEY, YOU REALLY PEEL OUTTA YOUR OLD SKIN UP THERE? THAT'S PRETTY GNARLY...
...AND KINDA HOT.
PERHAPSSS YOU'D LIKE ME TO PEEL YOU OUT OF YOURS... LIKE THISSS.
SLI-I-I-I-ICE
YOW.
NOTHIN' KINDA ABOUT THAT!
HELLUVA LOT YOU F*&KERS. SCREW IT, I'LL TAKE Y'ALL ON AND—

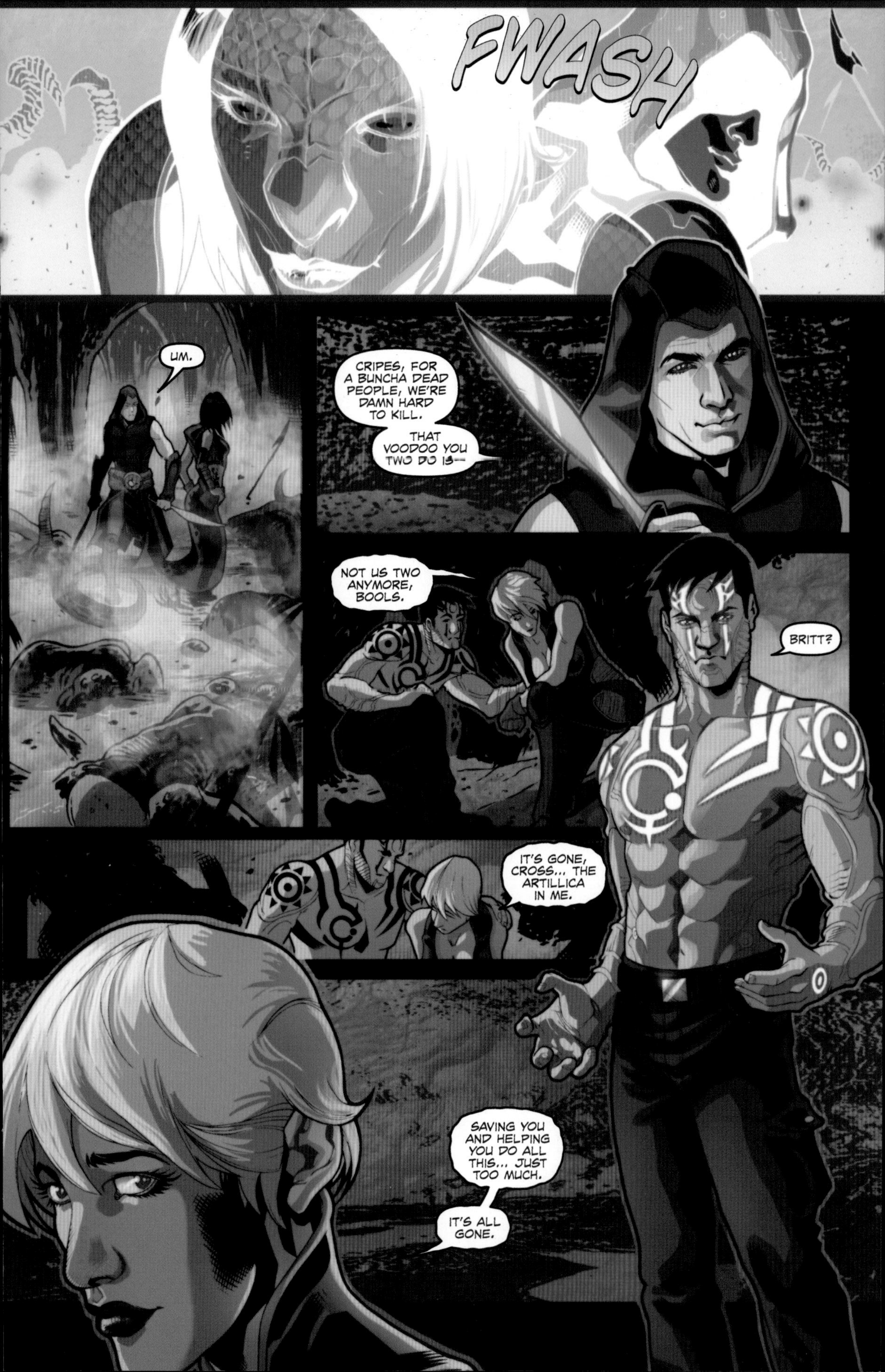
FWASH
UM.
CRIPES, FOR A BUNCHA DEAD PEOPLE, WE'RE DAMN HARD TO KILL.
THAT VOODOO YOU TWO DO IS--
NOT US TWO ANYMORE, BOOLS.
BRITT?
IT'S GONE, CROSS... THE ARTILLICA IN ME.
SAVING YOU AND HELPING YOU DO ALL THIS... JUST TOO MUCH.
IT'S ALL GONE.

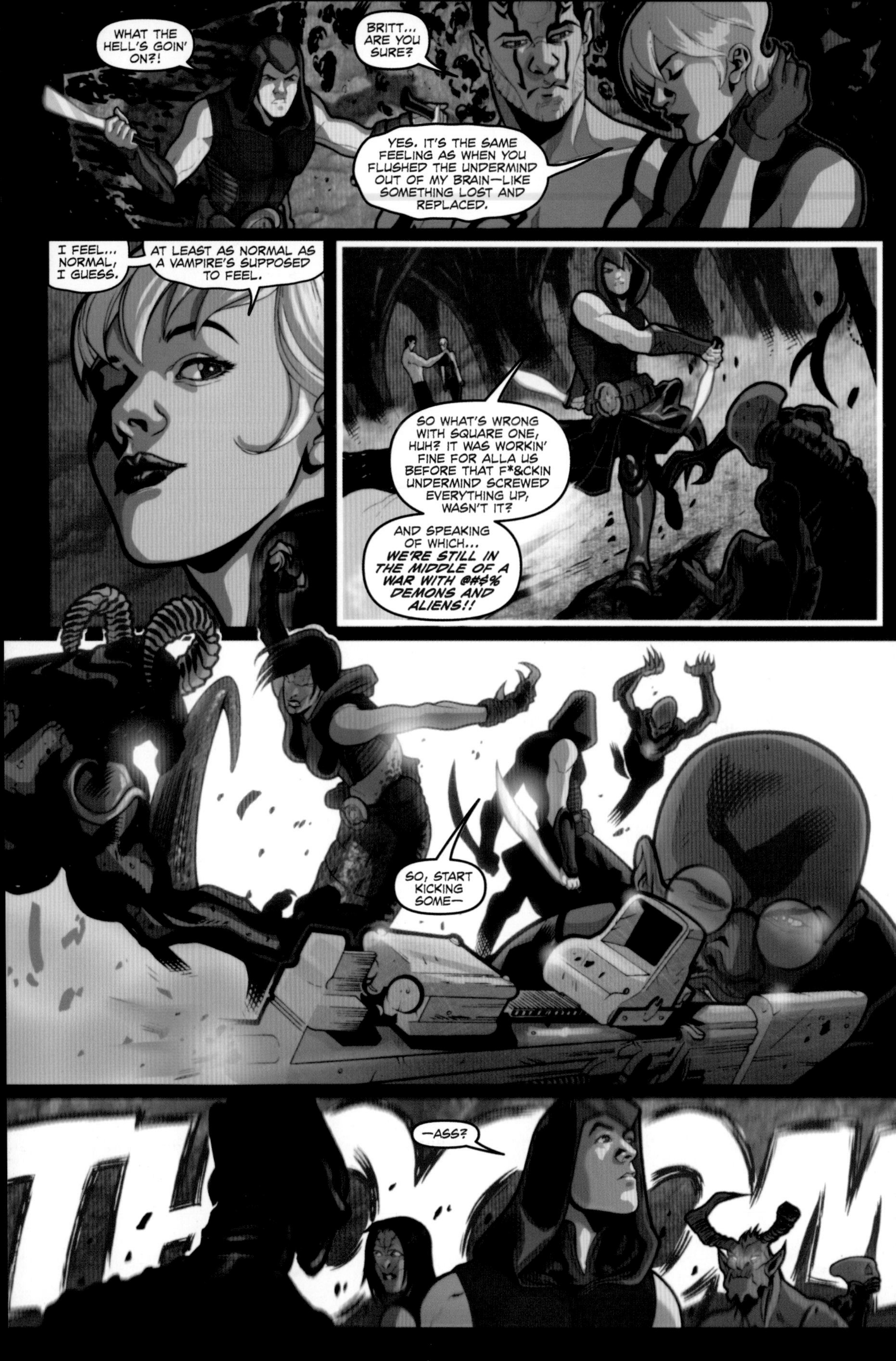
WHAT THE HELL'S GOIN' ON?!
BRITT... ARE YOU SURE?
YES. IT'S THE SAME FEELING AS WHEN YOU FLUSHED THE UNDERMIND OUT OF MY BRAIN—LIKE SOMETHING LOST AND REPLACED.
I FEEL... NORMAL, I GUESS.
AT LEAST AS NORMAL AS A VAMPIRE'S SUPPOSED TO FEEL.
SO WHAT'S WRONG WITH SQUARE ONE, HUH? IT WAS WORKIN' FINE FOR ALLA US BEFORE THAT F*&CKIN UNDERMIND SCREWED EVERYTHING UP, WASN'T IT?
AND SPEAKING OF WHICH... ***WE'RE STILL IN THE MIDDLE OF A WAR WITH @#$% DEMONS AND ALIENS!!***
SO, START KICKING SOME—
—ASS?

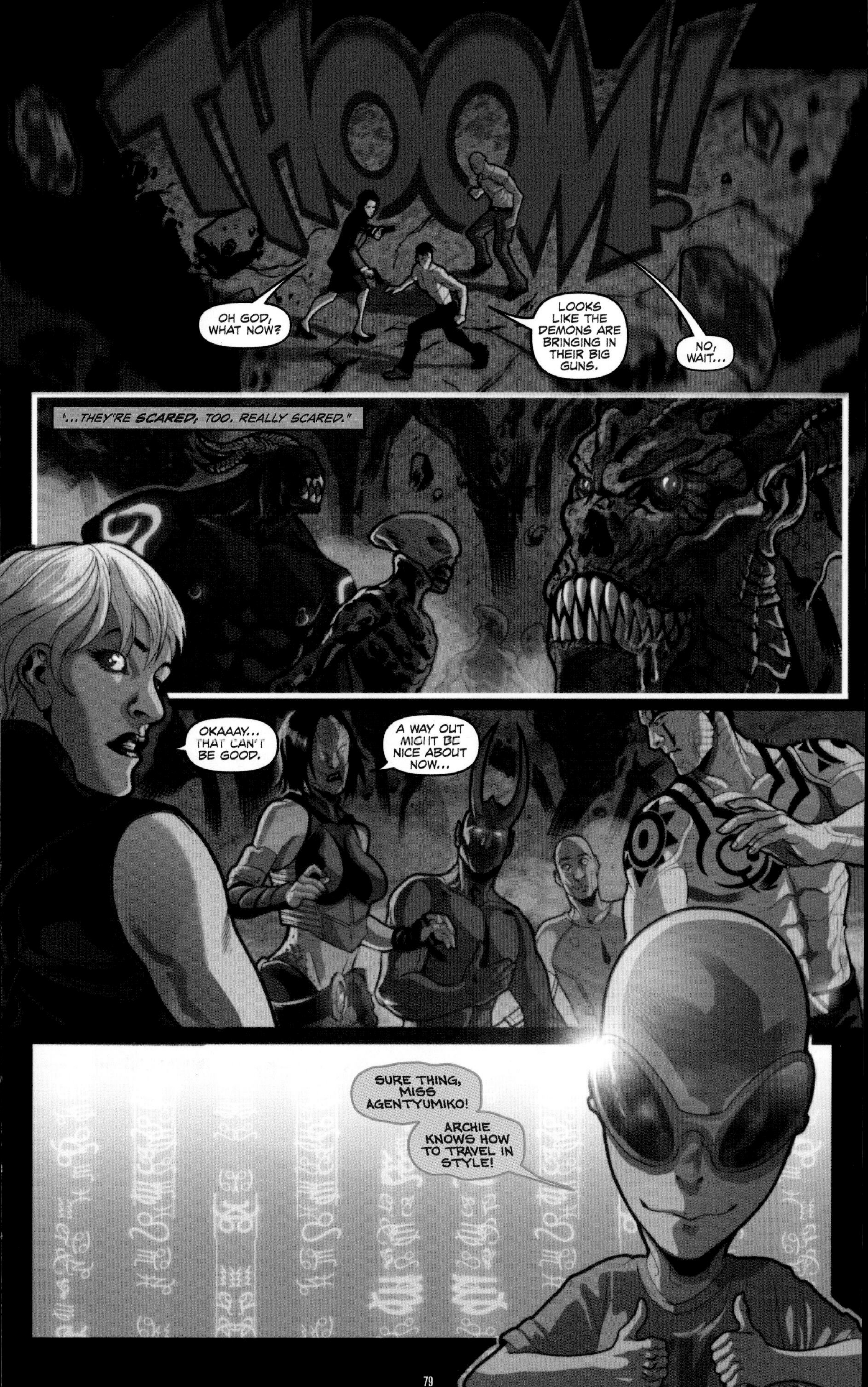
THOOM!
OH GOD, WHAT NOW?
LOOKS LIKE THE DEMONS ARE BRINGING IN THEIR BIG GUNS.
NO, WAIT...
"...THEY'RE SCARED, TOO. REALLY SCARED."
OKAAAY... THAT CAN'T BE GOOD.
A WAY OUT MIGHT BE NICE ABOUT NOW...
SURE THING, MISS AGENTYUMIKO!
ARCHIE KNOWS HOW TO TRAVEL IN STYLE!

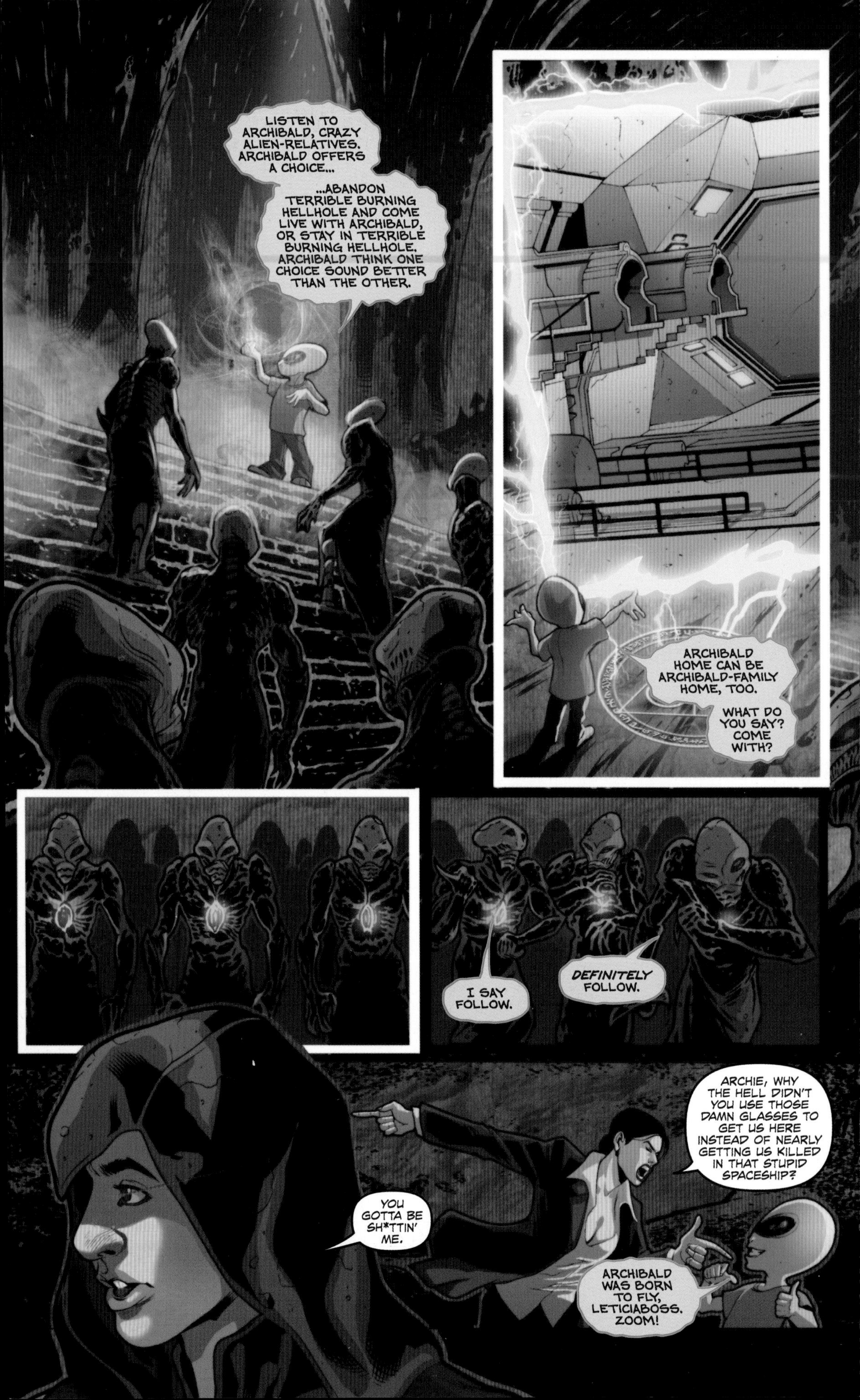
LISTEN TO ARCHIBALD, CRAZY ALIEN-RELATIVES. ARCHIBALD OFFERS A CHOICE...
...ABANDON TERRIBLE BURNING HELLHOLE AND COME LIVE WITH ARCHIBALD, OR STAY IN TERRIBLE BURNING HELLHOLE. ARCHIBALD THINK ONE CHOICE SOUND BETTER THAN THE OTHER.
ARCHIBALD HOME CAN BE ARCHIBALD-FAMILY HOME, TOO.
WHAT DO YOU SAY? COME WITH?
I SAY FOLLOW.
DEFINITELY FOLLOW.
ARCHIE, WHY THE HELL DIDN'T YOU USE THOSE DAMN GLASSES TO GET US HERE INSTEAD OF NEARLY GETTING US KILLED IN THAT STUPID SPACESHIP?
YOU GOTTA BE SH*TTIN' ME.
ARCHIBALD WAS BORN TO FLY, LETICIABOSS. ZOOM!

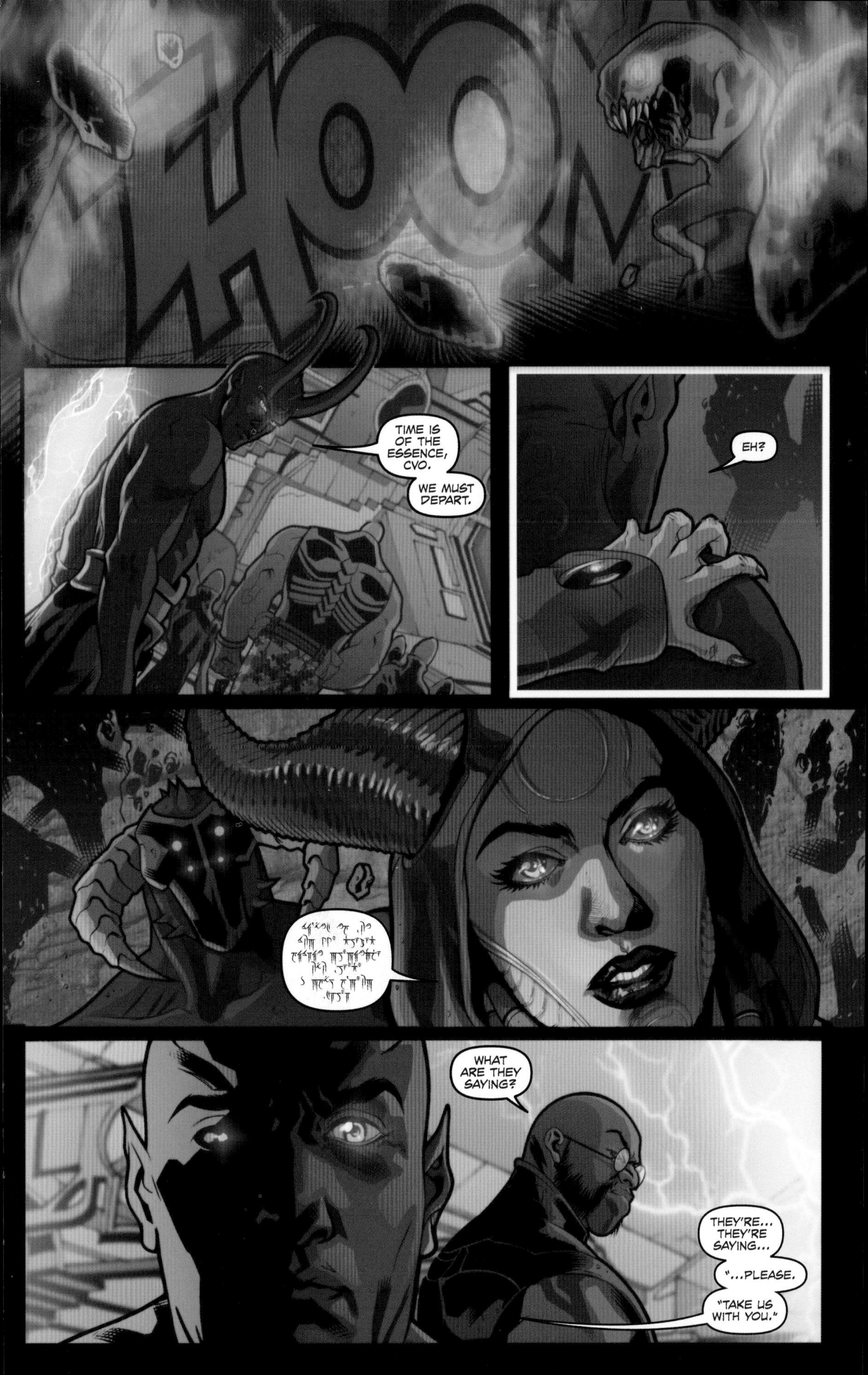

WHOOM!
TIME IS OF THE ESSENCE, CVO.
WE MUST DEPART.
EH?
WHAT ARE THEY SAYING?
THEY'RE... THEY'RE SAYING...
"...PLEASE.
"TAKE US WITH YOU."

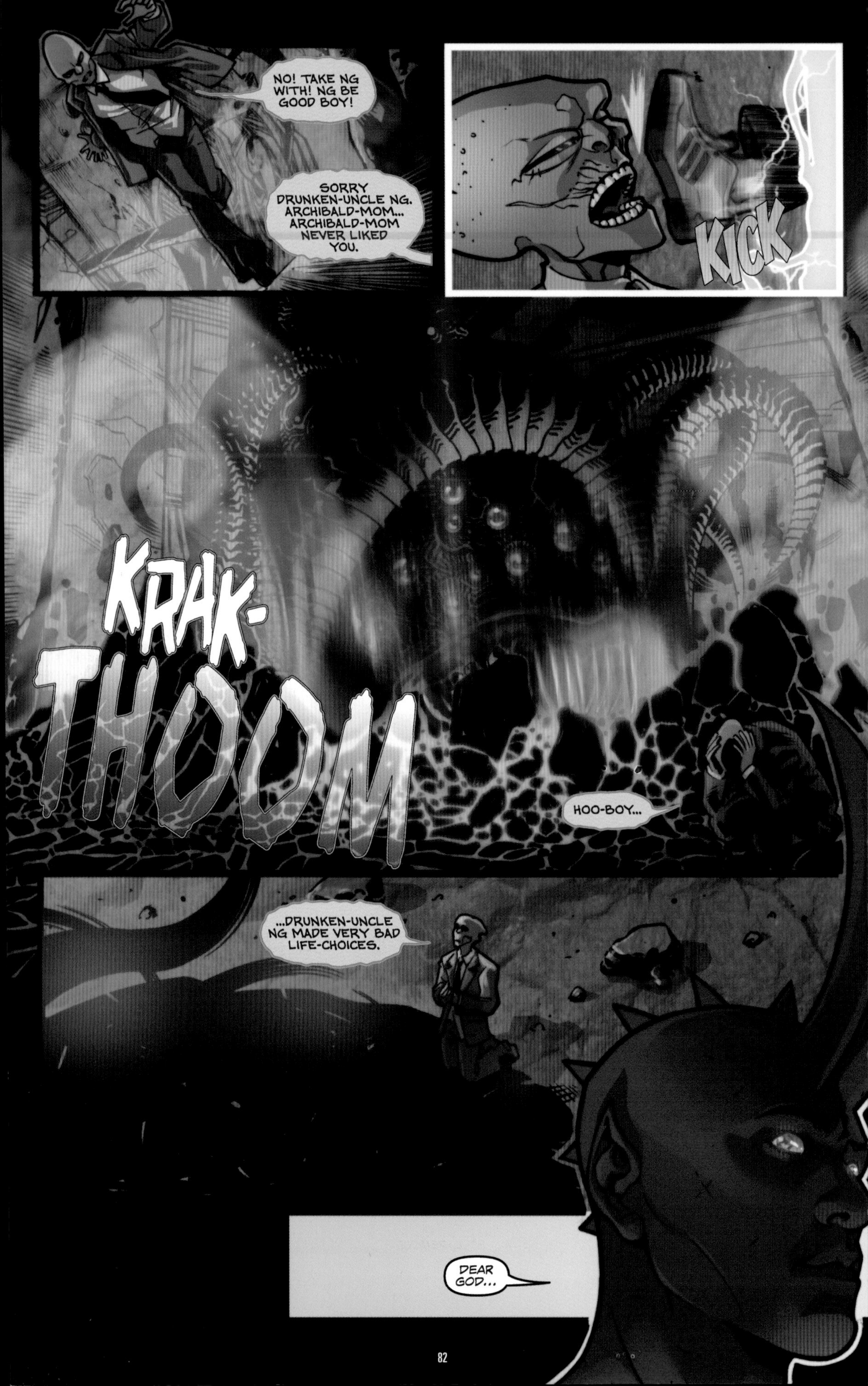

NO! TAKE NG WITH! NG BE GOOD BOY!
SORRY DRUNKEN-UNCLE NG. ARCHIBALD-MOM... ARCHIBALD-MOM NEVER LIKED YOU.
KICK
KRAK-THOOM
HOO-BOY...
...DRUNKEN-UNCLE NG MADE VERY BAD LIFE-CHOICES.
DEAR GOD...

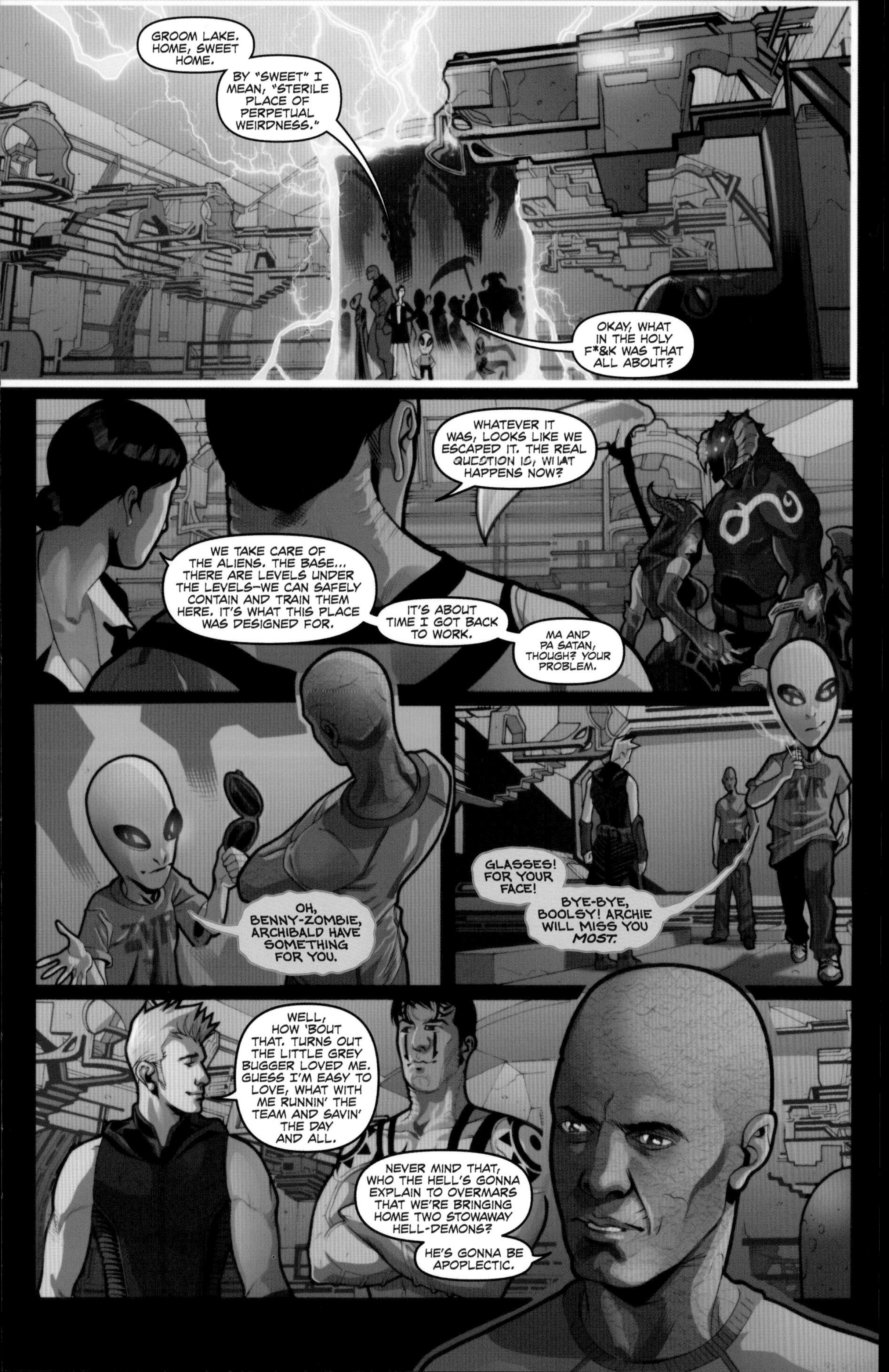

GROOM LAKE. HOME, SWEET HOME.
BY "SWEET" I MEAN, "STERILE PLACE OF PERPETUAL WEIRDNESS."
OKAY, WHAT IN THE HOLY F*&K WAS THAT ALL ABOUT?
WHATEVER IT WAS, LOOKS LIKE WE ESCAPED IT. THE REAL QUESTION IS, WHAT HAPPENS NOW?
WE TAKE CARE OF THE ALIENS. THE BASE... THERE ARE LEVELS UNDER THE LEVELS—WE CAN SAFELY CONTAIN AND TRAIN THEM HERE. IT'S WHAT THIS PLACE WAS DESIGNED FOR.
IT'S ABOUT TIME I GOT BACK TO WORK.
MA AND PA SATAN, THOUGH? YOUR PROBLEM.
OH, BENNY-ZOMBIE, ARCHIBALD HAVE SOMETHING FOR YOU.
GLASSES! FOR YOUR FACE!
BYE-BYE, BOOLSY! ARCHIE WILL MISS YOU *MOST.*
WELL, HOW 'BOUT THAT. TURNS OUT THE LITTLE GREY BUGGER LOVED ME. GUESS I'M EASY TO LOVE, WHAT WITH ME RUNNIN' THE TEAM AND SAVIN' THE DAY AND ALL.
NEVER MIND THAT, WHO THE HELL'S GONNA EXPLAIN TO OVERMARS THAT WE'RE BRINGING HOME TWO STOWAWAY HELL-DEMONS?
HE'S GONNA BE APOPLECTIC.

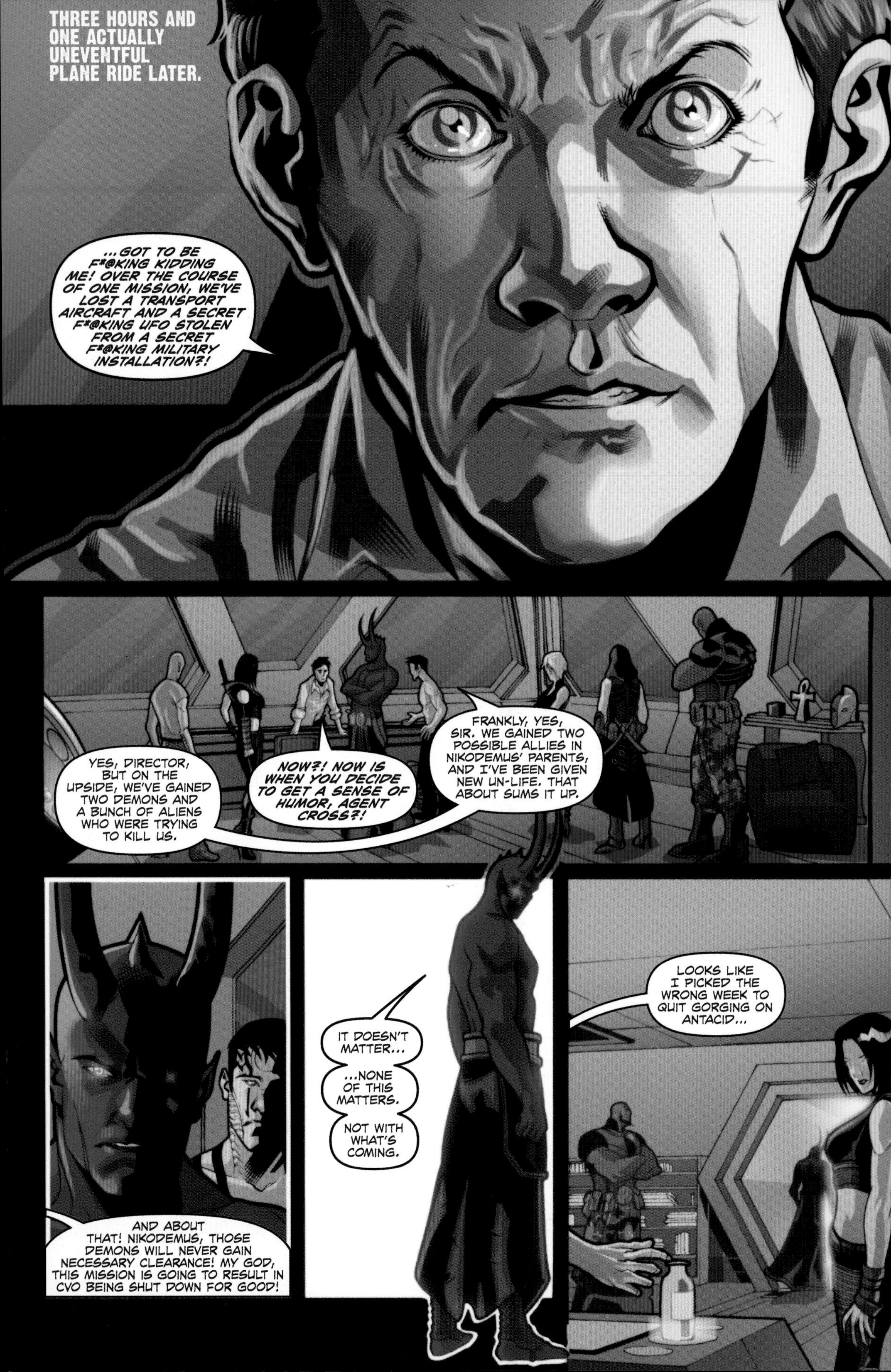
THREE HOURS AND ONE ACTUALLY UNEVENTFUL PLANE RIDE LATER.
...GOT TO BE F*@KING KIDDING ME! OVER THE COURSE OF ONE MISSION, WE'VE LOST A TRANSPORT AIRCRAFT AND A SECRET F*@KING UFO STOLEN FROM A SECRET F*@KING MILITARY INSTALLATION?!
YES, DIRECTOR, BUT ON THE UPSIDE, WE'VE GAINED TWO DEMONS AND A BUNCH OF ALIENS WHO WERE TRYING TO KILL US.
NOW?! NOW IS WHEN YOU DECIDE TO GET A SENSE OF HUMOR, AGENT CROSS?!
FRANKLY, YES, SIR. WE GAINED TWO POSSIBLE ALLIES IN NIKODEMUS' PARENTS, AND I'VE BEEN GIVEN NEW UN-LIFE. THAT ABOUT SUMS IT UP.
AND ABOUT THAT! NIKODEMUS, THOSE DEMONS WILL NEVER GAIN NECESSARY CLEARANCE! MY GOD, THIS MISSION IS GOING TO RESULT IN CVO BEING SHUT DOWN FOR GOOD!
IT DOESN'T MATTER...
...NONE OF THIS MATTERS.
NOT WITH WHAT'S COMING.
LOOKS LIKE I PICKED THE WRONG WEEK TO QUIT GORGING ON ANTACID...

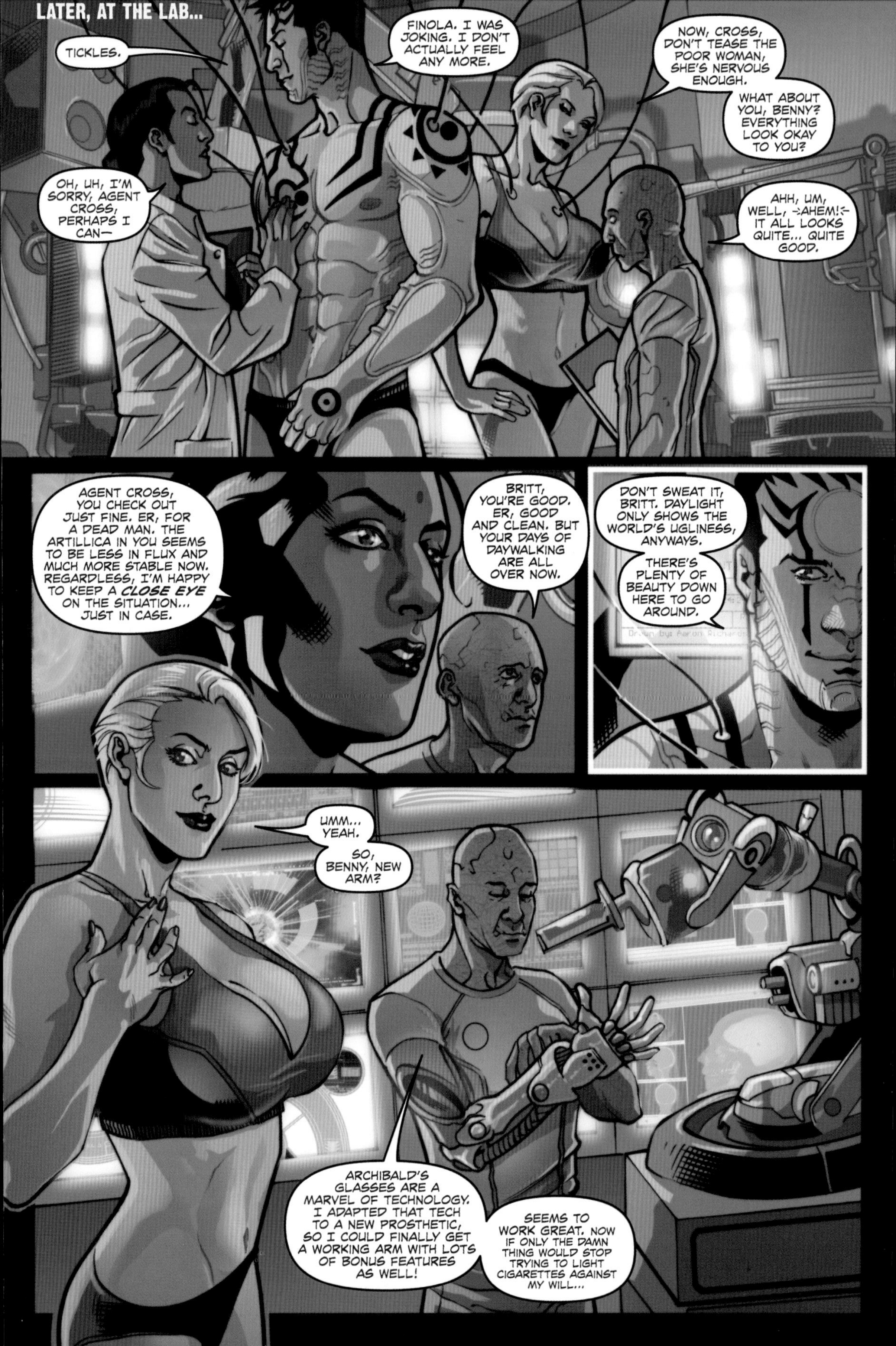

LATER, AT THE LAB...
TICKLES.
FINOLA. I WAS JOKING. I DON'T ACTUALLY FEEL ANY MORE.
NOW, CROSS, DON'T TEASE THE POOR WOMAN, SHE'S NERVOUS ENOUGH.
WHAT ABOUT YOU, BENNY? EVERYTHING LOOK OKAY TO YOU?
OH, UH, I'M SORRY, AGENT CROSS, PERHAPS I CAN—
AHH, UM, WELL, -AHEM!- IT ALL LOOKS QUITE... QUITE GOOD.
AGENT CROSS, YOU CHECK OUT JUST FINE. ER, FOR A DEAD MAN. THE ARTILLICA IN YOU SEEMS TO BE LESS IN FLUX AND MUCH MORE STABLE NOW. REGARDLESS, I'M HAPPY TO KEEP A CLOSE EYE ON THE SITUATION... JUST IN CASE.
BRITT, YOU'RE GOOD. ER, GOOD AND CLEAN. BUT YOUR DAYS OF DAYWALKING ARE ALL OVER NOW.
DON'T SWEAT IT, BRITT. DAYLIGHT ONLY SHOWS THE WORLD'S UGLINESS, ANYWAYS.
THERE'S PLENTY OF BEAUTY DOWN HERE TO GO AROUND.
UMM... YEAH.
SO, BENNY, NEW ARM?
ARCHIBALD'S GLASSES ARE A MARVEL OF TECHNOLOGY. I ADAPTED THAT TECH TO A NEW PROSTHETIC, SO I COULD FINALLY GET A WORKING ARM WITH LOTS OF BONUS FEATURES AS WELL!
SEEMS TO WORK GREAT. NOW IF ONLY THE DAMN THING WOULD STOP TRYING TO LIGHT CIGARETTES AGAINST MY WILL...

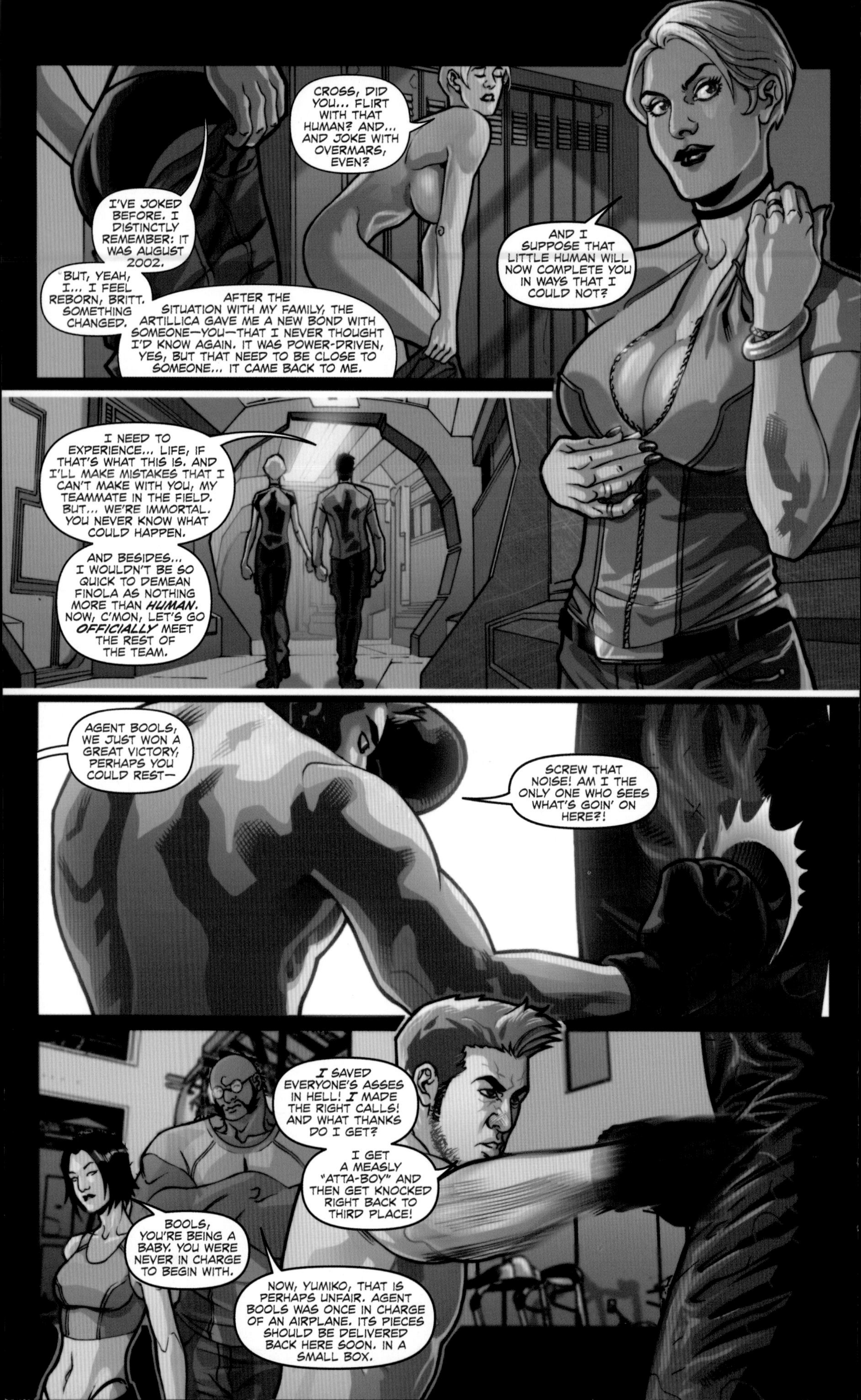
CROSS, DID YOU... FLIRT WITH THAT HUMAN? AND... AND JOKE WITH OVERMARS, EVEN?
I'VE JOKED BEFORE. I DISTINCTLY REMEMBER: IT WAS AUGUST 2002.
BUT, YEAH, I... I FEEL REBORN, BRITT. SOMETHING CHANGED.
AFTER THE SITUATION WITH MY FAMILY, THE ARTILLICA GAVE ME A NEW BOND WITH SOMEONE—YOU—THAT I NEVER THOUGHT I'D KNOW AGAIN. IT WAS POWER-DRIVEN, YES, BUT THAT NEED TO BE CLOSE TO SOMEONE... IT CAME BACK TO ME.
AND I SUPPOSE THAT LITTLE HUMAN WILL NOW COMPLETE YOU IN WAYS THAT I COULD NOT?
I NEED TO EXPERIENCE... LIFE, IF THAT'S WHAT THIS IS. AND I'LL MAKE MISTAKES THAT I CAN'T MAKE WITH YOU, MY TEAMMATE IN THE FIELD. BUT... WE'RE IMMORTAL. YOU NEVER KNOW WHAT COULD HAPPEN.
AND BESIDES... I WOULDN'T BE SO QUICK TO DEMEAN FINOLA AS NOTHING MORE THAN *HUMAN*. NOW, C'MON, LET'S GO *OFFICIALLY* MEET THE REST OF THE TEAM.
AGENT BOOLS, WE JUST WON A GREAT VICTORY, PERHAPS YOU COULD REST—
SCREW THAT NOISE! AM I THE ONLY ONE WHO SEES WHAT'S GOIN' ON HERE?!
I SAVED EVERYONE'S ASSES IN HELL! *I* MADE THE RIGHT CALLS! AND WHAT THANKS DO I GET?
I GET A MEASLY "ATTA-BOY" AND THEN GET KNOCKED RIGHT BACK TO THIRD PLACE!
BOOLS, YOU'RE BEING A BABY. YOU WERE NEVER IN CHARGE TO BEGIN WITH.
NOW, YUMIKO, THAT IS PERHAPS UNFAIR. AGENT BOOLS WAS ONCE IN CHARGE OF AN AIRPLANE. ITS PIECES SHOULD BE DELIVERED BACK HERE SOON. IN A SMALL BOX.

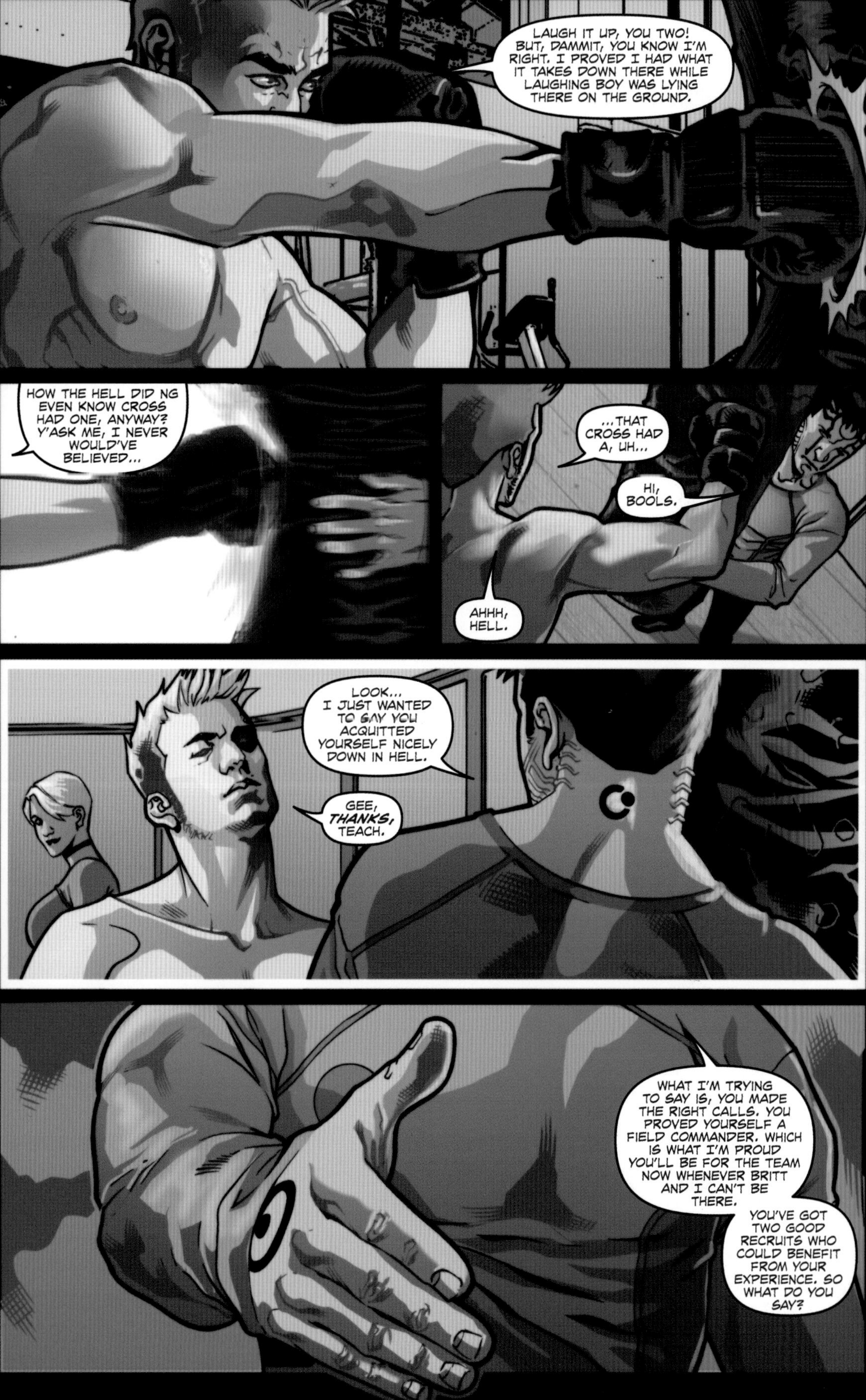
LAUGH IT UP, YOU TWO! BUT, DAMMIT, YOU KNOW I'M RIGHT. I PROVED I HAD WHAT IT TAKES DOWN THERE WHILE LAUGHING BOY WAS LYING THERE ON THE GROUND.
HOW THE HELL DID NG EVEN KNOW CROSS HAD ONE, ANYWAY? Y'ASK ME, I NEVER WOULD'VE BELIEVED...
...THAT CROSS HAD A, UH...
HI, BOOLS.
AHHH, HELL.
LOOK... I JUST WANTED TO SAY YOU ACQUITTED YOURSELF NICELY DOWN IN HELL.
GEE, *THANKS,* TEACH.
WHAT I'M TRYING TO SAY IS, YOU MADE THE RIGHT CALLS. YOU PROVED YOURSELF A FIELD COMMANDER. WHICH IS WHAT I'M PROUD YOU'LL BE FOR THE TEAM NOW WHENEVER BRITT AND I CAN'T BE THERE.
YOU'VE GOT TWO GOOD RECRUITS WHO COULD BENEFIT FROM YOUR EXPERIENCE. SO WHAT DO YOU SAY?

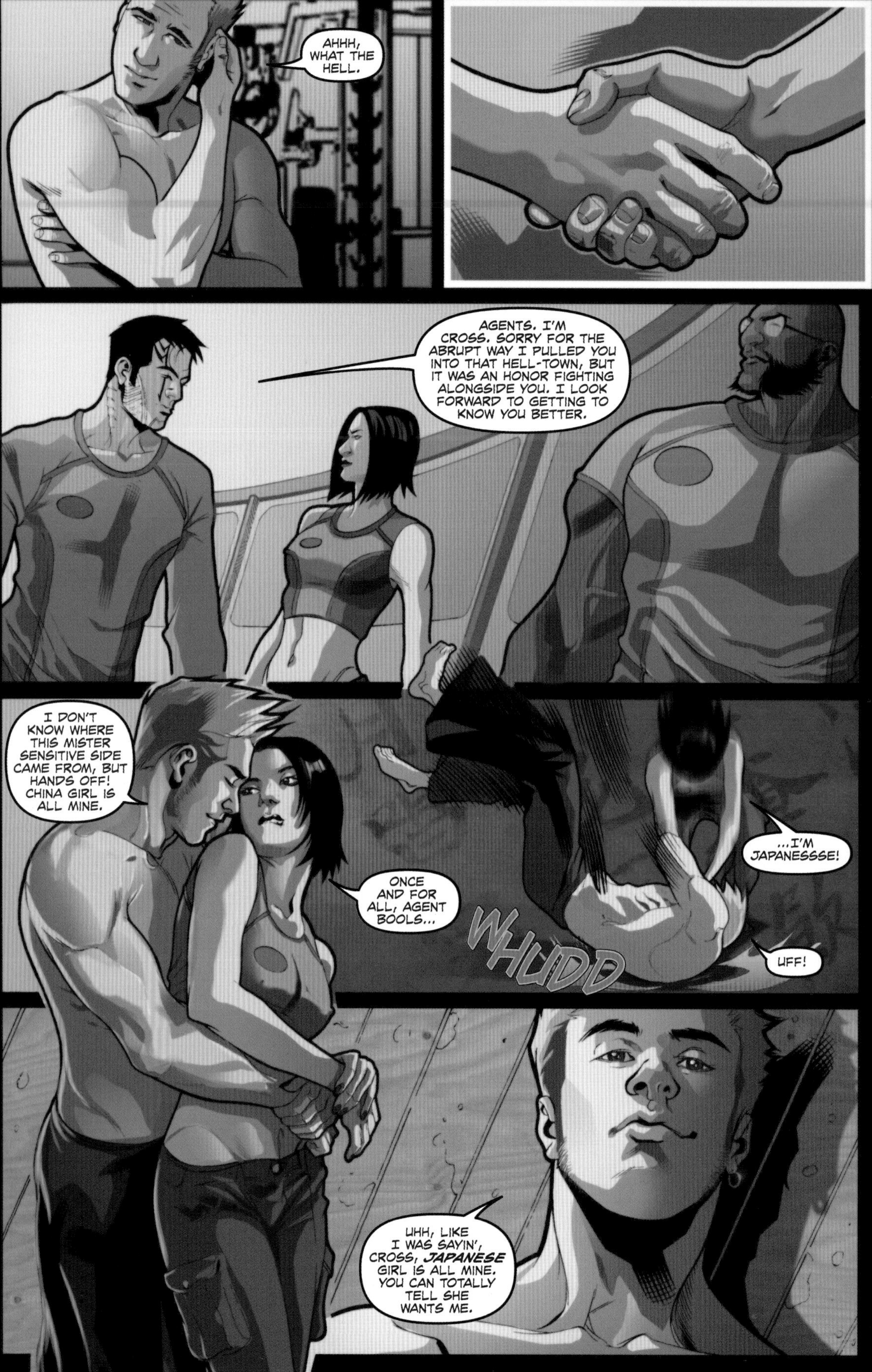
AHHH, WHAT THE HELL.
AGENTS. I'M CROSS. SORRY FOR THE ABRUPT WAY I PULLED YOU INTO THAT HELL-TOWN, BUT IT WAS AN HONOR FIGHTING ALONGSIDE YOU. I LOOK FORWARD TO GETTING TO KNOW YOU BETTER.
I DON'T KNOW WHERE THIS MISTER SENSITIVE SIDE CAME FROM, BUT HANDS OFF! CHINA GIRL IS ALL MINE.
ONCE AND FOR ALL, AGENT BOOLS...
...I'M JAPANESSSE!
WHUDD
UFF!
UHH, LIKE I WAS SAYIN', CROSS, JAPANESE GIRL IS ALL MINE. YOU CAN TOTALLY TELL SHE WANTS ME.

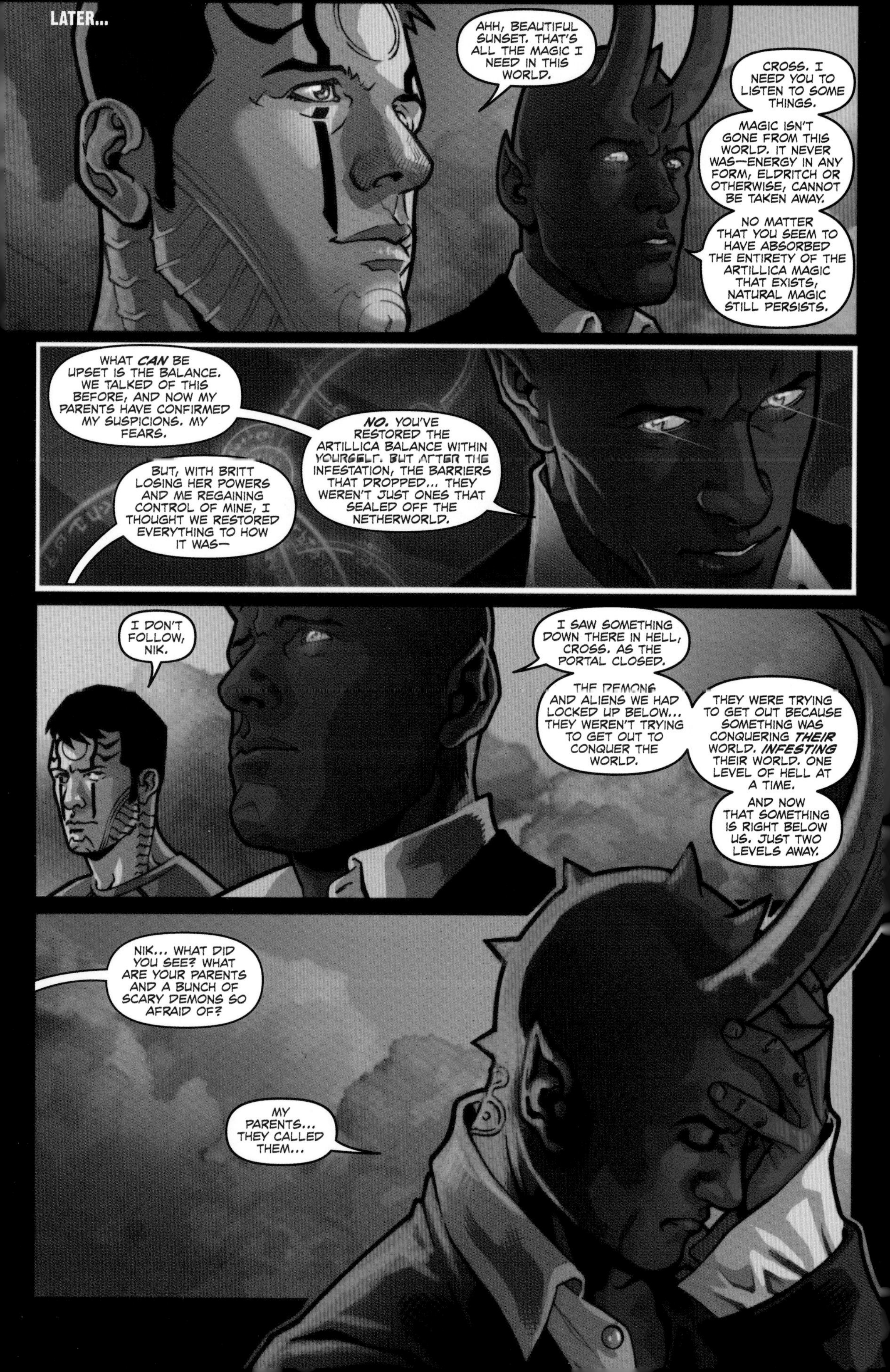
LATER...
AHH, BEAUTIFUL SUNSET. THAT'S ALL THE MAGIC I NEED IN THIS WORLD.
CROSS. I NEED YOU TO LISTEN TO SOME THINGS.
MAGIC ISN'T GONE FROM THIS WORLD. IT NEVER WAS—ENERGY IN ANY FORM, ELDRITCH OR OTHERWISE, CANNOT BE TAKEN AWAY.
NO MATTER THAT YOU SEEM TO HAVE ABSORBED THE ENTIRETY OF THE ARTILLICA MAGIC THAT EXISTS, NATURAL MAGIC STILL PERSISTS.
BUT, WITH BRITT LOSING HER POWERS AND ME REGAINING CONTROL OF MINE, I THOUGHT WE RESTORED EVERYTHING TO HOW IT WAS—
NO. YOU'VE RESTORED THE ARTILLICA BALANCE WITHIN YOURSELF. BUT AFTER THE INFESTATION, THE BARRIERS THAT DROPPED... THEY WEREN'T JUST ONES THAT SEALED OFF THE NETHERWORLD.
WHAT CAN BE UPSET IS THE BALANCE. WE TALKED OF THIS BEFORE, AND NOW MY PARENTS HAVE CONFIRMED MY SUSPICIONS. MY FEARS.
I DON'T FOLLOW, NIK.
I SAW SOMETHING DOWN THERE IN HELL, CROSS. AS THE PORTAL CLOSED.
THE DEMONS AND ALIENS WE HAD LOCKED UP BELOW... THEY WEREN'T TRYING TO GET OUT TO CONQUER THE WORLD.
THEY WERE TRYING TO GET OUT BECAUSE SOMETHING WAS CONQUERING THEIR WORLD. INFESTING THEIR WORLD. ONE LEVEL OF HELL AT A TIME.
AND NOW THAT SOMETHING IS RIGHT BELOW US. JUST TWO LEVELS AWAY.
NIK... WHAT DID YOU SEE? WHAT ARE YOUR PARENTS AND A BUNCH OF SCARY DEMONS SO AFRAID OF?
MY PARENTS... THEY CALLED THEM...

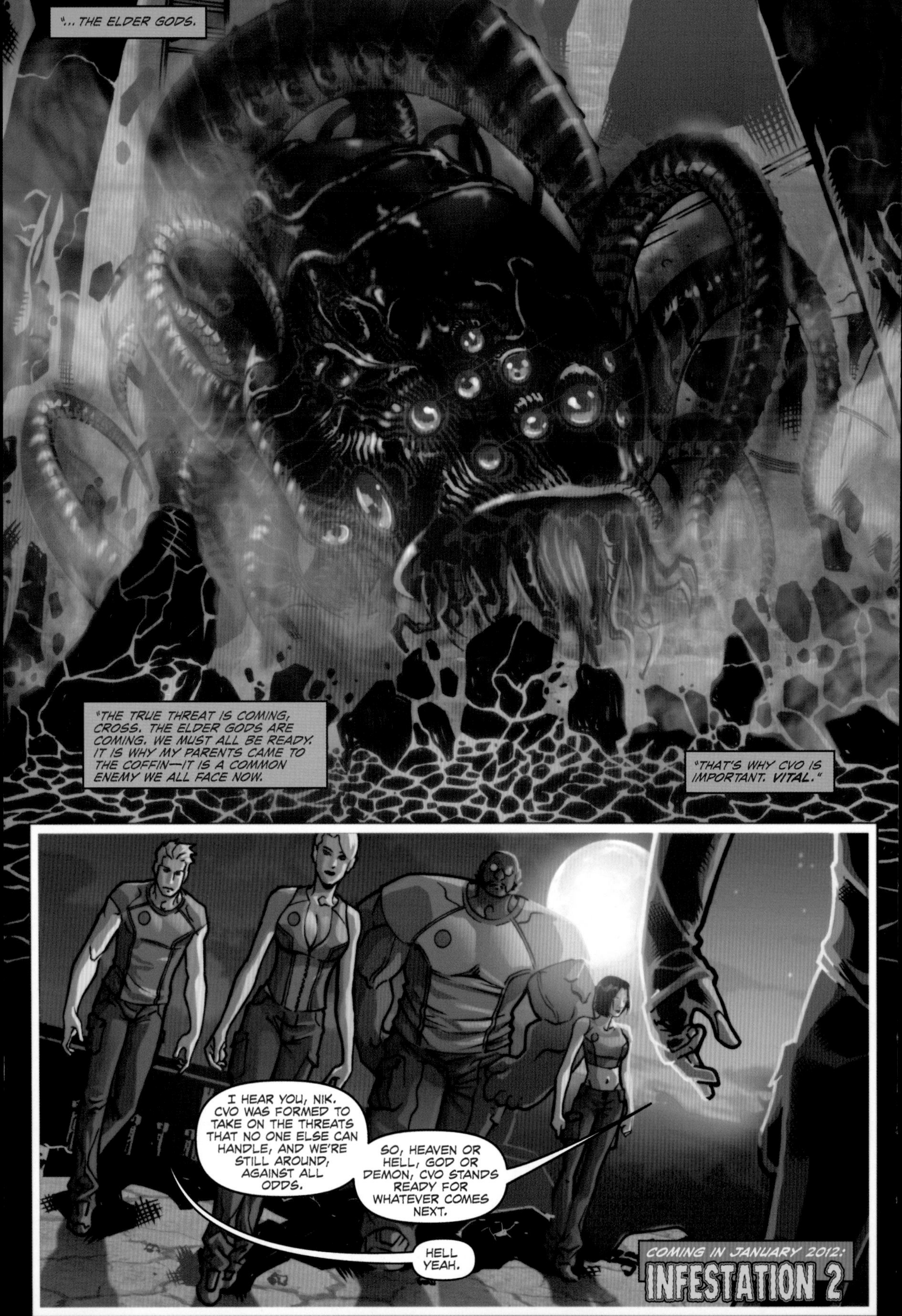
"... THE ELDER GODS.
"THE TRUE THREAT IS COMING, CROSS. THE ELDER GODS ARE COMING. WE MUST ALL BE READY. IT IS WHY MY PARENTS CAME TO THE COFFIN—IT IS A COMMON ENEMY WE ALL FACE NOW.
"THAT'S WHY CVO IS IMPORTANT. VITAL."
I HEAR YOU, NIK. CVO WAS FORMED TO TAKE ON THE THREATS THAT NO ONE ELSE CAN HANDLE, AND WE'RE STILL AROUND, AGAINST ALL ODDS.
SO, HEAVEN OR HELL, GOD OR DEMON, CVO STANDS READY FOR WHATEVER COMES NEXT.
HELL YEAH.
COMING IN JANUARY 2012:
INFESTATION 2

ART
GALLERY

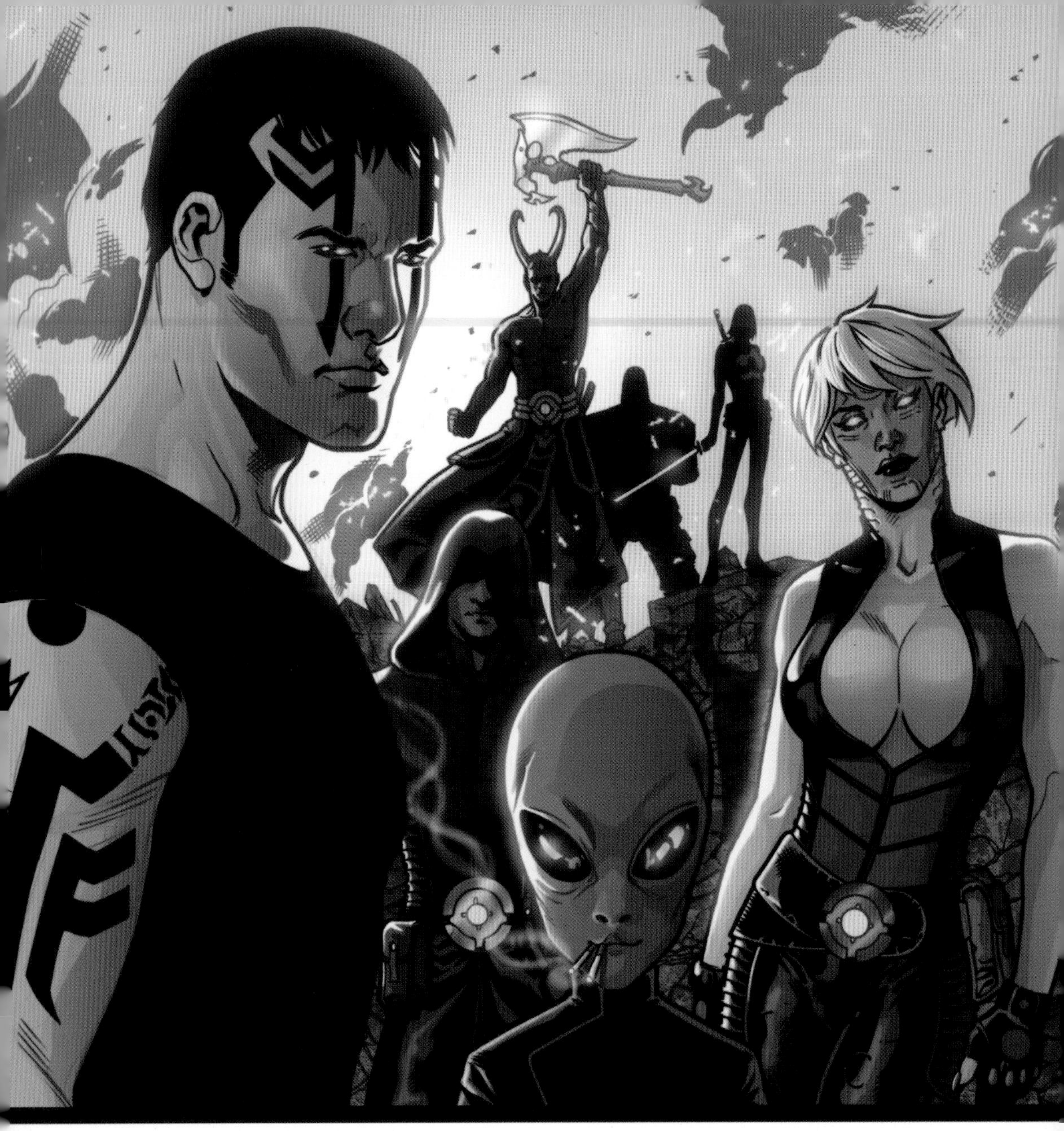

THIS PAGE:
Art by David Messina
Colors by ScarletGothica

NEXT PAGE:
Art by Davide Furnó

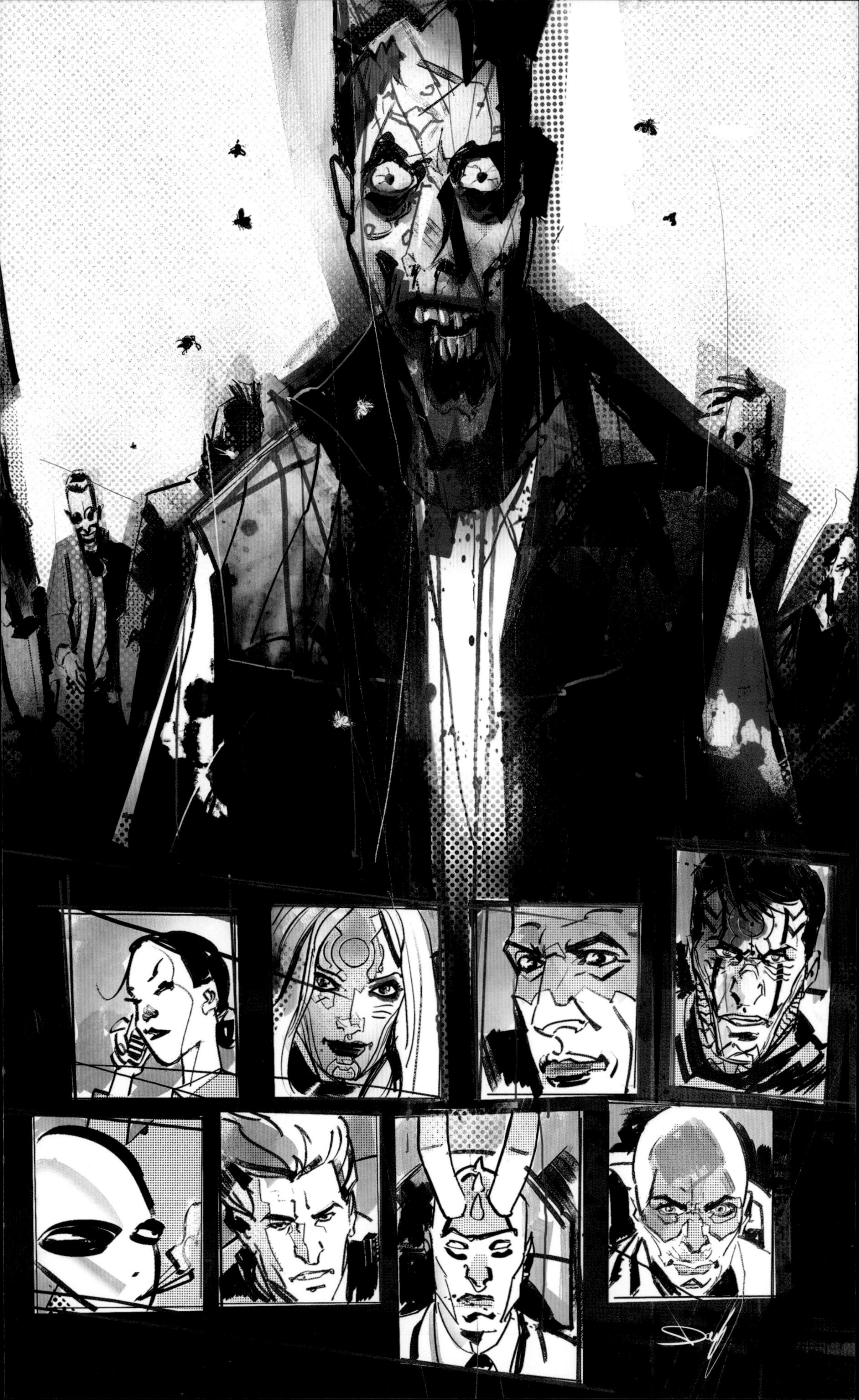

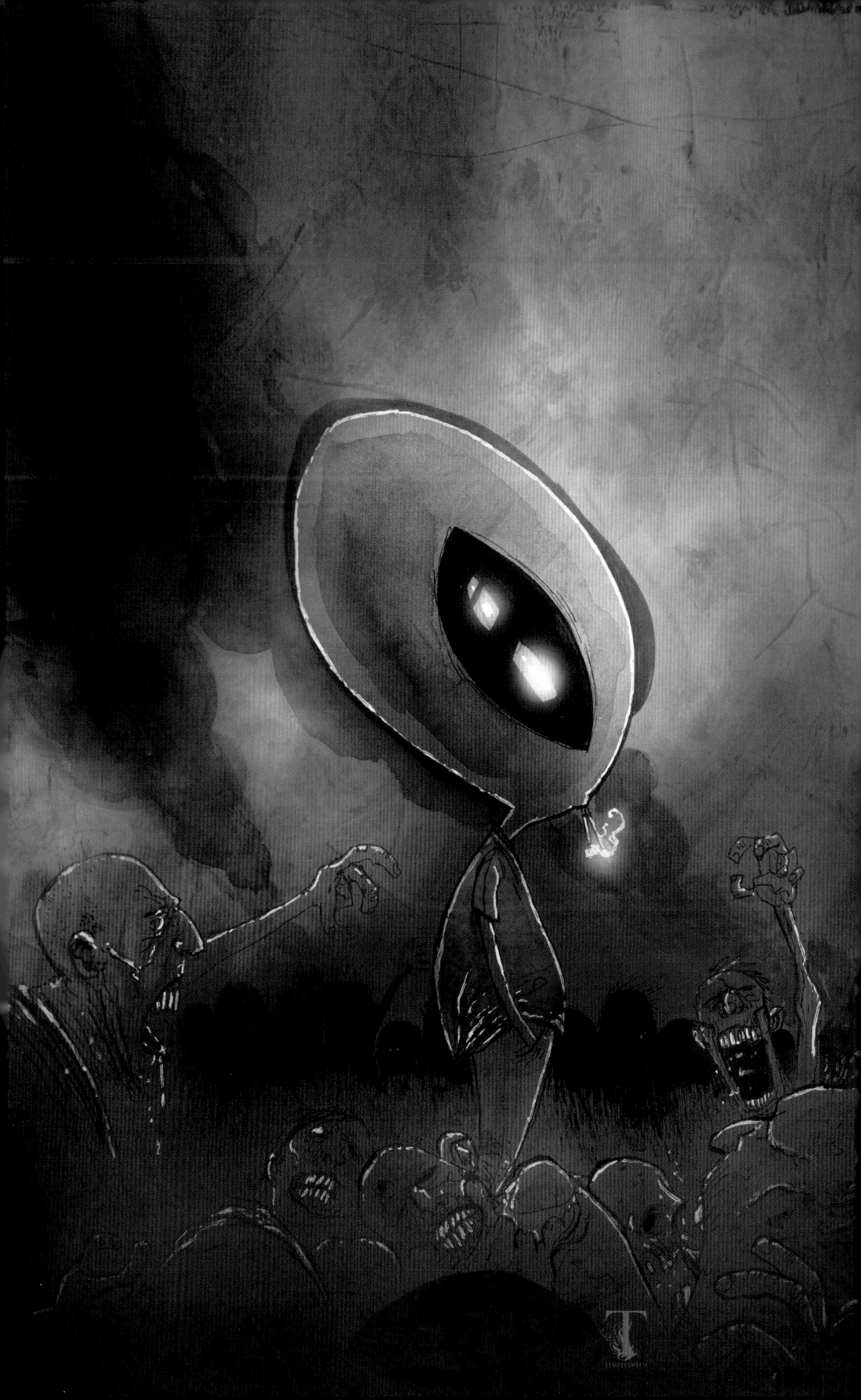

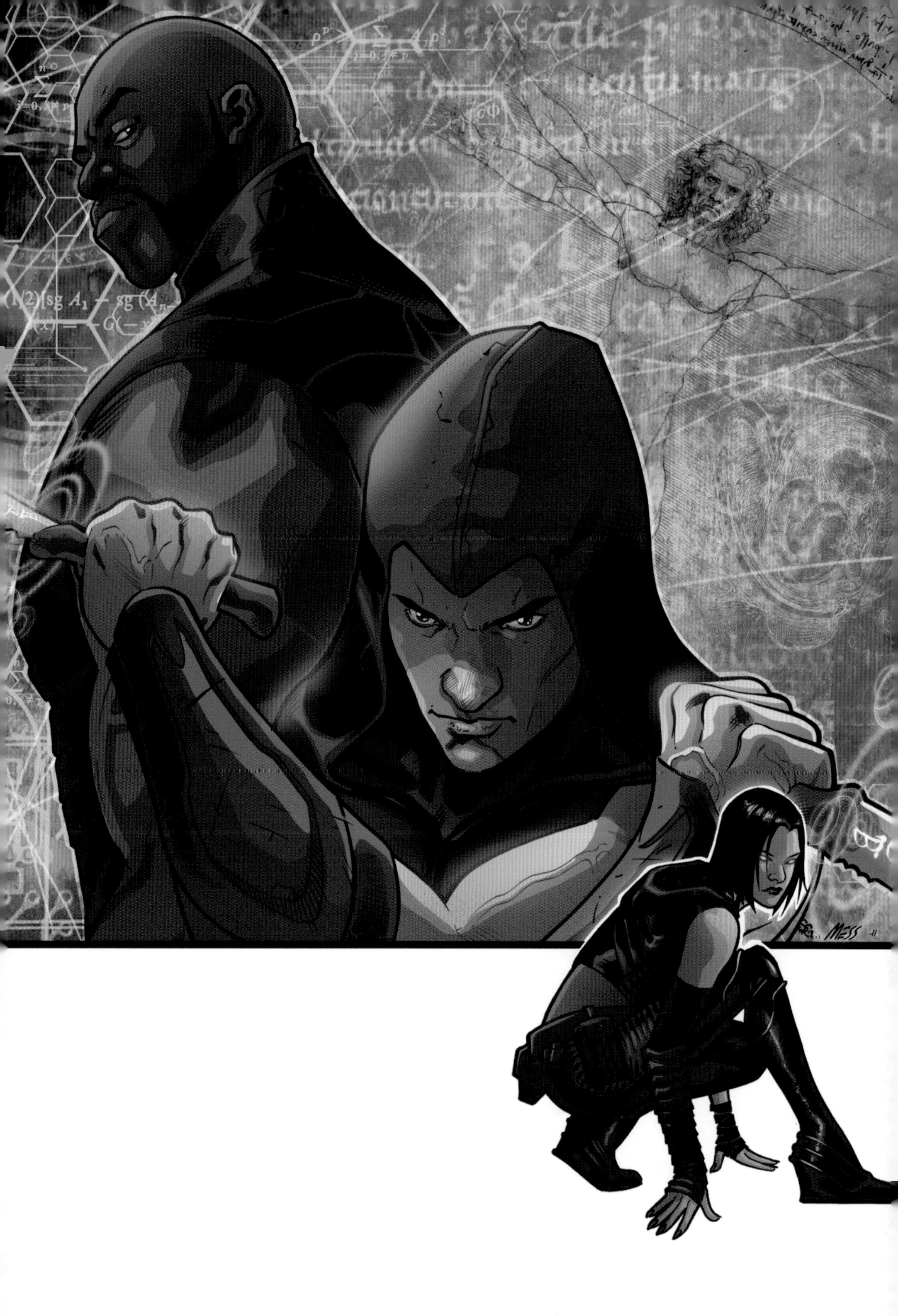
MESS

PREVIOUS PAGE:
Art by Ben Templesmith

THIS PAGE:
Art by David Messina
Colors by ScarletGothica

NEXT PAGE:
Art by Davide Furnó

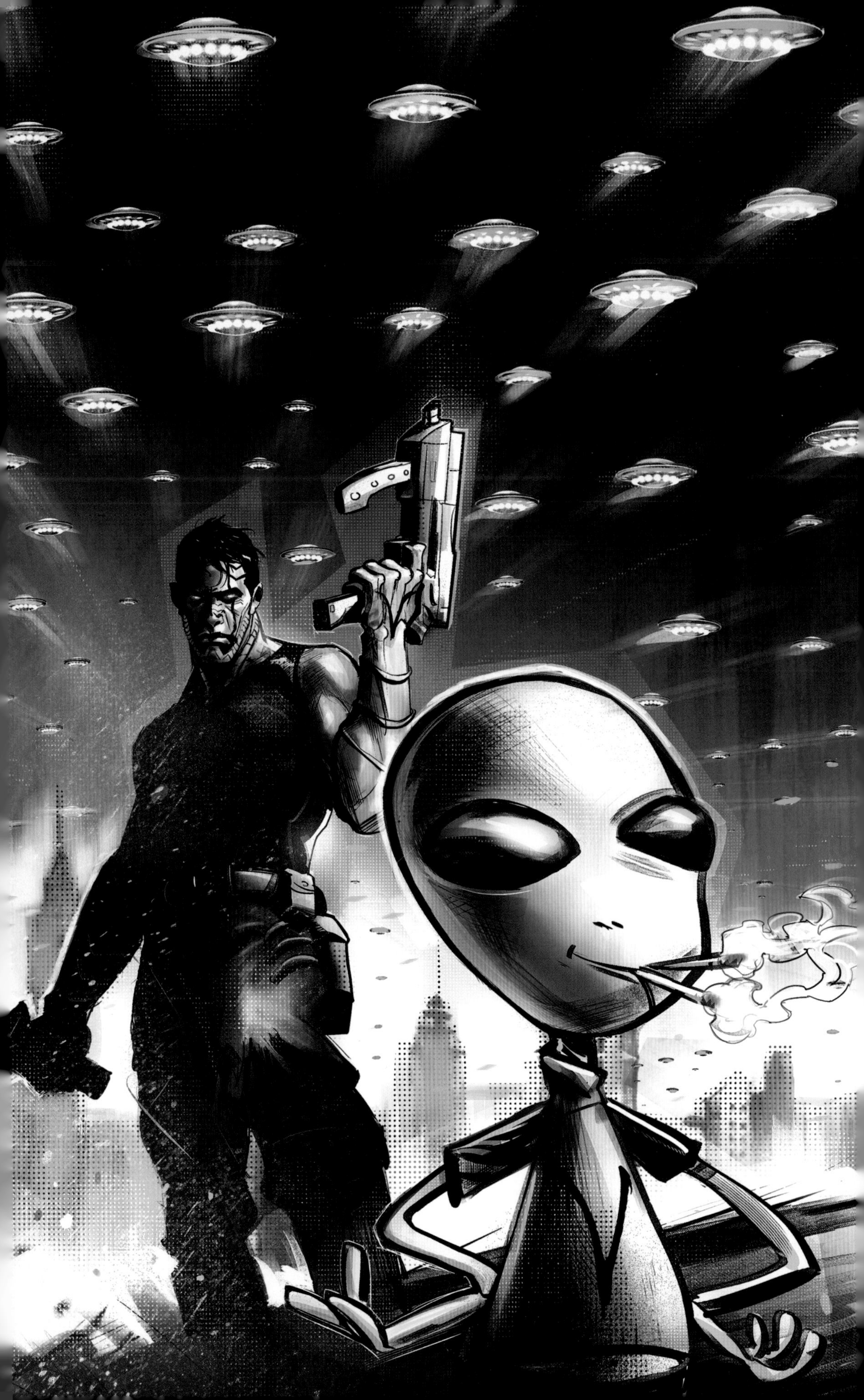

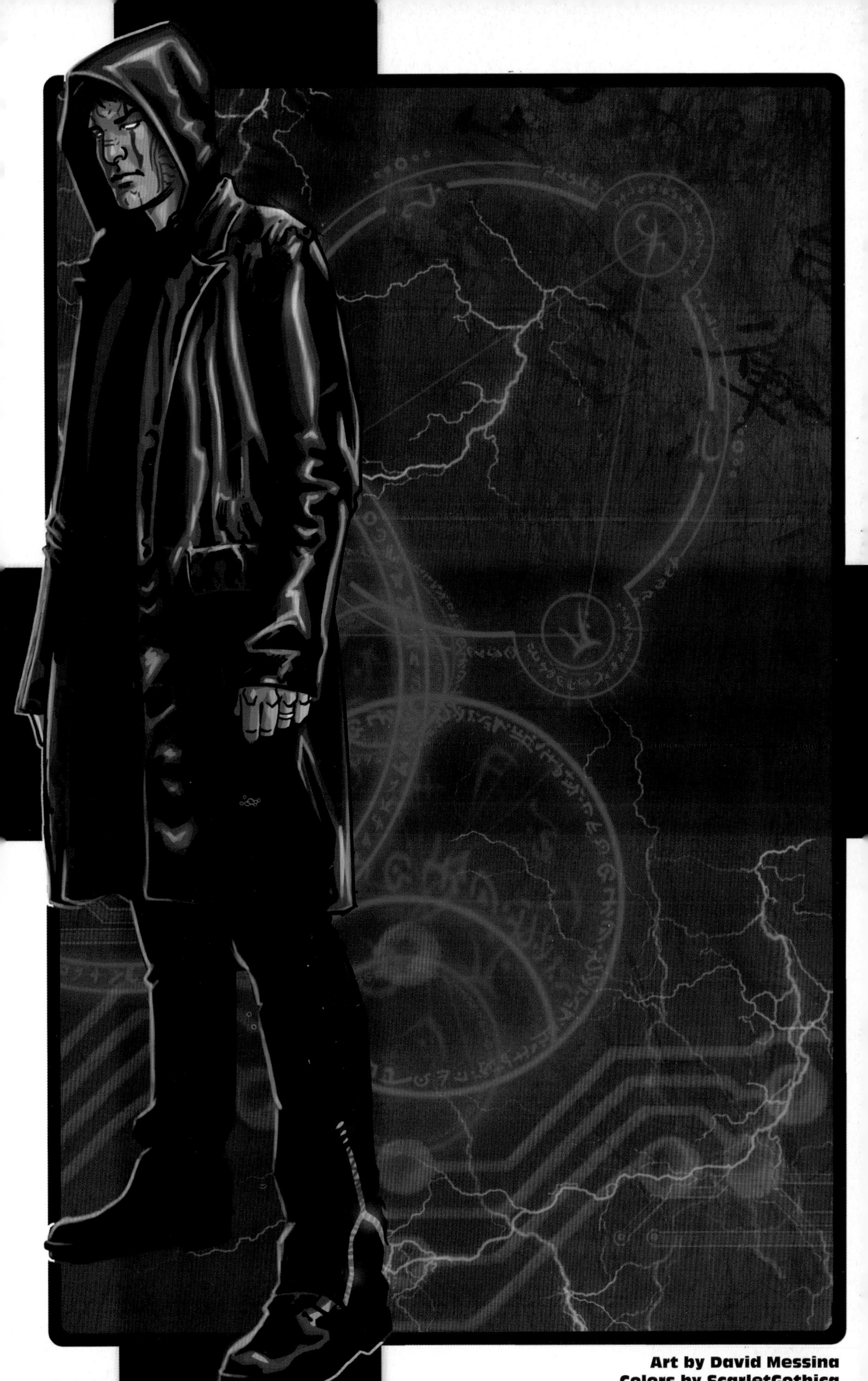

Art by David Messina
Colors by ScarletGothica

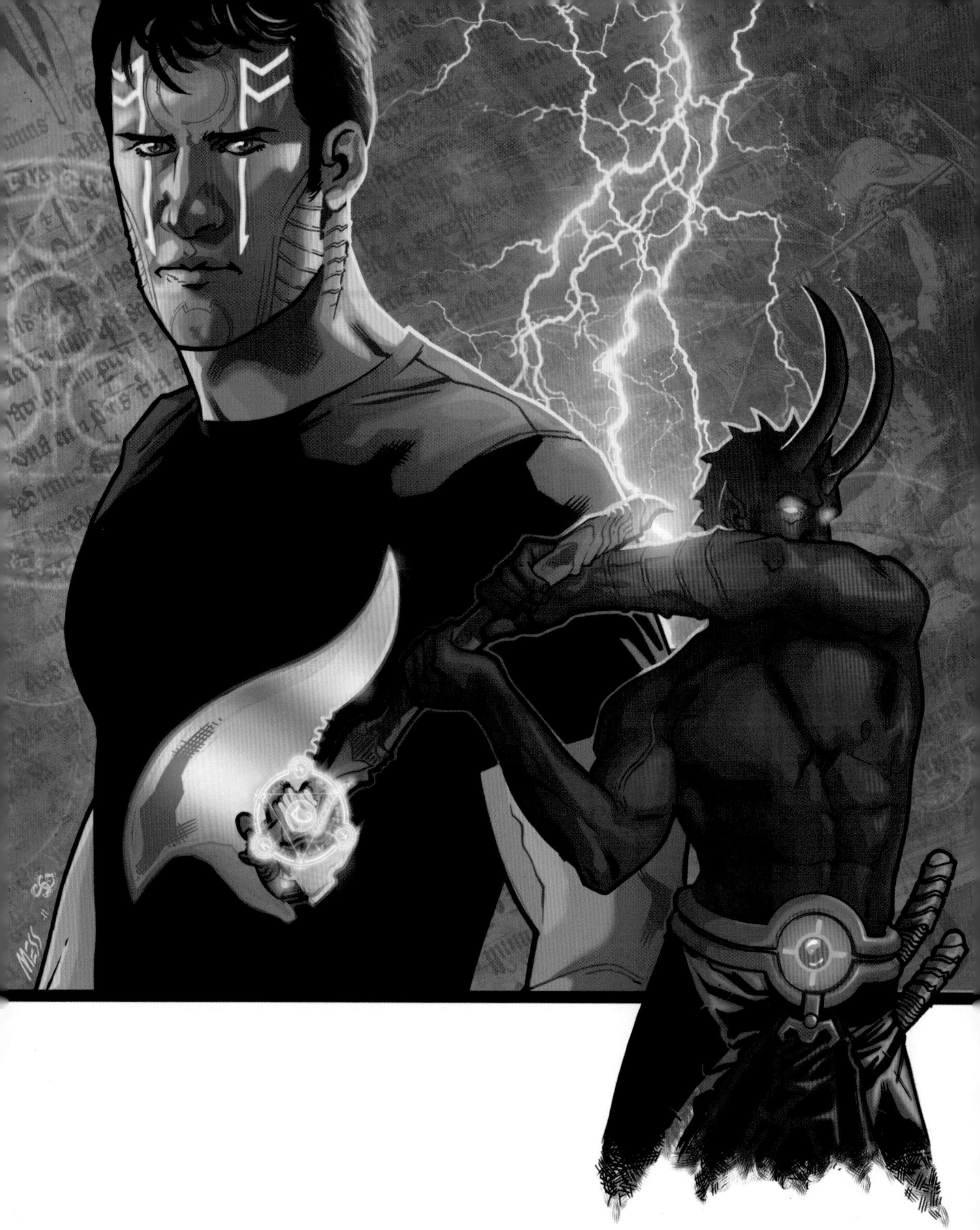

THIS PAGE:
Art by David Messina
Colors by ScarletGothica

NEXT PAGE:
Art by Davide Furnò

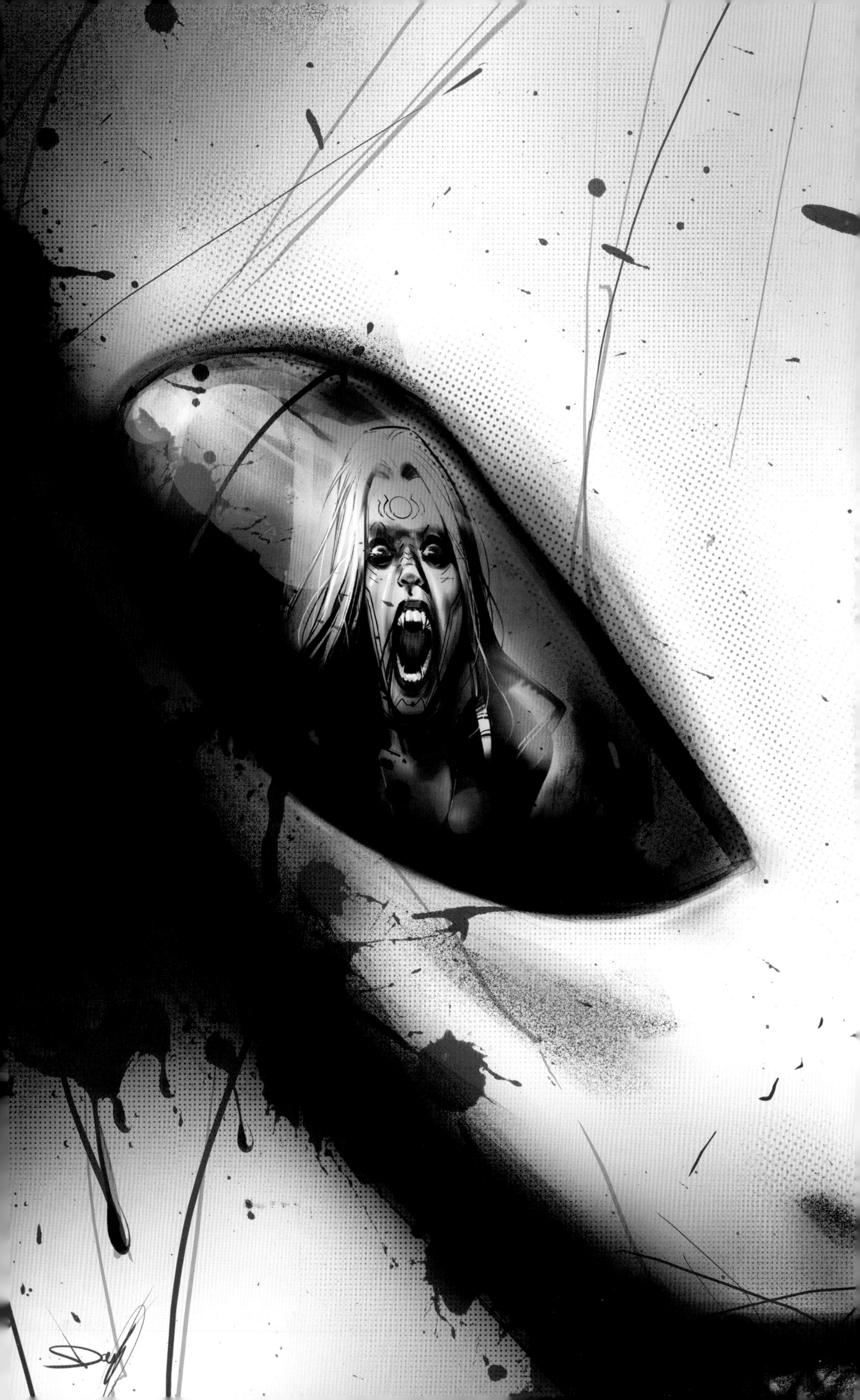

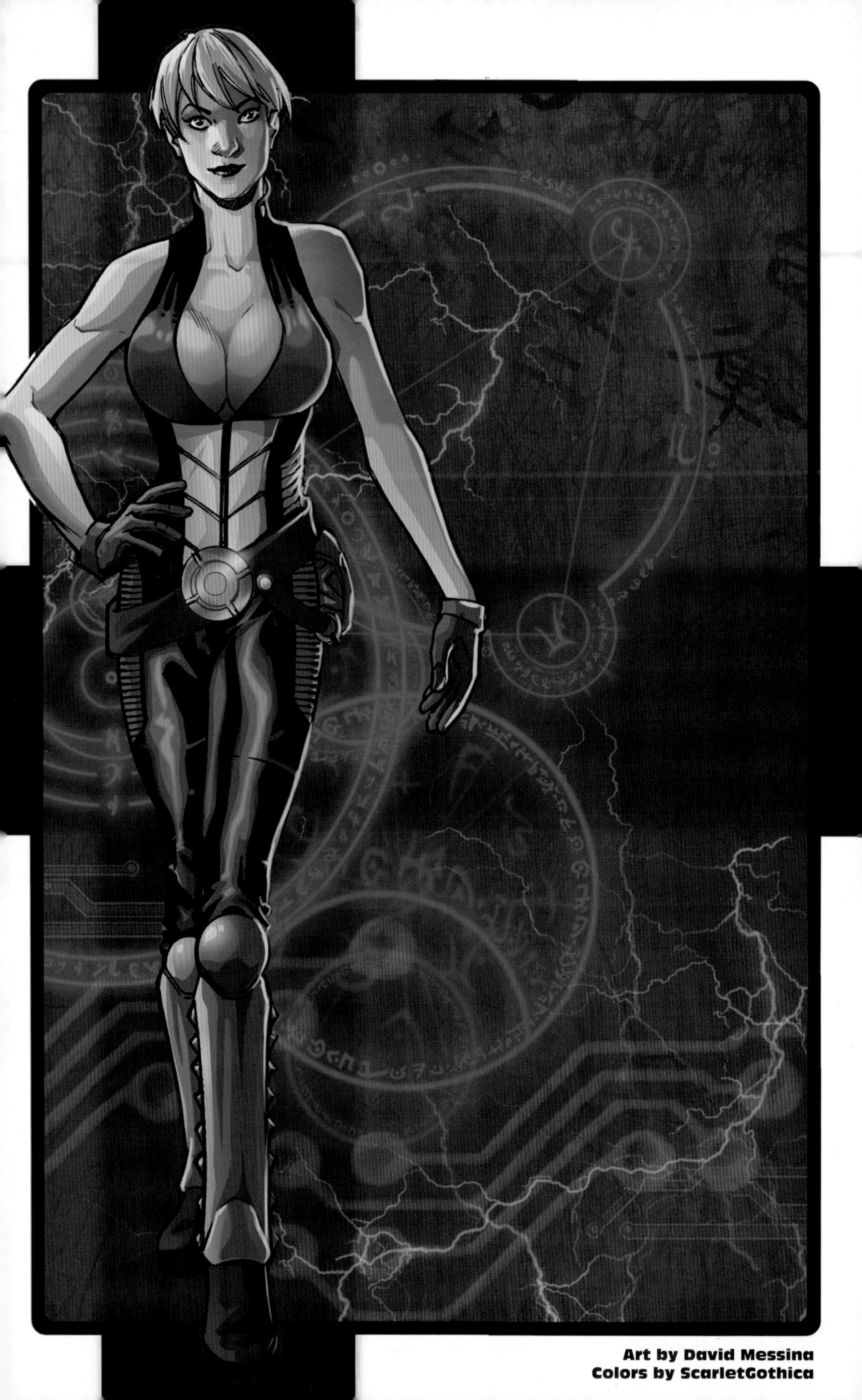

Art by David Messina
Colors by ScarletGothica

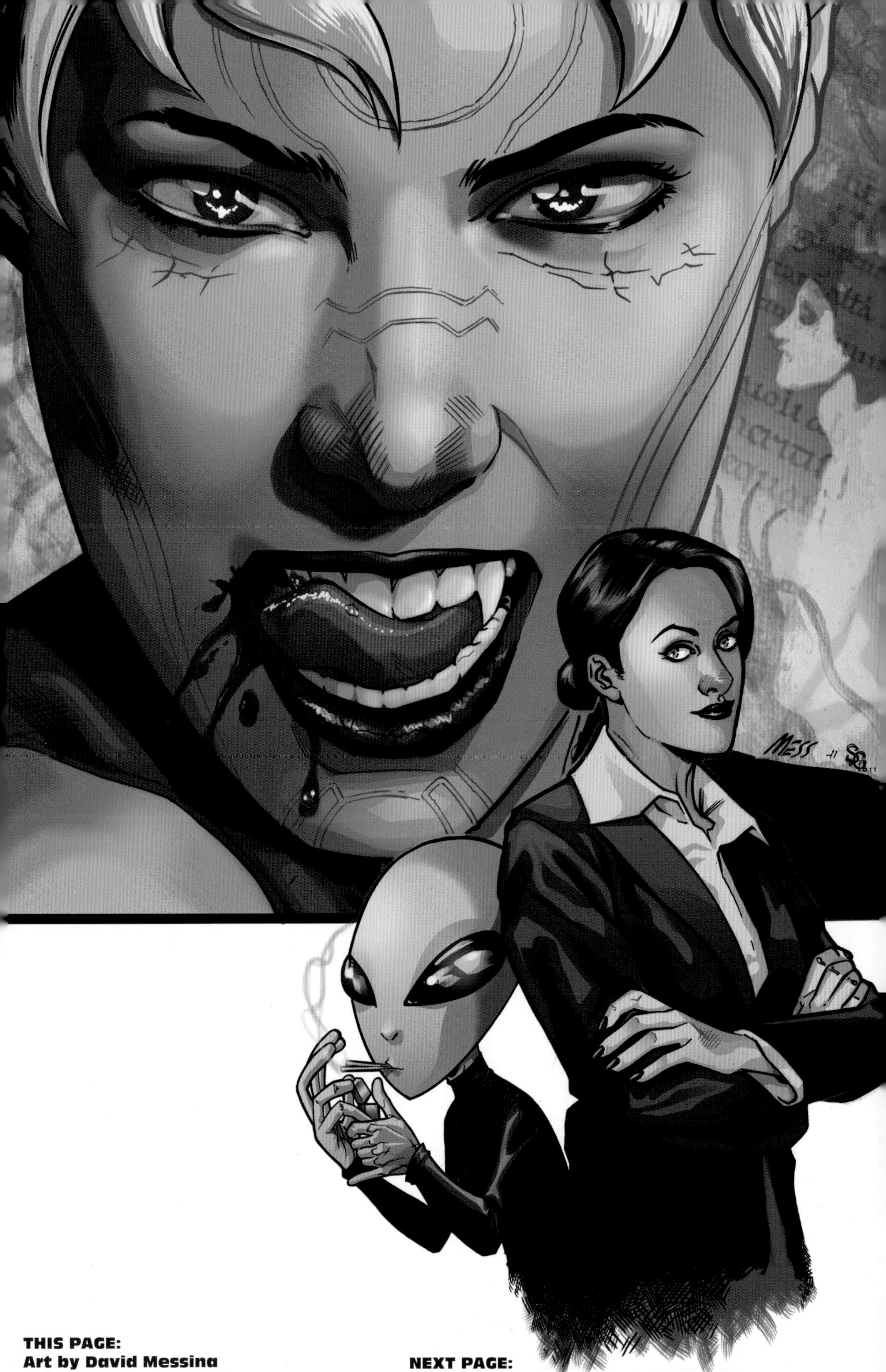
MESS -11

THIS PAGE:
Art by David Messina
Colors by ScarletGothica

NEXT PAGE:
Art by Davide Furnó

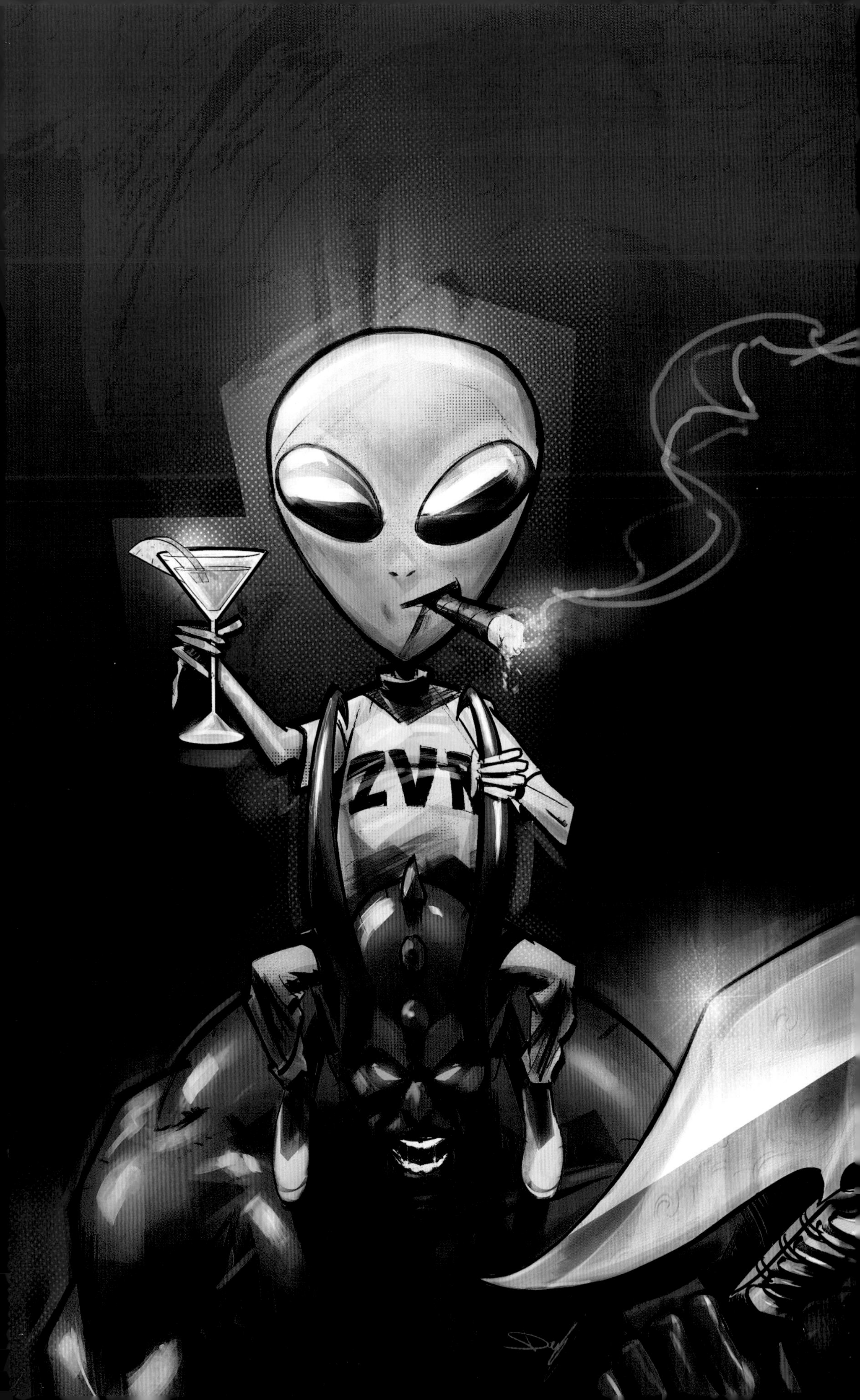

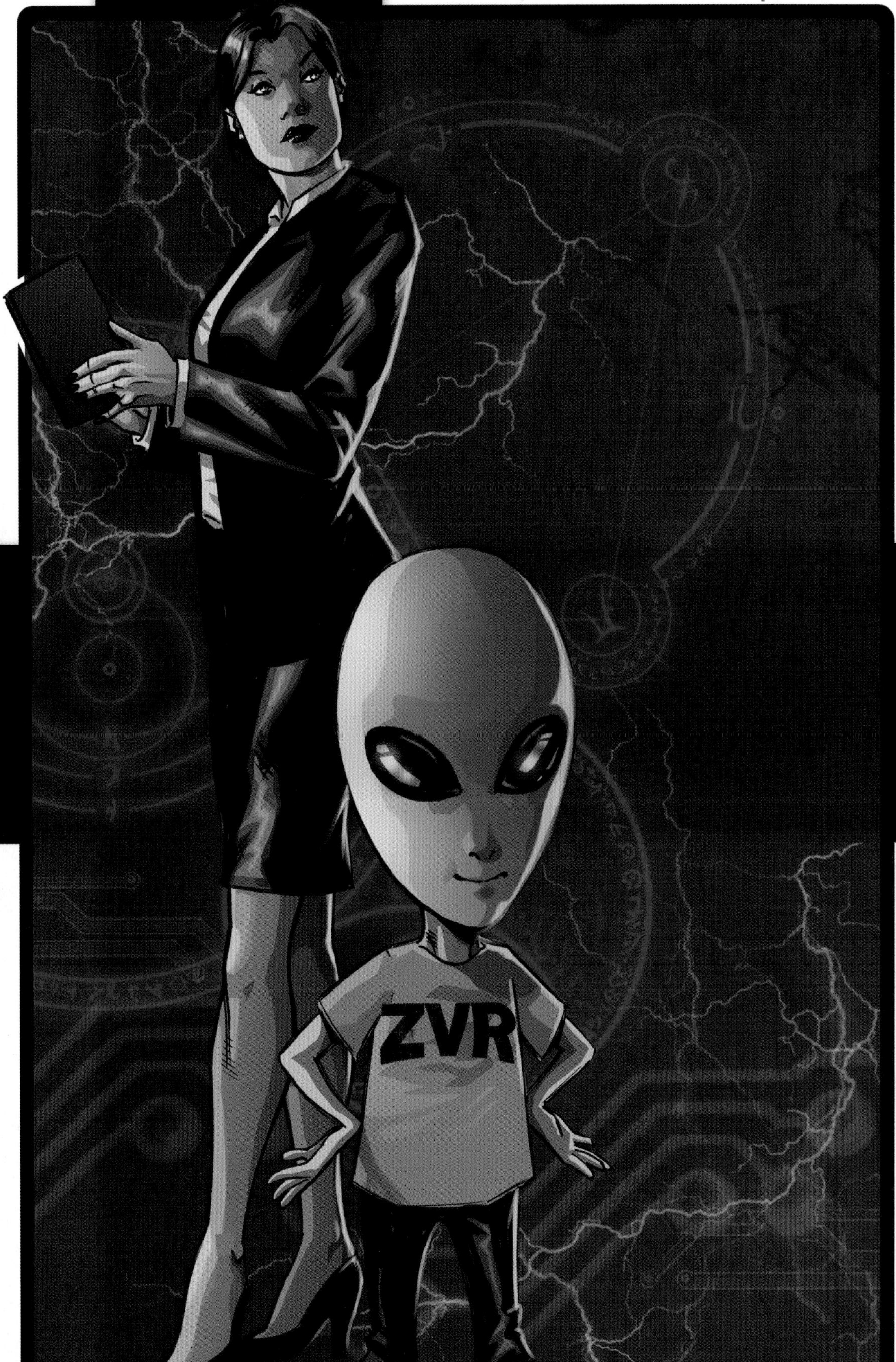
ZVR

Art by David Messina
Colors by ScarletGothica